INSIDE OUT:
Chronicles of a
Rock & Roll CEO

Mark Holden

Bath Hill Publishing

LONDON • VANCOUVER • LOS ANGELES

Published by Bath Hill Publishing
101 Principia Ct
Claremont, CA 9171

London, England • Vancouver, Canada • Los Angeles, USA

Library of Congress Control Number: 2016914260

Library and Archives Canada Cataloging in Publication Data

Holden, Mark, author
    Inside out : chronicles of a rock and roll CEO / Mark Holden.

ISBN 978-0-9952797-1-1 (hardback)

    1. Holden, Mark. 2. Rock musicians--Canada--Biography.
I. Title.

ML419.H726A3 2016   782.42166092   C2016-905846-8

Edited by Jim Grove
Cover Design by Don Bull
Design & Layout by Toni Serofin
Cover Photography by Jessica Haydahl

Printed and bound by Friesens in Canada
First Printing January 2017
Second Edition Printing March 2017

E-mail: info@markholden.com
www.markholden.com

FOR JANE, ELLIOT & ASHLEY
———

EDITED BY JIM GROVE

Preface

This book is about my life's journey. It's a story about the tapestry woven through triumphs, defeats, acceptance, intuition and instinct. It's about the effect you have on people and the lives you impact along the way. It's about the power of reinvention and creating things that will move and inspire people to connect with themselves and each other. And it's about never giving up.

When I was a young boy, I dreamed of becoming an architect. I was always fascinated by the concept of creating something beautiful. It may have started as a fort constructed of cushions from our living room sofa, forming a place of comfort and refuge where I could dream, where I could imagine beautiful buildings. There in my makeshift sanctuary, eyes closed, the elements would gather. One by one floating forward into view. From the foundations and the defining walls, to the placements of windows for maximum light to energize the inhabitants and frame the beauty that lay beyond. The concept of constructing something in my mind and then deconstructing it fascinated me. And still does. In my young mind, the possibilities seemed endless.

My imaginary creations were going to be timeless structures that would inspire everyone who stopped to enjoy their beauty.

I didn't end up becoming an architect in the traditional sense. I became a musician and an entrepreneur, but from an early age I used the same process my father and other great architects had followed. Applying the same principles to the process, I would often start with a simple idea – the outline of a business plan or a melody sketched out on the back of a napkin – and I would build from there. Breathing life and light into my ideas on the way to completeness. Creating things that would make the world a better place, I believed, was my destiny.

This book chronicles my life's journey and shines the light on three important things I've learned.

The first is to dream of what can be. If an idea still hangs together after several "wake ups", and you remain just as convinced as the day before, thinking you may be on to something, you probably are. Let your inner voice be your compass. Once you've set your intention and your course, go hard. The alternative will leave you wondering whether your vision was ever achievable.

The second is to have the courage to go it alone and take the road less travelled. The very things that make it scary and daunting are the same things that allow fluidity and freedom of movement, and the ability to thrive in the openness.

The third is to communicate—just keep talking, and listening. Sometimes it's the only way through.

I wrote this book because I feel that I have lived an extraordinary life. A life where I have changed directions and reinvented myself several times. Where I have lived the pursuit of my dreams, inspired by thoughts and ideas, fuelled by passion. And always with the same boundless enthusiasm and curiosity I had as a child.

With my story, I hope to inspire others with the courage to live their own dreams, and, if necessary, reinvent their own lives. Each of us will have a unique story. This is simply mine.

Contents

Yesterday is history, tomorrow is a mystery,
today is a gift of God, which is why we call it the present.

– Bil Keane

Beyond a Dream

Some experiences can cause us to wonder what powers might exist behind the veil of this physical world. For me, coming face to face with death was one such experience.

One evening in February 2000, my wife Jane and I returned home from a 40th birthday party for a friend of ours. It had been a great evening full of good conversations, boisterous laughter, and great music. After saying our goodbyes and heading home, we were left feeling abundantly happy to have been part of the celebration, and grateful to have shared a wonderful evening with close friends.

At about 2 a.m., I was awakened from what I had thought was a bad dream in which I had a horrendously sharp pain in my abdomen. It was a violent pain, and when I woke up, with my bed sheets drenched, I knew right away that it wasn't a case of simple indigestion. This was a pain that I had never experienced before.

I made my way to the bathroom and ran a bath, which in itself is a clear sign that something is wrong with me. Typically, I only take a bath when I am unwell or in serious need of soothing. I sat in the bath as the pain and nausea increased to a point just this side of passing out. I called out in a voice that must have been almost unrecognizable to Jane.

Knowing something must be seriously wrong, Jane jumped out of bed and opened the bathroom door. She could see that I was in agony, and she called for an ambulance immediately. I don't remember much after that point until reaching Lions Gate Hospital. They processed me through the emergency department asking me the usual questions—do you have any history, how much have you had to drink this evening, and the rest.

We had enjoyed some lovely wine that evening, so I responded honestly: "Perhaps four or five glasses of wine over the course of the evening."

I think this was a mistake. I think the triage nurse looked at me as if I was some sort of a party animal, throwing me one of those "It's-Saturday-night-and-we-got-another-live-one" looks.

The emergency room was particularly busy that night, and upon being admitted, I writhed on the gurney in a hallway, staring up at the ceiling tiles with bad fluorescent lighting that seemed to make everything look green. They administered a few oral painkillers, but they had no effect. They asked me over and over again:

"On a scale of one to 10, with 10 being the most painful, where are you now?"

"Nine point five," I replied again and again.

This went on for what seemed to be an eternity before they started a morphine IV drip. I started to feel a bit of relief, but at this point I was prepared to offer my entire kingdom to the powers that be in exchange for making this wretchedness go away.

They then switched to Demerol, and that seemed to help a little, but I was still quivering from discomfort. All the while, some part of me felt horrible that it was four o'clock in the morning, and Jane had to be in hospital with me, seeing me in this kind of condition, instead of home in bed.

At approximately 7 am that morning, they decided to give me an x-ray, and then they booked me for an ultrasound for the following day to see more of what was going on.

By the end of day three, I was in and out of consciousness and severely ill. The doctors were still trying to figure out what was wrong with me. On top of this, the hospital was extremely short of gastrointestinal doctors as all but two of them were at a conference. This may explain why it took four days for the doctors who were present to ask for a CT scan.

By this point, my abdomen had swollen up to a point where I looked like I was nine months pregnant.

When the doctors saw the images from my CT scan, they quickly discovered what was going on: I had a twist in my bowel.

Dr. Richard Lewis visited me and told me that they were going to have to operate. They scheduled me for surgery the next day in the late afternoon, confident that I could simply weather the pain for another 24 hours.

To this day, I still stand in awe and wonder at how incredibly relaxed they were about my situation. No sense of urgency whatsoever. I could sense that there was a "system" involved, and some sort of defined protocol for treating a patient with my symptoms. I get that. But taking almost five days to operate?

Unknown to everyone, including myself, my condition was actually much more dire than anyone realized. It would not become clear until they opened me up in surgery the next day, but my organs were starting to fail because I was toxic.

Through this process, I was steadily growing angry at the apparent nonchalance of the doctors and nurses. At one point said to Jane, "I think you should get me out of here and send me to another hospital where I can get faster treatment, maybe even the United States somewhere."

That would have been a mistake and she new it. She just nodded and let me rant in my feeble state.

And this is when things really started going sideways. That night, in a semiconscious state, I had what I guess you would call an out-of-body experience. It was beyond a dream, whatever it was.

I was lying in bed, and suddenly I felt a hand on my right shoulder, so I looked over to see who was touching me. My room was in a corner of the hospital on the sixth floor, and my bed was against an outside wall of the building. When I turned, I discovered that there was nothing there but the wall.

Then I think I drifted off. I found myself starting to sit up when one of the nurses came into my room and unlocked the wheels of the bed. It struck me that they would normally come in and be somewhat congenial, and they would start chatting as they prepared to wheel me down for x-rays or give me another shot of Demerol. But on this occasion, the nurse came in and she didn't say anything. She wasn't even looking at me as she went through her routine almost like a robot. She just moved the IV stand out of the way, and then she wheeled my bed out into the hallway and left me there.

From the hallway, I could see back into the room, and I watched the hospital custodian arrive. He was a pleasant and simple guy who looked like Weird Al Yankovic. I had become very accustomed to his quiet presence over the previous days. He started taking down the pictures that my kids had drawn for me, and collecting all of my get-well-soon cards and other belongings. And then he started carrying the flowers out of the room.

"What are you doing?" I said to him. "Those are from my kids! And why do the flowers have to go?"

He didn't respond. He didn't even look at me. It was like he couldn't hear me. He simply continued emptying the room.

I thought this was very strange. Everything felt like slow motion to me, and I was frustrated that he seemed to be ignoring me.

He finished emptying out my belongings, and then he started to mop the floor.

And then I woke up in my bed. Drenched in sweat. And I wept for the first time since I had been admitted to hospital, feeling a strange sense of comfort as my warm tears rolled down my face, bringing such a strange sense of relief as I looked to see everything in the room was exactly as it had been.

I imagined that I had experienced a dream, but it had seemed so real and life like that I felt that I had been shown something.

By this point, my condition had suddenly gone to a whole new level.

I was in extreme pain, and I felt like I couldn't move. It was as though I was buried in wet concrete.

I had to get up and get someone's attention. Summoning all that remained of my strength, and shaking off the delirium induced by my pain medication and sedatives, I lifted myself out of the bed and I walked down to the nursing station, teetering all the way, and leaning heavily on my rolling IV pole for stability.

The nurse there gave me a slightly confused and quizzical look. "Can I help you?"

I remember thinking, *Can I fucking help you?* My feelings of helplessness suddenly turned to anger. This nurse had been on duty and had watched my condition go from bad to dire in in a stretch of a few days.

I wanted to reply: *Why, yes, thank you. I'd like to go out and do a little shopping. Do you mind calling me a taxi?*

I stood there, a wreck of a man, with a tube shoved up my left nostril, leaning on my IV pole that was packing an on-demand morphine rig and a wide assortment of clear bags full of life sustaining fluids, barely able to stand on my feet. Seriously? What kind of a question was that?

"I don't think I'm going to make it."

There was anger in my voice, though I hadn't consciously intended it. I felt like I was dying. And I was not going to let that happen. I thought about all of the things I still wanted to do in my life, and I didn't feel this was my time.

The nurse just gave me a patronizing look and her best attempt at a sympathetic nod. It was clear that she didn't believe for a second think that I was going to die.

"I don't think I'm going to make it through the night," I said again.

She told me to go back to my room, and she would send someone down to see me.

As I stood there, I felt myself becoming weaker by the minute. I also felt myself becoming enraged, but I was too weak to say or do anything more. I turned myself slowly around, and I slowly shuffled myself back to my room.

As I got back into bed, a nurse appeared, gave me an extra strong dose of Demerol, and I fell into a delirious form of sleep.

When I awoke the next morning, I was grateful. I was still alive.

The doctor came by on his rounds, dutifully surveyed my chart, confirmed that I was in fact alive, and verified that I was scheduled for surgery for about ten o'clock that night. Again, I was afraid that I wouldn't last that long, but I had given up hope of trying to say anything.

Luckily for me, behind the scenes, other developments were unfolding that I didn't know about. I had a guardian angel looking after me in the guise of a woman named Oonagh McKinney.

Oonagh was the sister of my friend Jon, whose fortieth birthday party I had been attending. Was it coincidence or the planets lining up for me? It turned out that she was an operating room nurse at the hospital and she knew I was in there. She came on shift the day of my surgery, and she saw that I wasn't scheduled until ten o'clock that night. Apparently the late time was due to the fact that the surgical staff was short one scrub nurse that day.

"Look, we can get him in sooner?" she told the surgeon. "I'll just scrub for both surgeries. Let's just get this guy into surgery as soon as possible."

That made all the difference. Unbeknown to me, I was now fast tracked for my surgery.

Earlier that day, my brother Shane had called from Calgary, and we had a conversation quite unlike any other conversation we have ever had. I could hear concern in Shane's voice.

"Should I come out?" he said.

"Yes, I think it's a good idea," I replied feebly.

We didn't know what they were going to find when they opened me up that night, and in the event that I didn't make it, I wanted Shane there to help Jane with details.

Apparently Shane literally hung up the phone, drove to the airport in

Calgary, got on the next flight to Vancouver, and upon arrival walked outside and directly into an airport shuttle for downtown. He arrived at the corner of Georgia and Burrard Street in minutes, and within 60 seconds he caught a bus that took him directly to the hospital. He probably set a record for public transit from the Vancouver airport to the Lions Gate Hospital!

Just before 5 p.m.—about four hours after our phone conversation—the door opened and Shane walked into my hospital room. I was stunned. But before I could barely open my mouth to say hi, the OR nurse arrived to take me down to surgery.

"I'm so sorry," I mumbled," I have to go for surgery now."

"It's okay, Mark," Shane said simply. "Don't you worry. I'll see you when you get back."

I'm convinced that Oonagh's actions saved my life. They operated on me at about five o'clock in the afternoon, and when they opened me up, they found that a section of my bowel had twisted and ruptured. Until that point, they had suspected that it was an obstruction of some sort, but they hadn't known that it had ruptured. The surgical team ended up taking several liters of toxic fluid out of me. It was horrific. This was why I had been so distended for days.

While I was recovering a couple of weeks later at home, I went to see my personal doctor for a check up on my status. After he examined me, he told me how lucky I had been not to die.

"You know, if you had been 65 and out of shape, there's just no way you would have survived," he said, his gaze level with mine. "You just wouldn't have. The fact that you're in good physical condition and you have a very high pain tolerance, that's what got you through."

As Jane and I drove home from my checkup with my doctor, I was very quiet. I was reflecting on how close I had been to not making it, and how much I would have left behind me—Jane, my kids Elliot and Ashley, my friends, my dreams. And when I thought about the incredibly vivid vision that I had that night before my surgery, I felt certain that it was just not my time to check out. There was still so much to do.

Suddenly, I felt a new sense of purpose—and strangely enough, a profound sense of strength.

ONE

The Innocent

When I was four years old, my family lived in low-cost housing in the Fort Garry area of Winnipeg off of the Pembina highway. We lived very humbly, and I learned some hard early lessons about life there.

While my father studied architecture at the University of Manitoba, my mother struggled each day to maintain the household and take care of my brother Shane and me on limited income. It was very difficult for us financially owing to the fact that my father wasn't earning much income while he was in school, other than a few night shifts driving for Grosvenor Taxi. As with architecture programs everywhere, his studies were extremely demanding, and the professors at the University of Manitoba were infamous for intentionally burying their students in near-impossible quantities of assignments to try to get them to quit.

As kids during this time, we didn't have bicycles, and my family didn't own a car until I was about five years old. I clearly remember going with my mother to the hospital to get my tonsils out and having to take three different buses to get there. There we were, sitting on the bus, me a bit nervous with my little suitcase and my mom putting on her bravest face. It was winter in Winnipeg, and I remember stepping outside in the aftermath of the surgery to receive a blast of minus 30 prairie air on my very sore throat. But despite our discomforts, my mom never complained once about not having transportation.

One day, I was playing with my brother Shane at a giant construction dirt pile that was near the housing complex. This was in the days before video games and cable television, so a dirt pile, an old creek bed, or a scruffy patch of bush was the natural place for kids to gather and play. We were playing with some kids who had bicycles, and I remember being awestruck with their rides. There was one boy in particular who was probably a couple of years older than me, and he had a red bicycle. I thought it was *amazing*—because I couldn't in my wildest dreams have imagined ever having one.

As we were playing, I suddenly found a quarter in the dirt.

"Wow! I just found 25 cents!" I chirped.

My heart was suddenly pounding with excitement. In those days, that was a lot of money for a kid. My brother Shane and I each received one nickel each week as an allowance. Whenever we had a tiny bit of money, he would take me with him down to Devinski's store and we would buy penny candies. With one penny, you could buy three jujubes, and a quarter would get you an entire bag of candy, all under the watchful gaze of Devinski, a little bald man who always had a cigar hanging out of the corner of his mouth. When I found this quarter, it was like finding a goldmine. I just couldn't believe it. As soon as I announced my find, the boy on the red bike drew close to me.

"Wow! You found a quarter? Can I see it?"

"Sure!" I said, and I handed it to him.

"I need to get on my bike to look at it," he said.

I was only four years old. The model of innocence and naiveté. His request seemed perfectly reasonable to me. "Okay," I said.

He mounted his bike, and he pedaled away.

As I watched him and his buddies disappear, my consciousness struggled to process what was happening. And then I realized that I had been robbed. The boy had vanished. I stood there frozen, devastated. I didn't know how to react.

Some part of me died that day. But I didn't throw myself off a bridge. I slowly processed my grief and moved forward as kids generally do.

(Considering that I was only four years old, it was important that I chose to move forward.)

But money was now on my radar, as was theft and betrayal. And I knew I would have to take better care of myself next time.

Not long afterwards, I set out to start earning my own money. I was still thinking about the quarter I had lost, and my five-cents-per-week seemed pale in comparison. As grateful as I was, I wanted to buy my own treats at Devinski's store. I figured delivering newspapers would be a great place to start.

I had seen boys delivering newspapers in the neighborhood, and I knew that they collected money for their work. From what I could tell, the start-up costs were minimal and the barriers to entry were few, so I decided to get into the business. But how did it work? It was a bit of a mystery to me. I thought about it for a while until I thought I had it figured out.

I approached a friend of mind who had a little red wagon, and I asked him if I could borrow it. I explained that I was going to use it to deliver newspapers around the neighborhood.

With as much wide-eyed innocence as I had expressed that fateful day when the boy on the red bicycle rode away with my quarter, he said, "Okay."

I set out with his wagon and started going door-to-door on our short cul-de-sac. My little friend followed behind men like a curious puppy. I knocked on each door and asked if they had any newspapers. This is how I thought it worked.

Each time, I received the same response. They would look at me quizzically, trying to discern what I was doing, and then they would disappear briefly and return with their old newspapers. I said thank-you each time, and I placed the papers carefully into the wagon. Sometimes they would be folded neatly, and I would reflect with a measure of satisfaction, *that's a good one.*

I spent some time collecting until I had a big stack of newspapers. Then I started back around the block again.

I went back to the same houses and I knocked on their doors once more. When they opened the door, I would gesture to my stack of newspapers: "Would you like to buy a newspaper?"

Their facial expressions were comical as they realized what I was doing. I remember a couple of people chuckling, but I didn't understand why. I was just a guy trying to make an honest living.

Owing to the great generosity and amusement of my neighbors, I actually sold a few papers. I came home with a handful of pennies and nickels, and I figured I had made a big score. I grabbed my friend, and it was off to Devinski's to compensate him for lending me his wagon.

That was my first-ever foray into business entrepreneurship, but it gave me a good taste for understanding how money could be made by recognizing opportunity.

A few years passed, my family moved to Calgary. Then around age 10, I developed a renewed desire to make my own money. I surveyed my options, and I quickly discovered that newspaper routes were the number one option for boys in their early teens to earn hard cash. So I had been on the right track five years earlier.

My older brother Shane was 13 years old and he had a paper route. At one point, he started to become disinterested in doing it and he began asking me to deliver it for him occasionally. He wanted to hang out with his friends, play sports, and generally have a good time. I started delivering for him, and as the weeks passed, I ended up delivering his route about four days a week.

I thought about how I would like to have the route for myself, so I asked Shane if I could take it over. He thought this was just fine, and he agreed to hand it over to me. Then we found out that I had to be 12 years old to have the paper route in my own name. I felt completely deflated.

I thought about it for a while. I knew the route generated about a dollar a day, or about 25 dollars a month. So I came up with a deal for Shane.

"Look, what if I rent your paper route from you?" I asked him.

"What do you mean?"

"You keep the paper route in your name, and I'll give you five dollars a month to have the route. You won't have to lift a finger. I'll deliver the papers every day, I'll collect the money, and I'll take full responsibility. I'll give you five bucks a month just for keeping it in your name. And when I turn 12 years old, you let me put the route in my name, and I don't have to pay rent to you anymore."

His face lit up. "Deal!"

There were 43 newspapers on the route. I had two canvas delivery bags, so I would put about 20 papers in each bag. That was generally a comfortable amount if I swung one over each shoulder. Prior to my rental agreement with Shane, I had tied knots in each strap to shorten them, otherwise the bags dragged on the ground. It was uncomfortable because the knots would dig into my back. However, I didn't want to permanently alter the straps because the route and the bags still belonged to my brother.

When I took over the route with our new rental agreement, I had a special moment where I untied the knots in the straps. Now I could really do it right. I folded the straps over onto themselves to shorten them, and then I carefully stitched them up with a needle and thread. These were now my bags and this was now my paper route.

I felt immeasurable pride—and maybe just a bit of fear over the responsibility I had taken on—but I was excited to have ownership of my economic destiny.

As I grew over the next couple of years, I undid the stitching and lengthened the straps on a couple of occasions. I remember customers calling me "the little paperboy" and giving me big tips when I collected their subscriptions each month. They must have felt some degree of pity for me, or maybe it was just the cuteness factor of having a paperboy who was only slightly bigger than the bags he was carrying. I remember at Christmas time, there was one particular house where they would tell me to wait on the doorstep while they fetched me cookies or some sort of present. Those are warm memories.

By the way, I did get a bike of my own eventually. It arrived on Christmas morning when I was six years old in the form of a used blue CCM that was four inches too big. And while it wasn't the red CCM I had dreamed about, I enthusiastically set about learning to ride it by putting my leg through the frame under the cross bar.

I must have looked ridiculous but I didn't care. I loved that bike, and as the snow began to melt in April, a growth spurt put me within striking distance of actually reaching the pedals while properly seated.

And my experience getting robbed of my quarter when I was four years old would continue to linger with me. It hadn't made me determined never to trust anyone again, but the loss and betrayal would remain a pain in my heart's memory for years to come. It would also leave me wondering from time to time whatever became of the boy on the red CCM bike.

Meanwhile, my early entrepreneurial adventures with the newspaper business would predict one of the major emergent themes of my life.

TWO

A New Town

I was in the middle of grade three when my family moved from Edmonton to Calgary in December 1966. My father had accepted a job with the Calgary School Board, and there was a sense of excitement as we began packing up our home in Edmonton. Eventually, we were loading the car for the final journey south, and by New Year's Eve we found ourselves settling into a modest rental house in Calgary's Bridgeland neighborhood.

In short order, my brother Shane and I were enrolled at Stanley Jones School. The building was an austere neoclassical edifice from the time of the First World War built in 1913, and like most old school buildings of that vintage, it was permeated by the traditional smell of sweat, lunchboxes, and disinfectant.

My dad drove us to school on the first day, but thereafter we were left to make our way on our own. Though a little exploration during that first week of January, we soon found our preferred route and the most direct way to and from school. A very steep alley that led down the hill from our neighborhood to Edmonton Trail, a main arterial route that we had to cross to get to our school. Covered in compacted snow, it resembled an Olympic ski jump when you stood at the top of it. It was very steep and very slippery. The first day my brother and I discovered it, we were quite excited. There were bits of cardboard strewn around at the top of the hill and we quickly realized what they were used for. School books under our arms, we would launch ourselves on a piece of old cardboard down the hill at a lightning speed, often spinning round uncontrollably in the process. It was thrilling to start each school day with a solid shot of adrenalin—it definitely helped us in our transition to our new life.

At school, I had to go through all the usual adjustments that kids make when they change schools, including making new friends and learning the laws of the land. I slowly began to know the hallways, the kids, my new classmates. One of my first vivid experiences was recess. The school grounds were covered with compacted snow, and when you looked out across the playing fields, you would see seven or eight circles of kids standing around. Each of those circles was a fist fight. There would be two kids hammering away at each other in the middle, and the rest of the kids would be egging them on. I thought to myself: *Wow, Calgary is one tough town!*

I had never seen anything like it. In Edmonton, I had attended a brand new school that coincidentally my father had designed when he worked with the Edmonton School Board. Our neighborhood had also been new, and life was generally pretty squeaky clean. Calgary seemed to be the complete antithesis. Bridgeland was arguably one of the toughest neighborhoods in the city at the time. On the far east side of town you had Forest Lawn, on the west side you had Bowness, and Bridgeland sat right in the middle. The kids in each of these neighborhoods all guarded their own turf, and we would often hear about carloads of teens coming from one neighborhood to another and having massive rumbles.

In the shadow of the schoolyard violence and the strange new world I had entered, I slowly began to make friends. Two of them were a brother and sister in my class, Kenneth and Caroline. I first started noticing them when I observed that they often didn't have lunch, or their socks either didn't match or had holes in them. I also came to notice that Caroline was very much a mother figure to Kenneth. He had a bit of a speech impediment and a slightly challenged way of walking, and I think he had been held back a year. Despite being younger than him, it seemed that she was often helping him when he had difficulties. Some part of me recognized the tenderness that she displayed towards him, and I was very moved by it.

On more than a few occasions, they arrived at our homeroom class just as the final bell rang. Caroline was often wearing the same tired-looking oversized blue cardigan that looked like it might have belonged to her mother. She always seemed to have her head lowered as she entered the classroom, hiding her eyes from the stares of the other children. As she ushered Kenneth in the door, she would run her fingers through her unbrushed hair in an attempt to make herself a bit more pretty.

Kenneth, Caroline and I started to hang out at recess, and one day they invited me over to their house after school. They lived directly down the hill from the school in the heart of Bridgeland, so it was a simple short walk down to their house. I remember a deep sense of sadness coming over me when we got there. As we entered the house, I saw that half of the windows in the porch were missing and someone had taped cardboard over the holes. The inside wasn't much better. The entire house was run down and decrepit, and there wasn't a sign of a parent anywhere.

Sitting at the kitchen table on chairs that didn't match, Kenneth and I watched as Caroline made peanut butter and jam sandwiches for us. I can't remember whether we watched television or played games after our snack, but eventually it was time for me to go home. As I made my way down the street, I continued to feel a profound sense of lingering sadness. Their situation confused me. I couldn't understand how their mother wasn't present, and I was deeply disturbed that they had to live in such a rundown house. But of course, for them, that was their life—that was their home. They couldn't walk away from it like me.

I crossed Edmonton Trail to the alley. As I ascended the steep incline, I had to walk like a duck on the inside edges of the soles of my shoes to get any traction. As I approached the top of the hill with my head lowered and my eyes focused on my footsteps, my peripheral vision detected an assembly of legs waiting at the summit. I immediately sensed that this wasn't good.

I reached the top and was finally able to lift my head. There were about a half dozen boys blocking my path. One of them stepped promptly forward and swatted my school books out of my hands. I turned and watched them skitter down the alley, a cold sense of fear rising in my chest. I knew I was in for it.

They quickly surrounded me.

"Where are you going?" one boy demanded with an aggressive tone.

I tried to muster my calmest tone of voice. "I'm going h-h-home," I stuttered, partly from lack of oxygen as a result of the climb up the hill and partly out of fear.

"You have to fight one of us," one of the boys said. Remarkably, I felt slightly relieved—he wasn't asking me for my wallet.

I knew that running was not an option. This was their turf and I was seen as an outsider who needed to be made aware of that fact.

I had to make a quick decision. I glanced around and surveyed which of them was the biggest. I knew that if I fought one of the smaller guys, I would just end up having to fight the biggest one afterwards, or on another day. So I pointed at the tallest kid.

Someone murmured something and called him Morocco. He looked like a Morocco. I had no idea that Morocco was a country in North Africa, or even where North Africa was, but this guy definitely looked like he was from somewhere else.

What happened next is a blur to me. Morocco and I fought, but I can't tell you who really had the upper hand. We threw punches and wrestled back and forth, and it was clear that neither of us was going to give up. Eventually a neighbor woman came out of her house with a broom and broke up the fight.

Battered and bloodied, I clambered down the hill to retrieve my school books, and then I made my way back up the alley and home. When I went in the door, my mother and my brother Shane were there. They could see that I was battered and very upset. Shane asked me what had happened. He immediately insisted that we go back to the alley to track down the perpetrators.

It was time for a big brother vendetta. The thing was, all of these guys had been in grade six, and I was only in grade three. But they hadn't known that. I was about 10 inches taller than all of my classmates at the time, so these guys had probably figured I was older.

As we made our way back to the alley, I felt proud. Shane was in grade seven, and he was a pretty stocky guy, so I knew justice would be served. But when we arrived at the alley, no one was there. It was disappointing, but at the same time I felt vindicated. It was the thought that counted.

Funny enough, Morocco and his gang never bothered me after our fight. We would see each other from time to time, but everyone basically kept their distance. I think I must have earned enough respect—and instilled just enough doubt?—to make them think twice before challenging me.

Perhaps it was because I was feeling the change of city and school, and how such moves and life changes can often bring us more in touch with ourselves and those close to us. Of course at the age of 8, I had no knowledge or understanding of meta physical concepts or quantum theory, but something else happened in the first few months of my arrival at Stanley Jones School which would also come to connect me with what I now understand as proof to me of how we are all connected.

It was a grey Calgary morning with an unusually low cloud ceiling—I don't know why I remember this detail but it just stands out. I was standing at one of the three windows in our home classroom watering my bean plant. All of us had planted one single bean seed in a tin can planter a few weeks earlier as one of our science class projects. It was around 10 am, just before morning recess. I suddenly felt a very sharp pain in my heart. It was a sensation I had never felt before. I remember thinking, *hmmm…that was strange…I have never had that feeling before.* When I returned home from school that day, my mother told me that my little sister Brenley, who was 2 years old had been with my mother going to a doctor appointment earlier that day in a family friend's car. When they arrived at the appointment, little Brenley reached for the door handle in advance of my Mom and when the door handle was pulled open, Brenley's thumb was severed. When my Mom told me, I instantly thought back to the pain in my heart I had felt that morning. I remember asking my mom what time it happened—which I'm sure she thought was a strange question under the circumstances, and she said, *"oh it was about 10 am, just before our apt at 10:15"*. At that moment I knew, and I remember feeling a strange sense of connectedness. To be honest, at the time, it seemed a bit strange but cool.

Eventually, we moved out of Bridgeland.

Green Suede Boots

Spring came and we moved to a new suburb being developed on the edge of town. My parents had purchased a 50-foot lot with a plan to build a new house for us to move into. When we moved to our new place in the suburbs, I came to realize that Calgary was no different than Edmonton.

I remember showing up for the first day of grade 4 at F. E. Osborne School in Varsity Acres, fully prepared and ready for a few good rumbles in the schoolyard to secure my place in the social hierarchy. I clearly remember walking down the hall, ready to be singled out, but instead, I discovered that all of the kids were nice. *"How could this be?"* I thought to myself. I began to realize that my former neighborhood of Bridgeland had its own distinct character. The rest of Calgary wasn't that tough.

Now living the quiet suburban life, and free of the worry of choosing a safe route to hobbies. Remarkably, clothing and fashion was one of them.

Looking back now, I find it easy to imagine how I would be somewhat connected to fashion as a form of self expression. In my adult years, I was often surrounded by outside-the-box fashion-forward individuals when I was a recording engineer in Germany, a musician, and even a technology executive. But I actually had an affinity for stylish apparel ranging from cool jackets to distinctive shoes long before I started my own fashion design company. One of my earliest manifestations as a fashionista happened when I was nine in Calgary.

One day during the summer of 1967, between grade three and four, I went to the Hudson's Bay store with my mom. At one point, she drifted into the women's underwear section. Feeling just a bit awkward, I asked her permission to browse the men's department on my own.

I ended up in the men's shoe department in the basement of the store. And as I moved between the aisles of shoes, my eyes suddenly fell upon a pair of green suede cowboy boots.

They were tall, refined, and suave, and the suede seemed to absorb the light very softly. I was enthralled, and I immediately wanted to own them. There was no question for me—they were the most amazing boots I had ever seen.

A sales clerk was organizing the shoe display next to me. I turned to look at him, and my expression of awe must have spoken volumes.

"Wow"—I said almost breathlessly. "These boots are so great. They're *green suede!*"

He simply smiled and went back to organizing his shoe display.

I continued staring dreamily at the boots, and I thought about the guys in *High Chaparral*. In 1967, High Chaparral was a television western series that I watched religiously each week with my brother Shane. I thought the guys on *High Chaparral* were the greatest example of manhood ever seen, and I wanted to be like them. Riding horses and wearing cool boots and cowboy gear. I remember one of the characters, 'Buck', used to wear a very cool Poncho. I eventually got one myself.

As I stood in the shoe department mesmerized by the boots, I thought, "I bet these are the kind of boots that those guys wear in the show!"

Of course, I had no way of knowing, since our black and white television set provided no clue as to whether their boots were green, blue, black, brown, or aqua marine.

I said to the sales clerk, "I really want these boots. How much are they?"

"Nineteen-ninety-five."

It was a meaningful sum, but I realized it was reachable if I managed some clever fundraising.

"I am going to save my money and I'll be back."

I rejoined my mother, and I began plotting as to how I would earn the money to get those green suede boots.

I was already in the habit of making money by collecting pop bottles, cutting lawns, and doing odd jobs around our house or anywhere I could find. But I knew that wasn't going to get me enough money to buy the boots anytime soon.

For the next few weeks, I probably drove my mom crazy by repeatedly asking her if she had anything I could do to make extra money. I think she was always pleased with my enthusiasm and initiative, so she almost always managed to find something for me to do.

But my real break came when I discovered a special sales opportunity that could earn me some serious cold cash.

I remembered that I had seen an advertisement in the back of a comic book for a company called the Youth Sales Club of Canada. Something about earning money with part-time sales. I figured it was worth investigating further. So I went back to my stack of comics, scanned the tiny black print to find the advertisement again, and then proceeded to read each line carefully.

Apparently, if you sent them a letter, they would send merchandise for you to sell on your own, and then you sent them a portion of the sales proceeds. It was sort of like having a newspaper route, except you were selling other bits of merchandise. I figured if there was money in it, I had to give it a try. I wrote a letter to the Youth Sales Club of Canada and posted it.

Within a couple of weeks, a package came to my door. It was a shipment of greeting cards and a letter of welcome to the Club. They also threw in a green pen as my bonus for taking the job. I was *ecstatic*. It all seemed so official and prestigious! Suddenly I felt important, and I was fired up to sell greeting cards like no one had ever done in the history of consumer stationery.

I started going door to door in my neighborhood. I had decided I was going to do a blitz with greeting card sales, and I sold my brains out. My pockets quickly filled with coins and small bills.

All the while, I continued collecting pop bottles as well, and I did anything I thought possible to earn extra money.

After only a few days of receiving my first shipment of greeting cards, I had sold all of them, and I now had a shoebox full of money sitting on my dresser at home.

I had felt strong motivation, to say the least. I knew those green suede boots were waiting for me and I didn't want to risk someone else getting to them before I did.

The next step was to calculate the sales proceeds that I owed to the Youth Sales Club of Canada, and then send the money to their offices in Toronto. Here is how it worked: you *mailed* the cash to them in an envelope.

Seriously.

Those were different times, that's for sure.

About three weeks after I had first seen the green suede boots, I went back to the Hudson's Bay store in downtown Calgary. I walked into the men's shoe department feeling like a king. I was carrying about twenty dollars in my wallet, and that was huge money in 1967. At that time, my weekly allowance was a whopping 75 cents, so those twenty dollars basically represented a half-a-year's salary for me.

As luck had it, the same sales clerk was working that day.

I went up to him. "Okay, I got the money." I pulled out of my wallet and showed him.

His eyes went big, he did a bit of a double take, and then he narrowed his eyes and looked at me. "How did you get the money so fast?"

He was obviously curious to know how a nine-year-old boy could come up with twenty dollars so quickly, so I told him the story.

When I finished, he chuckled softly and smiled. "You're going to go places."

It was a very cool moment for me. Firstly, I felt extremely proud that I had seen something I wanted, and then I went out and earned the money, and now I was walking out of this store with these boots under my arm. And secondly, this adult just paid me a big compliment. I felt ten feet tall.

It was a huge boost to my confidence as a young entrepreneur. There was money to be had if I showed a little bit of effort and guile.

FOUR

First Band

Around the same time that I started strutting in my green suede boots, I also started getting interested in music in a big way. I had already been playing clarinet since I was six years old, so music had always been part of my life. After I started grade five at school, a series of events began to convince me that I wanted to do something more with music than simply learn to play the clarinet.

My mother taught piano lessons in the living room of our home. Our modest bungalow was always full of music. Most days when I came home from school, I would hear her in the living room with her students—99 percent of whom were girls—practicing scales and plunking through their first attempts at Mozart's *Minuet in G Major*. I suppose I could hardly help but have some of it rub off on me. My mother taught everyday after school for two hours, and she used the money to help support the family, but she also used it to pay for music lessons for all of her kids. I think having all of those girls around influenced me when it came time to choose which instrument I wanted to learn. I actually wanted to play the piano, but I associated it with being a girls' instrument, which is total nonsense, but I think my reaction was probably a natural part of being a young boy who didn't want his peers to call him a sissy.

In those early years, my dad was just beginning to build his career as an architect and money was tight. Our music lessons represented a huge financial sacrifice for my parents. However, given that music was something that my mother held as a cardinal value in life, she was determined to make sure that we had opportunities to study music one way or another.

From the very beginning of my music studies, it was clear that my experience was different from most kids. I seemed to *feel* music in a way that other kids my age didn't, and my practicing was more focused and intense. I also enjoyed analyzing songs that I heard on the radio, breaking them down in terms of compositional structure, rhythm, tonality, melody and more. I remember listening to a song on the radio with my friends, and exclaiming with great enthusiasm, "That is just such an amazing song!" And then being greeted by the blank, puzzled stares of my young friends.

I even purchased a transistor radio with the proceeds of my first paper route. It was small, about the size of a 20-pack of cigarettes. I would go to sleep every night with it under my pillow. I think it was a big part of the formative stage of my love of and connection to music.

After grade five started, it was announced that there would be an upcoming "battle of the bands". Kids started talking about how cool it would be to enter a band. For most of them, it was pure fantasy because few of them played instruments. But I actually knew a bit about music, and I also knew a couple of kids who played guitar, bass and drums. I was especially keen to be part of the action, so I was soon forming my first band.

I was the lead singer and my friend Ian Buchanan was the drummer. Ian was a very small kid with hair that looked like Davey Jones from the Monkees. Regardless of any drumming ability, he would have made it into the band on account of his looks alone. He could also play drums quite well, and he scored big points because his parents let us use his basement to rehearse.

We must have driven Ian's parents nuts as we squawked through our five or six song repertoire each week. Still, we were feeling pretty confident.

Our guitar player's name was Craig. He was a tall, skinny blonde guy who also scored points for looking the part. His hair was below his ears—which was considered hippie-like—and it was parted down the middle and dead straight. Craig had a serious acne issue, but we were more than convinced that all the coolness we were going to garnish as young rock gods would all but completely erase those zits in the eyes of the girls.

We didn't have a microphone or any real equipment to amplify my voice, so I used a Sony reel-to-reel tape recorder that had belonged to my grandfather. It had a very simple microphone intended for basic voice memo recordings, but it would actually amplify broadcast your voice when you spoke into it. It had a couple of small built-in speakers, so we cranked the volume knob and I used it as a PA system. My voice came out incredibly distorted, but it seemed to do the job.

Besides, we saw it merely as a short-term workaround. We were pretty certain that it was only a matter of time before we would be playing paying gigs with our own roadies and a professional PA system.

The first song that we learned was "Magic Carpet Ride" by Steppenwolf. In retrospect, the distortion on the Sony reel-to-reel probably helped my voice immeasurably on that tune. The second song we learned was "House of the Rising Sun" by The Animals. We stumbled and plodded through the verses like a thousand garage bands had done before us, and like probably twenty thousand have done since.

I don't think we ever made it to the battle of the bands. In fact, our group was so exceedingly short-lived that we didn't even get around to creating a name for ourselves. However, we had a brief spell of frenetic rehearsals that gave us an aura of coolness and purpose, and they also taught me some early lessons in performance and sound mixing.

And I was seriously bitten. In the handful of weeks that we rehearsed, I discovered that I really liked the feeling of being part of a band, and I loved the experience of creating music.

As the months passed, I continued to absorb popular songs on the radio, drinking them up as if by osmosis and marveling at how they were put together.

The first song that really stopped me in my tracks was "Lay Lady Lay" by Bob Dylan. I was 12 years old, and my mother and I were driving down a steep hill on Home Road into Montgomery, a nearby neighborhood. The car radio was playing, and when "Lay Lady Lay" came on, I absolutely froze in my seat. I thought, *wow, this is incredible.* The song transported me to an entirely different world. For those few minutes, I entered a euphoric state of suspended timelessness.

Shortly thereafter, I heard "Cinnamon Girl" by Neil Young for the first time. It knocked me over. The raw power in the guitar chords, the subtle passion behind the lyrics, the frailty of Neil's voice, and the plain simplicity in the entire composition that held it all together. These experiences sealed the deal for me. I started to feel that creating great songs would be the coolest thing imaginable. And as my teen years unfolded, that feeling played out through my growing desire to write and create my own music.

I wasn't dreaming of being a rock star, and I wasn't thinking about living in a fancy house or driving an expensive sports car. Those things never occurred to me. I simply wanted to write and create great songs that would make an impact. I simply wanted to move people in the same way that "Lay Lady Lay" or "Cinnamon Girl" had moved me. And to this day, I don't think any body of work has probably had such a profound impact on me as Pink Floyds' *Dark Side of the Moon.*

I clearly remember the first time I heard *Dark Side of the Moon.* Despite the fact that I was in an altered state of consciousness.

It was in Penticton the summer of 1973. I had hitch-hiked there from Calgary and met two guys from Vancouver, Les and Bernie, on the beach at Skaha Lake. I was 15 at the time, and Les and Bernie were both in their late teens, perhaps even early twenties. I was a big kid for my age and already shaving, so everyone always thought I was older than I was. After hanging out all day on the beach, they asked me if I had a place to crash. I didn't, so I happily accepted their offer to set up my pup tent on the lawn outside of their rented cabin at the Ogopogo cabins and campground.

There ended up being four or five of us, and we hung out together for a few days. They introduced me to my first real experiences with dope—not to mention copious amounts of beer. These guys would crack open a Heineken at nine o'clock in the morning and start smoking hash immediately. Bernie called this donning his rubber suit. I was a good sport and tried to catch the buzz alongside them, but after a few days I was completely wiped out from sleep deprivation and constant consumption of mind-numbing substances.

It was on the third night when we were sitting in the kitchen of the Ogopogo cabin. Les had backed up his Volvo 144 four-door sedan and opened the trunk to allow the rear speakers to blast all order of super-charged rock and roll directly into the cabin.

I remember sitting there, and running my tongue over my top front teeth from right to left. It felt like my tongue was vibrating like a strobe light. I became absorbed in the experience: *Wow—did my tongue just strobe?*

Suddenly, dozens of alarm bells started ringing and my heart leapt into my mouth.

Oh shit, we're busted.

I looked around at the rest of the guys. No one was moving. It wasn't the police. It was the song "Time" from *Dark Side of the Moon*—the opening sequence where the alarm clocks suddenly start to ring.

I'll never forget the shock it sent through my body. To this day, it remains a seminal moment for me in my understanding of music composition and the art of sound engineering.

I would learn years later that Alan Parsons, who had recorded the album, had gone into a number of clock shops in London to record all order of clocks and timepieces and then layered them together. The result was amazing!

It would still be years before I would really be able tackle the challenge of making my own records. I still had a lot to learn about music, and the business of music in general. But these early experiences with Dylan, Young, and Pink Floyd hooked me for life.

FIVE

Track Champion

With my eclectic background, some people seem surprised when I reveal that I have had a lifelong relationship with sports. It started for me when I was in elementary school, and has been a big part of my life ever since.

Cycling and running are my thing. I have been a keen runner for years, and I have also participated in races and cycled in various places throughout the world. Running and cycling have helped to ground me and maintain a sense of balance through the turbulence of making a living, raising a family, and pursuing all of my various entrepreneurial and passion-filled ventures. Through the years, I have come to realize that I need to nurture the connection between my mind and my body in order to optimize my health, both physical and mental. When I am fit and fresh off a great work out, I feel unstoppable. I know I am not alone in this—everyone on the planet has an intrinsic connection between mind and body—but some have realized it and some haven't.

Through the years, I have had the opportunity to compete in several international triathlons. I've done triathlon courses that range from the Olympic distance—the 1500 meter swim, 40 kilometer bike ride, and 10 kilometer run—up to the slightly more daunting Ironman distance—consisting of a 3.8 kilometer swim, 180 kilometer bike ride, and 42.2 kilometer run. For me, it's never been important to "win". I'm thrilled with simply being able to participate and complete one of these races, never mind placing in the top 10, or even the top 100!

It's about perseverance and self-discipline. And from my earliest days as a track athlete in middle school, these have been probably the biggest lessons that I have taken from sports.

As a kid, I had a couple of extraordinary experiences in sports and athletics that did a lot to shape my entire attitude towards life and adversity. I've drawn upon these lessons many times when I was confronted with a tough decision or a fork in the road.

The first significant experience happened in grade five when I was 10 years old. My family was living in Calgary, and I—along with thousands of other boys—was deep into Canada's greatest pastime: ice hockey.

It's safe to say I was one of the stronger players among my peers. I wasn't a great stick handler, but I was the tallest kid on the team and I was the fastest skater. I used to play defense because nobody could get by me with my long reach and my speed. Other teams would send their best forwards at me, and time after time I would simply smother their attack. They seldom even got close to our goal. Our goalkeeper might as well have been having a coke and a smoke in net, as I saw to it that the other team was never going to get a real shot on him.

During that grade five season, my father arranged a family trip to my hometown, Winnipeg for the Christmas holidays.

In those days, there was no way that your average Canadian family could afford a holiday in Mexico, Hawaii or the Caribbean. People stayed close to home. So it was no surprise that we were driving to see our relatives.

My dad had arranged for us to drive to Winnipeg for five or six days over Christmas, and this meant that I would have to miss a couple of hockey practices. I dutifully advised my coach of the dates that we would away, and I confirmed that I would be missing a couple of practices. He acknowledged what I had said, and I went to Winnipeg with my family.

It was classic. Four kids in the back seat, mom and dad up front. If you have ever had the pleasure of driving across the Canadian prairies in December, you know how the wind can blow constantly some days, and it can carry tons of snow. It creates a textured white blanket across the entire landscape—including the highway—and as the land is as flat as a pancake, it is almost impossible to see where the edge of the highway is. It can be quite nerve-wracking for the driver and even for a 10-year-old passenger!

We enjoyed our typically Canadian Christmas getaway with the extended family and then we drove back to Calgary. Upon our return, I dutifully showed up for hockey practice. As I arrived in the change room at the rink and started to lace up, one of my friends on the team advised me that I had been cut from the select team. I was now on the farm team because I hadn't shown up for those two practices.

First, I was confused. Then I was close to tears.

From what I could understand, the coach's son had always wanted to be on the select team, but he hadn't made the initial cut back in late October. Ever since the tryouts, the coach had been looking for any excuse to get his son onto the team. He even had him tryout as a goalkeeper, but there was no room for him. When I went away to Winnipeg and "missed" practice, it gave him a semblance of an excuse to kick me off. The coach's son was added to the team as the backup goalie, and I ended up with a team of kids who could barely skate.

Soon my upset turned to anger. I was only ten years old, but I phoned the coach to ask him for an explanation. To this day, I still can't believe I had the balls to call him myself.

"How can you put me on the farm team?" I said. "I'm the fastest skater on the team, I work hard, I always show up, I break up every play – how can you kick me off the team?"

"You missed two practices."

"But I told you that I was going to be away!"

"Well, that's just the way it is," he said simply. "You'll just have to play on the farm team for the rest of this year. We'll see where things are at next season."

One of those cocky, pat answers.

"You know what? You won't have to bother," I said. "I quit. I'm not a quitter, but I don't want to be part of this hockey team."

I just couldn't believe that adults could do something like that to a kid, and I knew that I didn't want to be part of it.

Starting that day, I turned my attention to the sports that were offered at school. I knew that they started having school teams in basketball and volleyball in grade seven, complete with team uniforms and all of the prestige that came with representing your school.

Most importantly for me, they would have a track and field team. I had always been the fastest runner in my class, and I couldn't wait to try out for the track team. I liked the competitive framework in track and field. If I won, I got all the glory, and if I lost, it would simply be on my head. I liked that idea. My successes would belong to me, and so would my failures.

It wasn't that I didn't want to be part of a team or a team player. My hockey experience had simply underscored for me the importance of taking full responsibility for myself.

I turned thirteen in March of grade seven, and a few weeks later I was changing into my shorts, runners and t-shirt to tryout for the school track team. I remember the first spots of grass that seemed to take forever to turn green after another long prairie winter, and the smell of the dank wet earth after the last remnants of snow had melted away.

At the tryouts, they lined us up in groups of eight to run the 100-meter sprint. The top three runners would advance to subsequent heats until the final few kids were selected. For me there wasn't much of a question of whether or not I would make the team, as I had demonstrated a lot of natural ability in phys ed class. It was really more a question of which distances were going to be the best for me. I made the team, and I soon found myself training with the four-by-100-meter relay team.

Our relay team was fast, and we did well at a series of qualifying track and field meets around Calgary that spring. We eventually ended up qualifying for the city quarter-finals for the city, and that was exciting for us. However, along the way, our track coach also had me try the 400-meter event. And I ran it well. In fact, I ran it so well that he decided that my new event was the 400-meter, much to my chagrin.

As anyone who has run the 400-meter knows, it's a hard race. It's basically a sprint all the way around the track. I was not very happy with this outcome, though no one would ever have known. I was glad to be on the team, and I accepted the fact that I was the best person to run the event, and I enjoyed some pride and esteem by having that recognition.

Besides, I figured out that there was a distinct advantage to running the 400-meter. Most of the fastest runners wanted to be sprinters, and they preferred the 100-meter distance because it was over quickly. It also had a lot of glory attached to it: the sprinters were always regarded as rock stars. From what I could see, this meant the competition for the 400-meter was thinning.

I ran the 400-meter at the city quarter-finals and I won, so I progressed to the city semi-finals. Then I ran the city semi-finals and I won there as well, so I advanced to the city finals at Glenmore Park.

On a scorching hot day in June, I took second place in the 400-meter city final, losing to a boy who went to Milton Williams High School just off of Glenmore Trail in Calgary.

I was reasonably happy with the result, and I was proud because my mom and dad had been in the stands to watch me. But I sensed that I could do even better if I wanted to. I thought to myself: next year I'm going to train even harder, and I'm going to win this.

Grade eight arrived, Christmas came and went, and I started to set my sights on the spring track season. Easter vacation was early that year, and as soon as we were back in school, I began training again.

There was still snow on the ground when I started running around the field at F.E. Osborn Jr High School in northwest Calgary by myself. Our house backed onto the school ground, so I started training on my own about a month before the track team had even started to assemble. By the time the school team began to train, I was in flying form. I could taste it that spring, and this time I was not going to see the back of any jersey in the City final. Nothing but that medal for first place.

And I worked hard. I trained and trained and trained. And one day at a noon team practice, our coach, Mr. Don Daum, shouted across the field to me. "Holden, get over here," he yelled.

I jogged over and I saw that he had the grade seven four-by-100-meter relay team lined up on the track. "Let's see you run your 400-meter against these guys."

I thought: *Oh God*. But I didn't want to say no, because this was the coach asking me.

"Uh...okay," I replied with more than a hint of hesitation.

I took my starting position on the track. And I waited for the signal from Coach Daum.

When he said go, I sprang so quickly from the blocks that you'd have thought someone had hit me with an electric cattle prod. I immediately began to accelerate past the first runner alongside me. Then the second, then the third, then the fourth as they stood in their transition zones waiting for the passing of the baton. And when I crossed the finish line, I was a full 10 meters ahead of their anchor runner.

Coach Daum looked at me. "I think you're ready."

We started the spring track season and I raced at all of the qualifying meets for the next month. Soon I was getting ready for the city quarter-finals again, and I felt more prepared than I had ever felt.

The quarter-finals were at Foothills Park that year. The meet was in the afternoon, and it was a perfect sunny day without a cloud in the sky or even a trace of wind. This was very unusual for Calgary, which almost always saw a steady breeze blowing. And I felt great.

We took our starting positions for the 400-meter. I put my head down, my body coiled like a spring. I breathed easily and waited in anticipation for what seemed like an eternity. The starter's gun rang out, and I shot out of the blocks.

I absolutely flew around the track. There were practically flames and sparks coming off the soles of my shoes.

And I placed second.

Second. I was devastated. After my results from the previous year, and after all of the training I had done since Easter, it felt like I had come last. I knew the top two finishers in each heat advanced to the next round, so I was through to the semifinals, but it provided cold comfort. I thought to myself, that's it. I can't even win the quarter-final? How can I have any hope of winning the city championship?

The worst part was the guy who beat me. His name was Brad Lomheim. I'll never forget him. He had blond hair that was cut just over his ears. In those days, long hair was just starting to happen. You had to fight with your parents if you wanted to have your hair go past your ears even a tiny bit. He had bangs with a wave in them, he was tall and skinny, he wore glasses, and he had the usual compliment of teen age boy acne. He went to Simon Fraser Junior High School. And he *smoked*.

The result shook me to the core. I left the meet in a trance, absorbed in dark thoughts.

When I arrived home, no one was there, and a strange dead silence permeated the house.

I slipped my shoes off at the front door and I went into the living room. I saw my mother's favorite chair in the corner. It was an upholstered armchair with a white background and floral print, and it rocked back and forth. It wasn't a recliner, but it was quite comfortable. She had bought it for herself at Sager's Maple Shop, and it was very popular with all of us, but this day it was all mine.

I sat down and put my feet up on the chair, which is something that I never did. But I instinctively drew myself up into a fetal position, with my knees to my chest and my arms wrapped around them. And I was in tears.

I sat there thinking to myself about what had happened. I felt like I was at a fork in the road.

I felt myself being pulled in two directions. One choice was just to quit track and start hanging out with my friends. I liked socializing, so maybe that was the thing to do. Start hanging out at 7-Eleven with the cool guys. It had been great doing track last year, and I had a laugh, and a bit of glory coming in second in the city finals, but maybe I wasn't really one of those people. Maybe I wasn't really so sporty after all. Maybe I just wanted to hang out with my buddies. I could easily dismiss the sporty thing and blow it off as simply a phase I went through.

Seriously, these were the thoughts that were running through my head.

And then on the other hand, I had this thought: if you think you've trained hard up to now, you haven't seen anything yet.

The reality was that the quitting option really didn't sit well with me. I couldn't see myself just hanging around and being one of the dudes. I had already started to establish a hunger for setting goals and then going after them.

So I chose door number two. I decided right then that there was no way that I was going to let this skinny guy who smoked beat me and destroy my dream to win the city championship.

I started training with renewed intensity and determination. The next day before school, I put on my dad's steel-toed work boots and ran eight-by-60-meter repeats on the school soccer field until I collapsed.

I continued the routine every day for the next two weeks leading up to the city semi-finals. One morning I ran thirty-two laps of the soccer field, which was about eight miles.

I trained very hard. I was possessed.

Finally, the day of the semi-finals arrived. I had to run three heats that Friday, and I was very nervous. We didn't run until about 4:30 in the afternoon, so I had all day to lose a bunch of energy. With proper competition preparation, all of us should have stayed off our feet for the hours leading up to the race, but in those days we didn't have a clue about pre-competition routines, and we just tried to stay busy. I was probably out having a slurpy and doing everything wrong.

But when we finally ran, I won hands down. I was given an inside lane, so that helped a little. But I had qualified for the city final for the second year in a row. And I had been able to do it by running my heat just fast enough to win. I didn't really have to stretch myself.

I was now on my way to the city final for the 400-meter event, which was scheduled for the very next day, Saturday, at about eleven o'clock in the morning.

This time I wasn't so lucky with my lane assignment. I was given lane number eight on the outside of the track. This is never desirable because you can't see any of your competitors as you are running, so it makes it very difficult to know where you are in relation to everyone else.

I had to create a strategy. I knew that I had a great stride in the straight stretches, so I planned to extend my stride on the back stretch as much as possible. If I was going to get out in front of my competitors, I had to get it done before the last turn. Once I entered that final curve, I knew I would be huffing and puffing, and my legs would be numb, and my lungs would be burning, and it would be a difficult enough job just to hold off any late drives for the finish line.

The race marshal summoned us to our starting positions, and I settled into the blocks in lane number eight. I cast one quick glance over my shoulder to see the field of runners in the lanes behind me as I heard the race marshal announce:

On your marks. Get set.

I exploded out of the blocks and powered through the first curve with the wind in my hair. I had to fight the temptation to look over my shoulder to check on the other runners. I always remembered the epic race between Roger Bannister and John Landy that had taken place in Empire Stadium in Vancouver on August 7, 1954 as both runners attempted the impossible task (at the time) of breaking the four-minute mile. Landy had made the mistake of looking over his shoulder at precisely the wrong moment, and Bannister had made his move and never looked back. The result was one for the history books.

I entered the last turn, and my breathing was quickly becoming hard and labored. I could hardly feel my legs as I came out of the curve into the final stretch. I could hear the other runners behind me, but I couldn't see how close they were. As I came into the final stretch, I took a chance and looked over my left shoulder. I was well ahead of everyone.

Still, I could feel that I might not last the final 70 meters. I pressed with everything that I had in my body, and when I lunged for the finish line, I almost collapsed. I was completely spent.

People were applauding and cheering, but I could barely focus as my lungs struggled for oxygen and the blood pounded in my head. I walked around trying to catch my breath and cool down, and then I walked over to the stands and waved at my folks. My teammates came to give me a pat on the back, and my coach approached me to shake my hand.

It was a powerful moment. My coach had always taken a special interest in me, and it meant a lot for me to get his acknowledgment. He had been yelling at the top of his lungs as I came out of the final turn and into the home stretch. He was looking at his stopwatch screaming, "You've got a record!"

I not only won the city final, but I broke the city record in the 400-meter for my age category. I won by a couple of seconds, and my closest competitor was 15 feet behind me. I set the new city record, and apparently it stood for several years.

It was truly one of the most rewarding moments of my entire life. I had come back from the brink of quitting to win the championship.

Brad Lomheim, by the way, got knocked out in the semifinals. It seems he had simply had a good day at the quarter-finals, whereas I had probably just had a bad day. But I didn't possess the training experience to realize that. Chalk one up for blissful ignorance.

So I probably hadn't needed to worry as much as I did after placing second in my quarter-final heat. Nonetheless, the shock had spurred me to push harder and reach higher, and the whole experience subsequently created a permanent shift in my attitude towards the obstacles and challenges in my life. Ever since then, anytime I have had to make a decision about whether or not to chicken out and take the easy route, or choose the difficult route in pursuit of an important goal, I have chosen to do the work.

And it all started with my hockey coach cutting me from the hockey team back in fifth grade. Perhaps things happen for a reason.

SIX

Primal Terror

I got up that Saturday morning in October with a sense of anticipation. The leaves were changing color in Calgary, and there was a cool crispness in the air that said winter was on its way. I was fifteen, and I had set my sights on an overnight camping trip on Victoria glacier, high above magnificent Lake Louise, Alberta.

I wanted to do something different, something brave, something that would test my mettle as a young man. So on this particular Friday night, instead of going to one of several house parties that were happening, I had decided I would stay home and prepare for my hitchhiking adventure to Lake Louise, two hours away in the Rockies.

I was well equipped. I left the house carrying a backpack, sleeping bag, tent, small camp stove, and a few cans of beef stew that I had wrangled from the basement food supply that my parents maintained in case of nuclear war or similar emergency. With my load harnessed to my back, I walked down Home Road into Montgomery until I reached the Trans-Canada Highway, the road to the majestic Rockies, and I put out my thumb.

During the summer, I had discovered that being polite had given me a distinct advantage over other hitchhikers. I employed the same technique this day by crafting a sign out of cardboard that simply said, "Please". As I had learned previously, when I held up this message with a smile on my face, it usually only took a few cars before someone pulled over.

I remembered an occasion that previous summer when I had hitchhiked to Penticton in British Columbia, and I got stuck in the town called Hope. The name was ironic as it was a notoriously bad place for hitchhikers to get a ride. That day had been no exception. Even with my "please" sign, I found myself still standing on the side of the road in Hope almost 36 hours later.

I finally decided to walk awhile and look for a fresh stretch of highway. Some minutes later, I came around a corner and saw road construction up ahead. There was a large sign posted which read, "Road construction ahead – proceed with caution".

I immediately had an idea. I flipped the "please" sign over and wrote something that I felt would get a quick response:

Hi – I'm Caution.

When the next set of cars straggled through the segment of road construction, it was almost the first car in line that stopped to pick me up. The driver said my sign was just too clever not to acknowledge.

Now in the Alberta autumn on the side of the Trans Canada, I was confident that my "please" sign should be enough, and it was. I quickly snagged a ride, and my host kindly dropped me off at the edge of the town of Lake Louise.

As the car pulled away, I turned around slowly to take in the scenery. The Rockies now towered above me, and I was surrounded by a vast expanse of emerald forest. I drew a long breath of the cool mountain air, and the awareness settled into my consciousness: I was on my own, in the mountains, and no one would be cooking my dinner tonight.

I slung my backpack onto my back, and I started walking up to the Chateau Lake Louise.

The Chateau Lake Louise sits on the shore of the lake, a gleaming monument of human civility in stark contrast with the surrounding wilderness. At the opposite end of the lake, Victoria Glacier rises above icy waters to straddle the mountainside. The glacier was where I was heading.

I walked the path around the lake, and then I ascended the trail to the glacier, passing the teahouse along the way. I arrived at the glacier by about three o'clock in the afternoon, and the daylight was already starting to fade. I knew I would have to move quickly to set up my tent otherwise I would be left fumbling in the dark and cold.

The tent was something my father had bought. It was called a "mountain tent" and it was designed to accommodate two people, presumably on their ascent to Everest or Kilimanjaro. I remember my dad being very excited about it when he brought it home because it represented the apex of camping equipment at the time. Looking back at it now, and comparing it with today's technology, it would be a lead anchor. It was made of heavy canvas, and it wouldn't have afforded much protection in a serious downpour.

It was kind of like a pup tent. It had a relatively tall peak at the entrance, and then it sloped down towards the back to a height of about eighteen inches. The idea was that there was very little air space where your feet were, a design feature intended to conserve heat by reducing the volume of airspace inside.

"What's neat about this tent is that it doesn't even have a tent pole," my dad had told me. "They're saving on weight. When you set up, you have to go and find a tree or a branch and make your own pole."

You were supposed to find a long stick or cut a branch, and that would be your main tent pole at the front. For the back, you were simply supposed to tie it to a nearby tree.

Well, something remarkable happened as I was setting up the tent.

I was on the top of the glacier, looking down at Lake Louise stretched out below me, and taking in this magnificent sight. But I knew the sun was setting, and it was already getting cold, so I needed to set up quickly.

And I suddenly realized: *Damn. I'm on a glacier well above the tree line. What am I supposed to use for a tent pole?*

I turned slowly around to survey the barren terrain. And there it was. No more than two or three hundred meters away, just above the trail where I had been walking, I saw a single, dead tree amidst the bare rock and glacial till.

It was just about the strangest piece of serendipity you could imagine. This tree was about two and a half inches in diameter, about six feet tall, and it was clearly deceased. It was missing most of its branches, and there wasn't a single pine needle left on it.

It gave me the strange feeling that some intelligence was watching out for me. It was like the universe had arrived at the office that morning, checked the day's agenda, and said, "This guy's going to need a tent pole, so we'll just plunk this down for him here."

It was the only piece of organic material up there, other than me and my beef stew. And I'm still not sure about the beef stew.

I took my hatchet and chopped the thing down. And suddenly I had my tent pole. It even provided enough material for me to cut a small pole for the rear of my tent, because there sure as hell wasn't another tree around to tie it to.

I got the tent and my camp set up, and then I sat down to survey the vast panorama in the last rays of daylight. It started to dawn on me what I had done and where I was.

I am on top of a glacier. Now what?

I decided to eat. I set up my little gas camp stove and heated up some beef stew, and I watched the twilight disappear as I dined. Below me, the Chateau Lake Louise slowly lit up. It sparkled in the deepening darkness at the end of the smooth black expanse of water. The air grew colder and my breath created clouds of vapor.

By eight o'clock, it was already night. So I crawled into my sleeping bag, and I drifted into a peaceful sleep.

Around midnight, I awoke suddenly. My senses were stirred by the sound of something moving outside my tent. A light crunching sound in the thin skiff of snow. Steadily and cautiously, something was walking around my tent.

Oh shit.

As a seasoned camper and a Boy Scout, I had taken the proper precautions to move my food about 30 feet away from the tent. I knew the usual practice was to hang it in a tree so it wouldn't attract bears and other animals, but of course there were no trees where I was camping.

I didn't know what was outside my tent, but I didn't think it was a bear. The footsteps seemed too light and delicate. But it wasn't a rabbit, either. It was definitely bigger than that.

It didn't make any sound other than the light, stealthy crunch of each footstep.

What was it?

I had never in my life been as frightened as I was then. I began to sweat despite the intense cold, and my heart felt like it was going to burst right out of my rib cage. I has thinking: if I have an encounter with a wild animal up here, I've got a two-and-a-half-hour hike down the mountain to the chateau. I'm screwed!

So I stayed as still and quiet as I could. I listened anxiously as my visitor walked around a few times. And then, finally, it left.

I was so full of adrenalin that it took a while for my heart rate to return to normal. Then, exhausted both physically and mentally, I fell back asleep.

At the first light of dawn the next morning, I got up and looked outside my tent. My tent was circled with a series of distinctive footprints in the snow. Cougar tracks.

As I looked at the size of the paw prints, I tried to imagine the cat that made them. If I had encountered this animal on the mountain trail, it could have been curtains for me.

The air was cold and crisp, and I was fully awake. I looked down at the lake beneath me, smooth as glass in the early morning, the pristine reflection of the chateau stretching across its surface. And I slowly felt a profound calm contentedness flow through me.

I ate a little food, and then I packed up my tent and made my way down the trail again. I felt triumphant as I walked back through the woods along the lakeside trail and came across the first day hikers on their way up the mountain. I made my way back to the chateau and civilization. From there, I headed down to the highway, and I stuck my thumb out to hitch back to Calgary.

I was sitting on my backpack on what I thought was the paved shoulder of the highway. In retrospect, I realize there was something a bit odd about this particular little stretch of pavement I was sitting on, but it didn't occur to me at the time. I was there for about fifteen minutes when an unmarked RCMP patrol car pulled up about two feet away from me.

I thought to myself: *Oh man, I'm in trouble.*

It was instinctive: If the police were stopping, I must be doing something wrong, right?

I could just hear the phone call: "Hello, Mrs. Holden. This is the Lake Louise RCMP. We have arrested your son Mark for hitchhiking."

I don't think hitchhiking was illegal at that time, but I naturally assumed that I must have transgressed some law. I had made it through the night on the glacier at 9500 feet, and survived a potential cougar attack—well, in my mind anyways—only to get arrested now for hitchhiking, or vagrancy, or something.

The officer got out of his car and walked up to me slowly.

"You know, this isn't the shoulder," he said. "You're sitting in the middle of a traffic lane. If you stay here you're going to get hit."

It turned out that I was sitting in the middle of a merge lane for an entrance ramp to the highway, and I hadn't noticed. I was just lucky that another car hadn't come along already doing fifty miles an hour.

"Oh my gosh! I'm so sorry, officer!" I said in a slight panic. "I'll just move onto the gravel shoulder. I'll be more careful!" I got up and started to move towards the gravel shoulder.

He looked me up and down, took in my camping backpack and sleeping bag. "Where are you going?"

"I'm going to Calgary."

"Do you live there?"

"Yes."

He motioned to his patrol car. "Hop in. I'll take you as far as Banff."

I threw my pack in the back and I climbed into the front passenger seat. Suddenly I was rolling down the Trans-Canada Highway towards Banff in an unmarked RCMP patrol car—my own personal police escort!

I told the officer about my adventure on the glacier, and he chuckled. He ended up being a really cool guy. Any prejudice or apprehension I might have felt previously towards the police was completely undone.

We were somewhere between Lake Louise and Banff when we came up behind someone speeding.

"If you don't mind, I might as well do a little work while we're driving," he said.

He reached down, grabbed a little red siren, and he plunked it down onto a metal receptacle on the dashboard. He hit a switch, and suddenly the car siren was wailing and the lights were flashing. He hit the accelerator and my body pressed back into my seat.

As we caught up with the other car, I felt like the cat that ate the mouse. How cool was this! It was like *Starsky and Hutch*.

He pulled the speeder over, gave the guy a ticket, and then we were on our way to Banff again.

He dropped me off at the traffic circle that marked the entrance to Banff, and I thanked him once more.

He chuckled. "Don't let me catch you sitting in the middle of the highway again!" Then he turned his patrol car around and headed back up the highway towards Lake Louise. I watched as his red taillights disappeared.

I hoisted my pack again and walked into Banff.

I went directly to a bakery I liked on Main Street. It was called Pop's Bakery, and it was a bit of a fixture in the town of Banff, but it's no longer there. I went in to buy a loaf of bread. Can you believe it? At the age of fifteen? Not donuts, not pastries, not cookies or cake.

Here's the backstory. They had this amazing multigrain bread with raisins and walnuts in it, and whenever I went to Banff I would buy that bread. This was long before the days of designer breads, whole foods, and any thought of things being organic or not.

Bread loaf in hand, I walked back up to the Trans Canada and stuck my thumb out again. I would take this loaf back to Calgary to share with my family. My Father particularly loved this bread.

I arrived home before dinner, and I recounted my adventure on the mountain and my encounter with the law. The next morning, my dad and I ate the bread with breakfast, and he thought it was amazing. He chewed thoughtfully and asked me more about my adventure in Lake Louise. After that breakfast, whenever we went to Banff, we would always make a point of going into Pop's Bakery together to buy a loaf of that bread.

My father was pleased that I had enjoyed my time in Lake Louise and that I had taken the initiative to go on my own. My mother, on the other hand, said she felt like she had aged ten years. I think I made the mistake of sharing the story of my encounter with the cougar with her, and of course she just about had a fit. God bless her, though. She had still trusted me enough to let me go in the first place, and she continued to let me do things that I'm sure were extremely difficult for her even after my Lake Louise trip. She was selfless enough to let me take those risks.

To this day, if someone were to ask me what has been the most frightening moment of my life, one of the top contenders would be that night on the glacier with the cougar. I've been frightened at other times during my life, and we all fear different things for different reasons, but that was just pure, raw, primal terror. I had never experienced anything like it before, and I can't recall any experience of similar magnitude since.

And then there was the tree. Finding that single, dead tree at the edge of the glacier above the tree line was just too weird. At the time, I didn't think too much about it, but it has since struck me just how remarkably coincidental it was that I found a single, solitary dead tree with perfect dimensions to use for my tent poles. I still think the universe was taking care of me.

SEVEN

Jane

The 1970s was the decade when North American college kids started to travel to Europe in big numbers. Prior to that time, European travel had been more or less restricted to a privileged few. Now anyone with a backpack, a sleeping bag, and the desire could save a few bucks and become a wayward explorer of exotic foreign locales, including me.

When I was 17, I took a semester off from high school with the idea of going to Europe. The year was 1975, and I had been talking with friends about travelling to Europe together.

As usual, everyone was totally into it when we first started talking, and there was a great buzz among us for several weeks that spring. But as had happened previously with many of our best laid plans, the enthusiasm fizzled out pretty quickly for many of the guys as they realized the costs involved, and the limited interest they really had in travelling with backpacks to places where no one spoke your language.

So once again, I found myself flying solo. But I was fine with that. I continued to lay out my plans to buy a round trip ticket to Madrid and a three-month rail pass which would give me complete freedom of movement in Europe.

I consulted some backpacking travel books, and I bought myself a copy of Europe on 10 Dollars a Day. (It would become my bible for that trip.) And on July 13, 1975, I flew from Calgary to Spain.

I don't know why I picked Madrid, other than the fact that I had always been fascinated by the name. That was about as much of a reason as I needed in those days. I had never been outside of North America, but with my backpack and a guitar in hand, I felt like I was ready to take on the world.

I arrived in Madrid in the evening. I passed through customs, collected by things, and I stepped out of the terminal building into the dry evening air of Spain. It was about 7 p.m., and the light shone with that beautiful 'magic hour' golden soft light.

I had been told not to trust taxi cabs because they often ripped off tourists. So I simply started walking from the Madrid Barajas Airport towards downtown.

I wasn't thinking too clearly. I hadn't thought to ask how far it was into the city, and I later found out that it was about 15 kilometers away.

I set off and soon found myself in a very rough neighborhood. I only walked a few blocks before some kids started throwing rocks at me. I definitely felt unsafe, so I quickly turned around and hightailed it back to the airport.

Upon arriving at the terminal building again, I discovered that there was a convenient and inexpensive shuttle bus to the train station where I wanted to go. Imagine that. An airport shuttle bus. These Europeans might know something about travel after all.

I didn't actually have plans to stay in Madrid. I had planned simply to arrive there as my port of entry into Europe. The first destination that I actually wanted to visit was Grenoble, France, but my plan was to arrive in Madrid and take the train to France. Crazy, but it shows how my mind worked as a teenager.

Choosing Grenoble had been the product of another odd bit of reasoning. Quite simply, Grenoble was the only city in France that I had really heard much about. I had an uncle who had lived there once, so the name was lodged in my brain. It's funny how we will sometimes grab onto the smallest thing to feel a sense of connection. I had also heard vague stories about strange cheeses, wine, pretty girls, and exotic accents in Grenoble, and that was enough to intrigue me.

I finally arrived at the Madrid train station, and I proceeded to make another display of my ignorance in travel.

Somehow I arrived at a small side entrance as opposed to the main entrance. However, I didn't know that. So I entered through the small side door, and I found myself looking over the tracks instead of the main passenger lounge.

I didn't think too deeply about it. I knew that there were no trains running until the next morning, so I sat down there in the dirty little alcove by the door and basically stayed awake all night. I'm not sure why I didn't go to a youth hostel, but I guess I didn't really know what to do. I was just a young guy who had never been to Europe, and I had neglected to think in advance about accommodation and food. I also hadn't learned to consult my travel guidebook yet.

I think I managed to grab a couple of hours of fitful sleep that night as I curled up in the alcove. In the early hours of the next morning, I slung my backpack over my shoulders trudged around the perimeter of the station until I managed to discover the main passenger area. From there I looked up and saw beautiful modern escalators and clean passenger lounges with soft, clean seats and carpeted areas.

If I had just explored a little bit more last night, I would have been ten times more comfortable.

That was my lesson on my first night in Europe: when you arrive in a new place, take a minute to scope things out. You might discover that there's something important just around the corner if you take the time to explore. This lesson would serve me well for the remainder of my trip and indeed my entire life.

I found a ticket booth, purchased my passage to Grenoble, and soon I was boarding the train north. I watched the suburbs of Madrid roll past my window, and then the arid plains of central Spain, and I settled into restful repose with the soothing sound of the tracks and the gentle rocking of the train.

Spanish trains were famous for being slow, late, and hot. This trip proved no exception.

It was around 11 p.m. when I arrived in Grenoble. On the train, I had met another Canadian who was travelling solo like me. His name was Peter, and he was from Windsor, Ontario. We decided that we would try to find a hostel. I pulled out *Europe on 10 Dollars a Day*, and we started looking for restaurants and youth hostels in Grenoble, along with what buses to take, prices, and all the other relevant details.

By midnight, Peter and I found ourselves standing at a bus stop near the train station. There was another guy waiting who looked like Al Pacino in the movie *Serpico*. Dark beard, curly hair, olive skin. He looked at us when he heard us speaking English.

"Where are you guys from?"

We told him we were from Canada, and it turned out he was from Lebanon. His name was Cham, and he was studying at the University of Grenoble. He was just a couple of years older than us.

"Where are you staying?" he asked finally.

We explained that we were going to the youth hostel, and he immediately made a gesture with his hands as if to stop us.

"Don't do that! Please, come and stay with me at my place."

He seemed entirely sincere, and there was a good chance that staying in someone's apartment would be more interesting and more comfortable than a hostel, so we jumped on the bus and went to his place.

Cham had a one-bedroom apartment. As soon as we arrived, he went straight to the kitchen. "You must be hungry," he said.

He opened his cupboards and his fridge, and he proceeded to empty everything onto the kitchen table. Absolutely everything. He didn't have very much, but he was offering all that he had to these two strangers from Canada.

Cham motioned to the table and looked at us with big, earnest eyes. "Please eat! You must be hungry from your trip."

He was right about that. So we ate an assortment of cheese, bread, olives and cold meat until we were full. After we had cleaned up, he motioned to some space on the floor in the living area where we could roll out our sleeping bags for the night.

As we settled down to go to sleep, he asked us about our plans for the next day. We were vague on what we planned to do, as we were basically just making it up as we went.

"Do you want to go camping tomorrow?" he asked. "Do you want to go camping up to the Bastille?"

The Bastille was the old fort that sat on the rocky hill directly above Grenoble, but it was also the name generally associated with the craggy hill itself.

"Sure! That sounds cool." It wasn't as though we had created any sort of firm itinerary for our travels, so this was a welcome invitation for an adventure.

The next morning, we went downtown to shop for food to take with us. In the market, I tasted Camembert cheese for the first time in my life and briefly wondered if it was supposed to be as gooey as it was. It was just one of the many things that would be a first for me on this trip, along with cappuccino and fresh tuna that wasn't from a tin.

We rode the gondola up to the top of the Bastille, and we took in the sweeping views of Grenoble and the surrounding valley. Cham pointed to some caves several hundred meters away that were carved into the mountainside about us.

"We'll sleep in those caves tonight," he said.

As we walked along the path crowded with locals and sightseeing tourists, I noticed a very well dressed young girl who was about my age or maybe a few years older. She was perfectly groomed. I especially remember her perfectly-fitting French jeans, tightly rolled at the ankle, and her cork platform sandals, plus a halter top made of some sort of woven natural fiber. It was a far cry from what I knew back in Canada. I remember thinking to myself, *wow, these French girls really know how to dress.*

To get to the caves, we hiked across a beautiful alpine meadow dotted with craggy outcroppings of rock. The caves had been part of the fortifications for the Bastille for centuries, and in my imagination I envisioned them once having been occupied by prehistoric man. Of course, I couldn't find evidence to support this theory, but I went with it anyway. And now they were accommodation for anyone who was adventurous enough.

We ended up camping there for two nights. All the while, it seemed as though we were hovering like birds in the sky over top of Grenoble.

The entire experience was amazing, but most of all, I couldn't believe our host's generosity. I was dumbstruck that we could be greeted by a complete stranger and treated with such consummate hospitality and kindness. This was right at the outbreak of the civil war in Lebanon, and the image of the country would soon become synonymous with violence, destruction and suffering. Yet here was this stranger named Cham who obviously had nothing but the kindest intentions. It provided me with my first glimmer of awareness that there were good people everywhere in the world, irrespective of color or creed.

I tripped around France for a couple of weeks after my camping trip with Cham, and then it was time to head north to Scandinavia. I had a rail pass, and I was intent on making the most of it.

I got to Oslo, Norway after days of sleeping while sitting up on trains, as well as crowded youth hostels in rooms with 12 guys, half of them snoring, I took a notion that I would go up to the tiny city or Narvik, which was about 200 miles north of the Arctic Circle. I had just missed the midnight sun, but I figured it would be really cool to go up there. At that time, it was the most northerly point that you could reach by train in Norway.

I bumped into another backpacker who told me that it was possible to buy a private sleeping birth on the train for an extra five bucks. I would get a bunk, and it would allow me to grab some decent sleep on the overnight trip. So that's exactly what I did. I left Oslo on the train and drifted deep into dreamland as the train rolled northwards. It never felt so sweet to get a good night's sleep.

After Narvik, I worked my way through a bunch of other countries, including Holland, Germany, France, Greece and Spain.

I loved Greece—the authenticity and warmth of the people, the exotic quality of real Greek food. Growing up in the Canadian prairies, the typical Greek restaurants had seemed to be a hybrid between modified Italian cuisine and a pizza parlor.

As I made my way into Athens from the coast, I walked straight into a student demonstration in Syntagma Square and experienced the remnants of tear gas. Painful stuff. It pretty much stopped me in my tracks. After sitting on the curb for some time waiting for the tears to stop, I made my way to a budget hostel called John's Place.

In the hostel, I languished on my bunk in a room on my down-filled sleeping bag in the 40-degree August heat. As I lay there perspiring and struggling to breath, I thought, *it's time to head for the islands.*

After exploring the Acropolis and the Parthenon, I made my way to the port of Piraeus and caught a ferry to Naxos. I camped on a beach on Naxos for a week, and then I made my way to Ios, known as the party island. It was one night on Ios that I actually fell asleep on a park bench due to over-consuming retsina, a wine flavored with pine resin having no recollection whatsoever how I got there. That was a first!

From Ios, I made my way to the island of Crete and the seaside holiday town of Matala. Everyone was talking about Matala. It was known for its beaches and the caves in the area, and it was also well known to young North American hipsters for the song "Carey" by Joni Mitchell. She wrote the song when she was there, and she sings a line where she refers to being "beneath the Matala moon." Even in 1975, it was already considered one of Joni Mitchell's best songs. I figured that was a good enough reason for me to go there. I spent a few days hanging out and enjoying the funky energy provided by the wide array of backpackers.

I made my way back up to Athens. I decided to skip over Santorini because it was packed with tourists. My travel criteria in Greece was essentially "islands without airports". I quickly discovered that if it had an airport, it would be overrun with tourists and commerce.

I made my way back to Spain and landed in Barcelona. I spent about a week in a town just south of Barcelona called Sitges. From there I had planned to take the ferry over to the Balearic Islands, Majorca and Ibiza, but I found that I was getting a bit low on cash and decided to head straight down to Morocco.

I made my way south to the town of Algeciras across from Gibraltar. From there, I took the ferry across the straits to the Spanish city of Ceuta on the coast of North Africa, bordering Morocco. Ceuta had a strange and lengthy history as a strategic port for many different cultures, including the Romans and the Carthaginians, but it had already been Spanish for about 300 years by the time I arrived. The presence of a Spanish city in North Africa continues to be a strange artifact of European colonial history.

Once I reached Ceuta, I caught the bus to Tetouan in Morocco. And that was my first experience with serious culture shock.

As we drove through Ceuta, it was clear from the architecture and the roadways that we were still in a European city. Then we arrived at the border with Morocco.

To cross the border, everyone had to get off the bus and walk through the small border crossing. We were asked to put our backpacks on a little conveyor with metal rollers, and the border guards basically slid them across the border. We passed through a gate on foot, collected our bags on the other side, and then we got back on the bus.

My senses were suddenly overwhelmed. In 1975, Morocco was still exotic and even a bit wild, especially for someone like me who had blue eyes and long blond hair half way down his back. And I was travelling by myself, so I really stood out.

The bus started rolling down the road again towards Tetouan. I peered out the window, and it was clear that we weren't in Spain any longer. There were goats and chickens wandering on the side of the road, and I saw men sitting by themselves with what looked like a burlap sack on their head, often with their eyes glazed white from vitamin deficiency. I was shocked and a bit freaked out by what I saw. As a middle class Canadian kid, and I had never seen anything like it.

We arrived in Tetouan around nine thirty that night. The bus was immediately swarmed by 15 or 20 little kids at the station. As the passengers exited the bus, the kids would basically try to grab each person's backpack and carry it for them, and then they would want money for their services. Many of the kids spoke phrases of English, Spanish, French and other languages. Using their limited command of a language, they would grab a bag and say, "I'll carry your bag. Where are you staying?" And they would hound passengers incessantly. Their job was to recruit travellers and take them back to stay at their family's pension.

One child asked me in Spanish, "Where are you from?"

When I answered Canada, he broke into perfect English.

"Which city? Vancouver? Toronto? Montreal?"

These kids were only about seven or eight years old, but they spoke Spanish, they spoke French, they spoke German, they spoke English. It was remarkable.

It happened that I had arrived during Ramadan. While riding another bus from Tetouan to Tangiers a few days later, I became better educated about this important Islamic religious holiday.

I didn't know much about Ramadan other than the fact that it was very important in the Arab world. During the bus ride, I was sitting at the very back in the middle of the rear bench seat, facing straight up the aisle. Where I was seated, anyone getting onto the bus would get a full view of me.

I happened to be hungry. So I pulled out a loaf of bread and a tin of mackerel. I rolled back the lid of the tin, grabbed a piece of bread, and I started making myself a sandwich. Suddenly, I became aware that the entire bus was staring at me. And not with warmth in their eyes. I didn't understand what was going on, but I was half expecting one of the men to run their hand across their neck in a throat-slitting gesture.

There was another backpacker on the bus, a Dutchman, whom I hadn't noticed previously. He carefully crept to the back of the bus to talk with me.

"You know, they can't eat until sundown, so you really shouldn't eat in front of them," he said quietly.

I immediately put my loaf of bread away, sealed up my can of mackerel as best as I could, and put them both away. It hadn't occurred to me what was going on, nor that I wasn't supposed to be eating at that time.

Of course, it's one of the essential restrictions of Ramadan. Between sunrise and sunset, you are supposed to fast.

It was just another classic example of me being a kid and not knowing the culture. But it remains a vivid memory. I can still see the shocked and dismayed faces of the other passengers, looking at me as if to say, *what on earth are you doing?*

Morocco was an amazingly rich cultural experience, but it wasn't without its travel hazards. While there, I became very sick with dysentery. As I boarded the ferry back to Algeciras about 10 days later, my stomach was distended and I was very weak. If my mother had known the shape I was in, she would have likely been hysterical. I guess there are small blessings in being out of sight and out of mind.

When the ferry arrived in Algeciras that evening, I was disoriented and too weak to even care about looking for a hostel. Instead, I simply found a quiet spot on a grassy boulevard and bedded down for the night. I was literally sleeping between two roadways, but I didn't care. There was little traffic at night, and I just couldn't be bothered to walk any more.

The next day, I wandered around until about five o'clock in the afternoon. I drank and ate carefully, and I could feel my strength slowly starting to return. For some reason, it didn't occur to me that I might want to get to a hospital to get some medicine to help with the symptoms.

My next destination was the Canary Islands and Tenerife, and the ferry was leaving that evening at eleven o'clock.

What was about to happen would prove to be one of the most important events in my life. Because of someone I was about to meet. It was September 13.

I went to the Algeciras ferry terminal at five o'clock, and I took a place in the line to buy a ticket for the ferry to Las Palmas de Gran Canaria. For some reason, I was whistling the disco song "The Hustle" by Van McCoy. I can't begin to imagine why I was whistling it. It had just been released and was getting lots of radio play, so I guess it was stuck in my mind.

Presently, I felt a tap on my shoulder, and a voice asked me, "Do you speak English?"

I turned around a saw a girl. So I replied cautiously, curiously, in my best sultry baritone, "Yes..."

Her name was Rose Patterson, and she was travelling with a friend. Her friend was a girl named Jane Turland.

My focus immediately went to Jane.

It turned out that Rose was the more outgoing of the two, and over a few glasses of wine many years later, I would learn from Jane and Rose that Jane had sent her over to talk to me and find out who I was. My attraction to Jane was immediate. Like the movies, it was love at first sight.

Jane was wearing a pair of cut-off denim shorts and a blue plaid linen shirt tied in a knot at her waist. On her head, she had an aqua-colored print scarf. Her beaming smile lit up the room.

It quickly emerged that we were all from Canada. Jane and Rose were from Vancouver. It also turned out that they were both going to the Canary Islands like me, so we stood in line together. After we bought our tickets for the ferry, we hung out together and related where we had been in our travels, and we bought groceries and fruit for the journey.

We went back to the terminal around ten o'clock that night. By now I was convinced that this girl Jane was just amazing. I was head over heels. And she would tell me later that she liked me right away as well, but she was cautious since she had basically just met me on the street, and she also had a boyfriend back in Canada. As for myself, I wasn't looking to get into a relationship. But I started to have new thoughts around this as I spent more time with Jane.

As we waited in boarding area for the ferry, we observed three transvestites who were also waiting to board the boat. They were German, and all three were dressed in luxuriant evening gowns. Las Palmas had a reputation for being a magnet for the gay population. It had tons of clubs and gay nightlife, so these three guys were on their way to enjoy a holiday in Las Palmas. You couldn't help but notice these guys. One guy looked like he was most of the way through a sex change procedure, and the two others looked like they were on the verge with evidence of hormone treatments. One of them wore a flowing pastel blue chiffon gown, and another had a skin-tight body suit which left nothing to the imagination. They looked as though they were getting onto the Love Boat and they were ready for action.

Meanwhile, the three of us were travelling in backpacks, flip-flops and cut-offs.

We boarded the ship, and we showed the stewards our E-class tickets, which were the cheapest class down below the waterline. Jane and Rose were assigned their cabin, and I was assigned mine. I took my backpack and my guitar and I walked down three flights of stairs. It seemed like I was descending into the very bowels of the ship. I finally reached the E deck, and I walked a long aisle through a few bulkhead doors until I found the door to my cabin.

I swung the door open to see my roommates for the voyage. The three German transvestites.

I looked at them. They looked at me with expressions that seemed to say, *Oh my! This is going to be fun!*

I closed the door and I walked back upstairs.

I went to the ship's purser, who was a very pretty and petite young Spanish woman. I explained as best as I could in my feeble Spanish who my roommates were and that I couldn't stay in that room. She started laughing.

Just then, as luck would have it, Rose and Jane came upstairs from their cabin. After explaining what had just happened, they too joined in on the laughter at my expense and were kind enough to offer me a place in their room as they had an extra bunk. The purser was having so much fun with the situation that she acted in mock hesitation about switching the rooms. After a little more laughter, she officially made the switch. It was settled that I would stay with Jane and Rose for the next two nights during the trip to the Canaries.

After arriving in Las Palmas, we caught another ferry to Tenerife. On the approach, it seemed to rise out of the Atlantic like a volcano. I soon learned that this was because it was indeed the home of the third-largest volcano in the world, Pico de Tiede. So my eyes weren't playing tricks on me.

We ended up staying together in a little town called Los Cristianos, and we continued to the island of Gomera together. The Canary Islands were beautiful in themselves, but my entire experience of the Canaries was illuminated by the presence of Jane. I was soundly head-over-heels and I seemed to be floating through each day in a constant state of bliss.

Eventually, I began to run out of money, so I needed to plan my return to Canada. Conversely, Jane and Rose were actually just at the beginning of their European trip, so we were forced to say goodbye. By now it had become clear to Jane and me that we were interested in each other, but I told her that this was basically farewell. We both knew that she had a boyfriend in Vancouver that she had been with for six years. (Rose had mentioned this fact more often than I would have liked.) I was determined to respect that relationship even though I was seriously smitten.

The day that I said goodbye to Jane in Santa Cruz on October 3, 1975, I told her that I planned to return to Calgary to work, save money, and then travel around the world. I told her that I would come back through the Pacific, and then up through Mexico and California to British Columbia, so I would go and visit her in Vancouver in a couple of years.

Of course, it broke my heart to even say those words. Because the thought of not seeing Jane for another two years was the last thing I wanted. But I was trying to be brave.

We parted, and the next day I flew back to Calgary.

EIGHT

Household Bliss

I wrote to Jane a few times while she was still in Europe. We had agreed on a couple of places where I could send her letters during her travels. I sent one of the letters to a place called Mama's Store in Matala, Crete. And remarkably, she actually received it. There was no postal code, and there was no real address. It was simply addressed "Attention: Jane Turland, Mama's Store, Matala, Crete." When Jane arrived in the town with Rose, the letter was waiting for her.

There was no question that Europe had been a transformative experience for me. I don't want to say, "I found myself," because that expression has never held meaning for me. I figure that you are wherever you are. As well, I don't think you can "find yourself" in one single movement. Learning who you are is an ongoing process, and you can argue that it continues for eternity. But I certainly discovered things while I was in Europe, and I became comfortable with being alone with myself. That was meaningful enough.

I moved back with my parents and I started looking for a good day job so I could begin rebuilding my depleted bank account. I also joined a top 40s cover band called Rock and Roll Express playing Tenor and Alto Sax. We started gigging regularly around Calgary and covered versions of songs by groups like the The Commodores, Average White Band, Tower of Power, and Bruce Springsteen.

One day in December just before Christmas, the phone rang and my mom called downstairs to me.

"Mark—phone."

"Who is it?" I listened intently to hear what she would say.

"She says her name is Jane," she shouted back. "From Vancouver."

I flew up the stairs so fast that I swear my feet didn't even touch them.

Shortly after her return to Vancouver, Jane had felt that I might be the right guy, and she broke things off with her boyfriend of six years. I felt the blood rush to my head. I could hardly believe what I was hearing. I had become very philosophical about our destiny and I figured that it would happen between us if it was meant to be.

And now it seemed that it was. I remember thinking, "Maybe it is meant to be." We agreed that she would come to visit me in Calgary in February.

Our reunion was extraordinary. By that point, I was living in a very modest basement suite with a guy named Hans Sahlen who played bass in our band. Hans had a heart the size of Texas, but on the night that Jane arrived, he enjoyed visiting so much that it was around three in the morning when I think he finally picked up on our wanting a bit of "alone" time and headed off to bed, leaving us to reconnect.

The following month, I went to Vancouver to see Jane, and by then she had decided that she wanted to move to Calgary. That really tells you something when a person leaves Vancouver for Calgary. Either she was deeply in love with me, or she really needed a change of scene.

In June 1976, I rented a van from my friend Brock so I could help Jane move to Calgary. It was a old Ford Econoline 100 and it wasn't pretty, but it did the job. After we finished our gig at 1 am on a Friday night in Calgary, I jumped in the van and began driving to Vancouver. I drove all night and arrived at Jane's house in the early afternoon on Saturday. It was about a 12-hour drive, but I didn't feel any fatigue whatsoever. It was like mind over matter. We spent Saturday packing the van with her stuff, and then we left Sunday morning for Calgary.

About halfway between Vancouver and Calgary, the van broke down and we had to be towed to the nearest town. A new fuel filter relieved me of $150 and we were ready to set out for Calgary again. None of it bothered me in the least—it was all part of our new adventure together.

Jane got a job at Holt Renfrew in Calgary while I was working in construction during the day and playing in the band at night. I was getting money together so I could go to school the following September at the Southern Alberta Institute of Technology to study film and television.

We were happy to be living together, but the apartment lifestyle of our 16th floor pad at Pentland Place was not really my thing. As autumn passed, we talked about getting married and buying a house, though not necessarily in that order. All we knew was that we wanted to be together.

I was a big believer in buying a house as fast as we could. We didn't have enough saved for a down payment, so I borrowed a few thousand dollars from my father and we put an offer on a tiny little place in West Hillhurst in Calgary on a thirty-three foot lot. We offered $43,500 and got it.

The deal was due to close on December 30, and we discovered that there were favorable tax incentives if we got married before the new year, so we figured we would take advantage of them by setting our wedding date for December 27. I didn't see marriage as a business enterprise, but since we were planning to get married anyways, I was certainly up for paying less taxes.

As winter descended on Calgary, I was laid off my construction job around the middle of December. This was no surprise—it's pretty common practice in the construction industry to shut down during the coldest part of the winter. And I wasn't too worried, as we had planned ahead and saved enough to pay for the wedding and cover the mortgage for the next few months.

The day after I was laid off, I called our mortgage company, Crédit Foncier, just to make sure everything was on track with closing the sale. I remember calling from a pay phone at an indoor Mall in Calgary at about four o'clock in the afternoon, and I had all of the paperwork in front of me.

"By the way, what does this mean, this 'conditional acceptance' for funding?" I asked the woman on the phone.

We had been granted a conditional acceptance with a few "subject to" clauses, but being new to the real estate game, I didn't really understand what that meant.

I'll never forget what she said to me.

"It's subject to you completing the work that we have laid out."

My heart almost stopped. "What work?"

She told me that there was a document that outlined a number of repairs that needed to be done on the house for the financing to be approved. I had not received this list of 'deficiencies', and I had to remind myself to continue to breathe as she very nonchalantly read through a list of the issues over the phone.

There were three things they wanted us to do. First, we had to re-roof the front side of the house. It was an asphalt shingle roof, and this was December in Calgary. It was minus thirty outside!

Second, all of the fascia boards and the soffits were currently exposed, and they wanted them to be enclosed.

Third, in the basement, there were two walls that were dirt. These had to be retained with expensive pressure treated lumber.

My eyes were glazing over. First of all, I didn't have the money to do the work, and second of all, I didn't have the time to do it. How could I possibly do this before we closed on December 30?

I said to her, "What happens if I can't do this?"

"You lose your down payment," she said emotionlessly.

I just about choked.

"Well, that can't happen," I said.

Five thousand dollars was a lot of money in 1976. There was no other option. I had to make this work somehow. To finance the house repairs, we would have to use our credit cards and any additional cash we could scrape together. I think we also sold a few things to generate a bit of additional cash.

The first thing I tackled was the roofing. I had found some other temporary work during the day for money, so I had to work on the roof at night. I worked over three nights, on my own in the dark in minus thirty. And I slid off the roof a few times. Thankfully, the snow was a meter deep and cushioned my fall. It was actually kind of fun, and I tried to see the humor in the whole situation.

I didn't win the affection of the boys who lived next door. They weren't much older than me, and their dad was a Scotsman named Terry McGovern who had immigrated to Canada back in the 1950s. He admonished them in his thick Scottish brogue, "Now *that* is a hard worker, boys—*that's* what you need to do! Look at that guy—he's out there in the middle of winter!"

On another night, my older brother Shane—I think telepathically sensing the jam I was in—showed up and helped me to build the retaining walls in the basement. All this while, the old owner of the house still had occupancy, so he was still living there with his wife and four little kids. He felt so sorry for me that he came downstairs one night and helped as well. I hadn't realized that he was a carpenter, so I was very impressed when he walked in with a full tool belt, hammer and all.

I finished the roof, I retained the dirt, and enclosed all the fascia boards and soffits in pressure treated lumber. I also installed some aluminum eaves troughs. I'll never forget doing those. My hands were so cold, I couldn't hold on to anything—the drill, the screws, the aluminum. It was just ridiculous.

But in the end, we pulled it off. We completed all of the repairs on time and we didn't lose our down payment. The bank came out and inspected the work, they released the funds, and we moved in. And all of this happened just before our wedding date of December 27.

The wedding was fraught with equal drama.

When I went with Jane to Vancouver in September 1976, we told her parents that we were going to get married and it didn't go over well. I was a musician with long hair and an earring, and they were convinced that I couldn't provide for their daughter. Consequently, they did not support our decision to get married. It was up to us to organize and make all the necessary arrangements for the wedding. Given our state of sheer bliss, we were fine with it.

I told her mother, "I know I can provide for Jane. I know that I can do this."

She replied dismissively, "How can you possibly say that."

Under the circumstances, it was probably a perfectly normal question.

"Well, I just know that I can." It was a simple answer. What else could I say? I loved their daughter. I could see no other path before me.

We proceeded with our wedding plans.

In keeping with our financial limitations, we had arranged to be married at my parents' home in Edmonton. We set off on the four-hour drive around five o'clock on Christmas eve. Jane had tried getting off work early given that it was Christmas Eve and we were getting married in three days, but her boss didn't feel this was a suitable event to warrant early departure that day. Meanwhile, I had sat in our 1967 Volkswagen beetle behind the Holt Renfrew store since three o'clock that afternoon in the hope that she would appear. I was fuming when she got to the car. I wanted to go in and wish Mrs. Muirhead a very merry Christmas, but Jane calmed me down and we set off for Edmonton in minus 35.

Just to add a little more drama to our journey, the car's gas-powered heater—temperamental at best—decided to stop working that day. In light of the goings on in the previous weeks, I remember thinking sarcastically, *Oh, now the gas heater has stopped working—why not?* So I brought along a down sleeping bag to keep Jane from freezing. By the time we reached Edmonton, my feet were both numb, and we had scraped the inside of the windshield a thousand times as a result of the frost from our breath.

A Mormon bishop from Calgary, Val McMurray, agreed to perform the ceremony as he was a long-time family friend. He and his wife drove to Edmonton at their own expense And despite their objections, Jane's parents did in fact attend. Jane and I were both glad for that. Their presence suggested the hope for some form of reconciliation at some point.

Our wedding music was tremendous. My parents had a friend who was an incredible pianist, and her husband was an opera singer who had graduated from the Juilliard School of Music in New York They performed a number of songs, mostly in the classical vein, along with Jane's processional. It was sublime.

I had a funny moment with Val just prior to the ceremony.

I had been greeting guests at the front door, and I decided to go downstairs to use the bathroom. I knocked on the door.

Val was inside. "Who is it?" he said.

"Oh!" I said. "I'll be right out."

Val opened the door and looked at me with a smile. "Mark, I'm so glad to hear you say that. I was getting worried. Until now, you didn't seem nervous. Now I know you're actually human."

I went back upstairs and took my place. We had about seventy-five guests, so it was standing-room-only in the living room where I waited for Jane. Her processional was *Brian's Song*, the title track from the James Caan film. The song was very popular throughout the 1970s, and it always promised tears. Today was no exception. The music began to play as Jane descended the stairs, and there was soon no shortage of wet eyes. My own included.

We said our vows, we signed the registry, and we celebrated with our friends and family. It was as beautiful a wedding as if it had been at Buckingham Palace. That's real love. Beyond time and place.

As a present to ourselves, Jane and I bought cross country skis and drove to Banff for three days of skiing. We might have gone to Hawaii if we had the money at the time, but I wonder now if we didn't have a better honeymoon amidst the snowy pines and mountains.

I have a vivid memory of going up to Sunshine Village, a stunning ski resort in the Rockies. I thought it would be cool to take a picnic and ski deep into the backcountry. We took one of the lifts up, and then we began a cross country trek through deep virgin powder. We found an ideal spot at the top of a small rise and we put down a ground sheet. I prepared a pot of tea with melted snow, using the small gas camp stove that I had carried with me on my trip to Europe in 1975. The tea and sandwiches tasted amazing. There was something about having a picnic at 9,000 feet after skiing for three hours that seemed to make everything taste so much better.

That spring, I went back to work in construction, and Jane continued working at Holt Renfrew. We saved our pennies, and in September 1977, I started attending the Southern Alberta Institute of Technology for film and television studies.

We hadn't spoken with Jane's parents in the nine months since the wedding, and even the short amount of time spent with them at the wedding had been predictably awkward and uncomfortable. Then suddenly, they decided to visit us for Thanksgiving.

When they arrived in Calgary, I had a weekend project planned to build a tool shed in our backyard. It turned out that Jane's dad, Doug, loved these sorts of projects. He helped me to build the shed, and slowly conversation began to flow between us. In one of the time-tested traditions of real male bonding, we even went and bought power tools together from the local building supply store.

It ended up being a beautiful weekend for all of us. History would come to testify that this was the pivotal weekend where everything became reconciled. Jane's parents got to know me, and when they heard the story about what we had done to get the house, such as falling off of the roof, and how close we had come to loosing our down payment, they started to appreciate that there was more to me than they had previously thought.

At one point, Doug went into the house while we were working on the shed, and he said to his wife, Mary: "I think Mark's a keeper."

To be fair to Jane's parents, they had both come from very traditional upbringings, and they had both followed traditional courses of study and careers. Mary was a nurse, Doug was an engineer, and they both had graduated from the University of British Columbia. They had waited until they completed their degrees before getting married, and then they bought their first home together in North Vancouver. They had two children—one boy, one girl—and Doug spent his entire career at the same job at General Electric until he retired at age fifty-five. They basically lived the "perfect" life. So when they met me with my eccentricities, the hair, the earring, my attraction to the music business, and without a recognized career, it naturally gave them cause for worry! It was completely understandable.

Now everything was put behind us. We became family that Thanksgiving, and now—almost four decades later—Jane's parents still think I'm the greatest.

NINE

Sound West

W hen I was in Scouts and Venturers as a kid, our leaders used to organize different field trips around the city so we could occasionally glimpse something more than just canoeing and camping. It was on one of these occasions, when I was 13 years old, that my Venturers troop went on an excursion that would begin to shape just about everything that has happened to me since.

In the autumn of 1971, our troop leader, Mr. Richard Gailey, announced that we would be going to visit a modern recording studio. "Where they make records," he said.

Mr. Gailey was a former executive at Walt Disney Studios and was Dean of the Film, Television, and Arts program at the Southern Alberta Institute of Technology in Calgary. Naturally, he had a contact at this local studio, the only professional studio in Calgary, who arranged a tour for us.

My ears perked up. It hadn't been too long since my grade five buddies and I had tried to enter the battle of the bands at school, and it had been very recent when I heard "Lay Lady Lay" by Bob Dylan and I was feeling very inspired. I had music and songwriting very much on my brain, and now this studio tour added another dimension to explore. I was still just a kid, and I was keen to know, what exactly happened behind the scenes to make a song into a *record*?

A week later, we were at Sound West Studios. My eyes were the size of pie plates and I absorbed everything like a sponge.

We toured the front offices briefly, and then we went into the control room and examined all of the equipment. Hundreds of buttons and knobs, cables and wires all over the place, a 16-track tape machine with two-inch magnetic tape, and the feeling that you were at the helm of the U.S.S. Enterprise with Spock and James T. Kirk. It was incredible. I even loved the smell of half-stale cigarette smoke and electronic components slightly over heating. I thought to myself: I'm going to work here one day.

As a consequence of that tour, I started to fantasize about becoming a sound engineer, and one day making and producing records. I became mesmerized by the thought, and I began to make myself a student of sound and production techniques.

In those heydays of Pink Floyd, Yes, Led Zepplin, and other bands with extraordinary depth of sound, I found that there were certain sounds and recordings that I just absolutely loved. I became a student of the recording process. The creative things that were being done various reverbs, echo chambers, phasers and flangers, and how they effected the guitars, the drums, the keyboards and vocals. All of it fascinated me, and I could tell when a song was well recorded.

I didn't know much, but I would often listen intently to a record for hours on an old massive pair of headphones that I had obtained in a trade with a buddy for some bike part or pair of jeans. These headphones had volume controls on each ear. A feature I never quite understood. Why you would want to turn one ear down and not the other? I wanted full blast! In both ears!

As I listened, I tried to understand and dissect the layers of sound, and I tried to imagine the recording techniques that had been used. It was like a story that I heard about Jerry Lee Lewis. As a young man, he was very poor and didn't own a piano, so he would lie under the floor of the church while the choir practiced, and he would "air play" the piano parts that the accompanist was playing. I sort of did the same thing with recording techniques.

By the time 1977 arrived, and as I prepared to go back to school, I had given a lot of serious thought to what I was going to study. I concluded that if everyone could study what they were truly passionate about, they would become very good at what they had studied. I knew that my passion was to create, and therefore I figured my greatest gift to myself was to follow my passion for creation. I enrolled at The Southern Alberta Institute of Technology to study film and television.

It wasn't an easy life. Jane worked at Holt Renfrew and I continued to play at night to make ends meet with Rock and Roll Express.

At one point, our band was signed to a five-week gig at an Italian restaurant in Calgary called White Spot. They hired us for a five-week run leading up to Christmas, six nights per week. We played from nine o'clock until two am. I had to be at school every morning by 8:30 am. It just about killed me.

I remember one night, we were ready to go on stage, and our bass player Hans wasn't anywhere to be seen. We were already about ten or fifteen minutes late, too.

Presently the restaurant manager waved to us. He was holding up the phone.

I went over to the bar and he passed me the receiver. "Hello?"

It was Hans. He was calling from the hospital. He had been running to catch his bus and he tripped on a support cable for a telephone pole. These cables used to be relatively common on telephone poles. He didn't see it in the snow, and he tripped on it as he was running with his bass. He landed on his elbow and completely mangled it. So he was out. We would have to play that night without a bass player.

We were all very afraid that they were going to fire us and take our money back because we had been paid *in advance*. I don't know why, but for some reason they paid us at the start of each week. This was highly unusual in the club business—well, in any business for that matter. And although the owners were very professional, you would definitely not want to cross them.

As it turned out, our worries were unfounded. We played fine without a bass player that night, and we found someone else to fill in for the subsequent nights. Money was too tight to mention for all of us—Hans included—so a few days later, 24 hours after undergoing surgery and with 2 screws holding his elbow together, he was back playing because he couldn't afford to lose the wages. The cast on his left arm was so heavy that we had to prop his arm up with a microphone stand so that he could play.

Around that time, I was hired to play my very first session as a studio musician. This session led to a series of events that would effectively set the course of my future in music, recording and creative arts.

I was hired to play sax on a couple of songs for a vocalist named Linda Curtis who was recording her first solo LP. The producer's name was Doug Wong. Doug hired me because he liked my playing and he knew I could read music. I was also given a strong reference from another sax player friend of mine, Neil MacCallum. I'll always owe a debt of gratitude to Neil for this.

For years, I had been dreaming of working as a studio musician as much as I had been dreaming of writing my own songs. In those days, horn sections were big in top 40 rock, soul and funk bands, so I was right in my element as a saxophone player. Bands like Tower of Power, Chicago, and Blood, Sweat and Tears all leaned heavily on horns as a major part of their sound. I was a big fan of Tower of Power in particular, and specifically Lenny Pickett, the tenor sax player who presently leads the Saturday Night Live band.

I went into the studio at Sound West on a Saturday morning about at ten o'clock. Doug wanted me to play a baritone sax part on one song and a tenor solo on another.

I was so nervous that I didn't sleep the night before. As a session player, you know you're being hired to deliver, and they're also paying huge money for the studio time, so you have to produce a performance that makes it onto the record. Failing to do so is not an option.

If you're a really seasoned session player, you don't worry about it. But

I was new to this. I thought I was pretty good, but I didn't know if I was really good enough. I couldn't help but worry whether or not they would say, "Wow! We love that! It's awesome! It's on the record!" or simply "You're awful and you'll never work in this town again."

We did the baritone sax part first. I sat down on the stool in the studio and put on the headphones. As they started to roll the tape, I looked down and saw that my right leg was quivering.

I thought to myself, *Okay, Mark—settle down.*

I took a deep breath and I started to play.

After a few run-throughs, we got it done in two or three takes. I made it all the way through the baritone part without a hitch, quivering leg and all. I felt great. Then it came time to do the tenor solo.

The song was the Drifter's 1962 classic, "Up on the Roof".

Of course, "Up On the Roof" had already been covered several times by different bands and vocalists over the years. I was familiar with a particular recording of the song that featured a tenor sax part, and I wanted to play something different.

It didn't go well.

We did a series of takes, and none of them worked. I became increasingly worried. After about 10 or 12 unsuccessful takes, Doug asked me to come in to the control room to "listen back". We listened to a few playbacks and everyone decided to break for coffee refills. I was feeling the tension and decided to sit down on a couch which was in front of the mixing console to sort myself out.

After a few minutes, Doug returned to the control room with the drummer, who for some reason was present at the session. They were evidently unaware that I was in the room. The drummer said to Doug, "Do you know any other sax players?"

I was absolutely devastated. *They're going to hire someone else.*

I froze for a moment. I didn't know what to do. Then I stood up.

The drummer said, "Uh-oh." He lowered his eyes and his face went a bit red.

Without a word, I left the control room, and I went to get a coffee. But he knew I'd heard what he'd said.

I was crushed. I went outside with my coffee, lit up a cigarette, and pondered my predicament. I couldn't see any other option than to go back to the session and pretend I hadn't heard anything.

When I went back into the control room, Doug had decided to move on to another track and said, "No sweat, Mark—we're going to move to guitar overdubs, so I'll give you a call later."

I packed up my stuff and I went home.

I arrived at an empty house. Jane was working that day, and it was deathly silent in the house. I had that same feeling as when I took second place in the 400 meter quarter-finals when I was 13 years old. I felt like I was the only person on the planet.

I was awash in emotion and uncertainty for the rest of the day, and eventually I came to a decision. I called Doug Wong.

"Doug, I am very, very sorry it didn't work out today," I said. "If you give me just one more chance, I'll come in again and I promise I'll nail it. I know you're busy, but maybe we could tack it onto the end of another session that you're doing. If I could just have one more shot. I don't want to be paid for it. I just want to play a killer part that will make the record better."

Doug paused and seemed to reflect for a moment. "Alright, Mark, you've got it," he said. "Come back next Wednesday at six o'clock."

I carried a lump in my throat every day leading up to the next Wednesday. I was extremely nervous. But I showed up at the appointed hour, a bit weak in the knees, and I nailed it on the first take. I was almost in tears—half joy, half relief—as we listened back and everyone in the room gave the two-thumbs-up.

A couple of days later, Doug Wong apparently began to share the story with the owner of the studio, Peter Bentley, by saying, "You won't believe this guy."

Peter replied, "What do you mean?"

And Doug told him the story.

Peter said, "That's the kind of guy that I want to work for me."

Peter immediately offered me a job at Sound West. Six years after I had toured the studio with my Ventures troop. I was ecstatic. I had dreamed of working in a studio and recording great records, and now I would have my chance.

I wasn't paid at the start. I began as an intern-assistant engineer, just learning the ropes. But I was there—I was working at the only professional recording studio in town.

Over the next few years at Sound West, I learned a lot about sound recording and making records. It turned out that I ended up getting a lot more than I had bargained for. The studio business grew steadily more difficult, and the equipment at Sound West began to fall into disrepair. All of the engineers had to learn how to fix the equipment on our own and how to troubleshoot problems on the fly without flinching in front of the clients. These were my early lessons in "grace under pressure" that would prepare me for the next step in my musical journey.

A transatlantic flight to Germany to answer a job ad...

TEN

We are Two Rockers from Frankfurt

Over the course of the next year and a half, I slowly worked my way up the ladder at Sound West in Calgary. First, I started getting paid as an assistant engineer, and then one day, after a couple of senior engineers left, I suddenly found myself promoted to chief engineer. I was *incredibly* happy.

All the while, I was still playing with Rock and Roll Express, and Jane and I were managing financially. But still only just. So one part of me always had an eye open for new opportunities.

I also began to feel as though I needed to get some international experience. A lot of local artists who were thinking of recording at Sound West seemed to question the validity and cache of local engineering talent like myself. They seemed to turn their noses up at anyone who was "from here". It was sort of like that expression, "Anyone is an expert 50 miles away from home."

So I was primed when, in April 1979, I saw an advertisement in Studio Sound magazine.

We are two rockers from Frankfurt with a studio. We are looking for an engineer motivated...

The wording in the ad was peculiar. I could only guess at who might have written it—a couple of guys named Hans and Franz who had done compulsory high school English in Bavaria?

There was a phone number and an address in Frankfurt. I was curious. What if there was a chance that I could work in Germany?

That could be cool.

I figured it couldn't hurt to explore the possibility. I put my resume together and sent it in the mail.

Two weeks later, I followed up with a phone call to the number listed in the ad. I ended up connecting with an English guy named Nigel on the other end who was one of the engineers at the studio in Frankfurt. The studio was called Hotline.

He was impressed that I had taken the time to call, and that I had submitted a resume in the first place. We arranged to do an interview by phone.

A couple of days later, on a Thursday morning, I talked with Nigel and his workmate Armin. They took me through a few questions about my background and experience, and it soon became clear that they liked me. But there was one little snag.

"It's been great talking with you, Mark," said Nigel, speaking in a very deliberate, measured, and more-than-slightly condescending tone that reflected his education in the Public school system in England in Henley-upon-Thames. "We really like your attitude and your experience. But I hope you understand, but we can't really hire you without meeting you first. And you're in Canada."

"Well, I sort of anticipated that would be the case," I replied. "I've already booked a flight to Frankfurt. I am leaving Monday and I'll be arriving Tuesday."

"You—you're just flying over?"

You could almost hear him fall off his chair.

"Yeah. I thought this might come up, so I bought a ticket and I'll be arriving on Tuesday."

It was true. I had already bought my ticket, and it had cost me a $650, which was a lot of money in 1979. But I was serious about this opportunity. I was prepared to take some risk to have a real shot at this job.

Nigel and Armin were suitably impressed. They may have even felt put on the spot. It didn't matter to me—because suddenly we were setting up a meeting time.

Then the next day, Nigel called me back.

"Mark, it turns out that our chief engineer, John Lloyd Hughes, and our studio manager, Norbert Friedl, are going to be in London at the APRS—the Association of Professional Recording Studios trade show," said Nigel. "It's being held at the Connaught Rooms on Great Queen Street in Holborn. Would you be able to fly to London instead and stop to meet with John and Norbert? And then continue to Frankfurt?"

"Sure," I said. "No problem." In those days, it wasn't entirely cost prohibitive to change plane bookings, and I was happy to be able to accommodate my prospective employers.

That Monday, I jumped on the plane in Calgary and I was suddenly on my way to a job interview in London. I'd never been to London, and I had absolutely no travel budget. I was making the trip happen on a shoestring.

I arrived at Heathrow, collected my bags, and I got on the tube for Holborn station. Actually, it was slightly more complicated than that. First, I had to ask for directions to take the tube from Heathrow to *whole-born*—the normal pronunciation for anyone from North America. I asked a woman in the arrivals area, but when she began to answer me, I couldn't understand what she was talking about. It turned out that she was talking about a place called *hull-bun*, and then I suddenly realized that she was talking about Holborn.

"Ah yessss! Hulburn!" I clarified, doing my best to feign an English accent.

I was soon on the tube heading to Holborn, and shortly thereafter I emerged into the streets of the London borough. I immediately set out to find a hotel room. My hope was to find a place to sleep that wouldn't exhaust the little money I had.

I proceeded to walk the streets of Holborn along Great Queen Street in search of accommodation. I walked for hours. It was intolerably hot and humid—coming from the dry Canadian prairies, I wasn't accustomed to it. And the smell of diesel exhaust from the London cabs was so strong that it burned my eyes. I was already completely exhausted after being up all night on the flight from Canada and numb with jet lag.

I hadn't used a travel agent, and of course there was no internet or GPS on a smartphone to help me find a hotel. I quickly became discouraged by what I found.

All of the hotels were astronomically expensive in relation to my meager budget, which was about 25 pounds per night. However, after dragging myself around to about ten different hotels, I finally found one that I could barely afford.

When I checked into my room, I discovered that I could touch the walls on both sides if I stretched my arms out. "Welcome to London," I said sardonically. It was basically a closet with a sink in it, and there was a shared bathroom with toilet and shower at the end of the hall.

I was jetlagged and whacked out of shape, and I had to go to an interview the next morning. The whole scenario was daunting.

I decided to go out and try to find some dinner. After staggering around the streets of London a while more, I found a small pub off a back alley. I went inside, found a stool at the bar, and ordered a pint. I was wearing a long-sleeve black t-shirt—standard issue for rock and roll sound engineers at the time—with a big Superman logo on the front of it.

The bartender looked at me and smirked.

"You don't look like any Superman to me."

A couple of nearby patrons stopped talking and turned to watch us. I felt like I was in a western movie where the bartender asks the drifter how he's going to pay for his whiskey.

I raised one eyebrow, leaned over the bar, and replied in an intentionally dark baritone:

"Looks can be deceiving."

He laughed and passed me my beer.

So the good news was that I hadn't lost my sense of humor through all of this. I still laugh today when I remember that episode in the pub. I was completely exhausted and starving, yet I still managed to laugh and create laughter for someone else.

After the pub, I went back to my tiny hotel room, had a decent sleep, and was ready to meet with Norbert and John the next day.

They asked me a host of questions about sound engineering—many of them quite challenging—to test my technical prowess. To my surprise, they also asked me personal questions. You could tell that they wanted to get a better sense of what I was like on a personal level.

At the end of our two-hour meeting, John turned to me.

"You know what. We like you. Based on this interview, we think you should continue on to Frankfurt."

Until he said that, I hadn't known that it had been possible that I might get turned back at the border!

Nonetheless, we established that I would continue to Frankfurt, and I would meet the other guys at Hotline Studios at about three o'clock in the afternoon on the coming Saturday. I didn't think anymore about it. I was there, and I had passed the first hurdle.

I spent the next couple of days checking out London and the APRS show. Again, as money was tight, I had to make my own walking tour of London, punctuated by the occasional pint and another cheap takeout from street vendors for sustenance.

It was Saturday when I flew to Frankfurt. The challenge of finding my way in London with the woman describing 'Hulbun' paled in comparison to what I encountered in Frankfurt. For starters, it was an entirely different language and I knew about six words: *eins*, *dwei*, *drei*, *vier*, and *nein danke*.

I met a long string of people who seemed to look at me as though I was a complete imbecile. As I attempted to ask for directions in fractured English and German, they would furrow their brows and look at me in that grave, pragmatic manner that seemed quintessentially German to me. At the same time, I was anxious about phase two of my interview and I had gone for a third night without much sleep. By the time I sorted out the bus, and a street car, and found the studio, I was about an hour late. And I felt like a zombie.

Now I was extra stressed and anxious. I thought: *I've flown half way around the world on my own dime and I've blown my chance by being late.*

I found a note on the front door of the studio. My heart skipped a beat as I pulled it off the door to read it.

To our wandering Canadian engineer,

We missed you. We are awaiting your arrival.

You can find us at the Café Groessenwahn across the street

I looked about me and scanned for the café. I walked up and down the street and eventually found it on the corner. I walked in and could smell that unmistakable blend of stale beer and strong tobacco—everybody smoked in those days—with a hint of bleach thrown in for good measure. Very much like the bars where I had played so many gigs back home.

I must have looked a bit like a deer in the headlights as I heard a very proper English voice call out, "Are you Mark?"

I looked over and saw Nigel and Armin. Nigel was a medium-height, pasty-white guy with curly red hair and a big gap between his two front teeth. Armin was tall very lanky with solid jaw bones and very dark circles around his eyes.

We exchanged greetings and they insisted that I join them for a pint before we started the interview. In my exhausted condition, this was the last thing I wanted to do. As it was, I was drawing on all of my strength just to stay awake. Drinking a pint might just finish me off and leave me as a heap of rubble.

"Of course," I replied. "I'd love a beer."

This was their day off, and they were on their second Pils. I quickly discovered that both of them had great senses of humor. Nigel spoke with a certain air of sophisticated aloofness that initially struck me as arrogance, but I quickly came to see that it was simply an artifact of his English-public-school upbringing, and not a true reflection of his character.

We finished our beers and went back to the studio. They began to put me through the technical portion of the interview process.

We walked into the control room. I had a "holy shit" moment. The mixing console was about fourteen feet long. It was one of the first Solid State Logic consoles ever made—it was called an Acorn. To this day, SSL is one of the two big manufacturers of solid state mixing consoles used in multi-track recording. The other is Neve. Both made in the UK.

It was incredibly intimidating for me because I had never worked on a console that size. It was also laid out completely different from the MCI console that I used in Calgary. This behemoth made the MCI in Sound West look like a toy.

"Here's a roll of tape," said Nigel. "Lace it up on the machine, get yourself organized, and we'll be back in fifteen minutes to do a rough mix on a track."

They left the room. I swallowed hard. I lit a smoke and tried to gain my composure.

I laced up the two-inch tape on the Lyrec 24-track tape machine, another piece of equipment that was completely strange to me. The Lyrec was made in Denmark, and I had neither seen nor heard of one before, let alone operate one. Nonetheless, I muddled my way through, and I proceeded to set my recording levels to start shaping the mix.

When Nigel and Armin came back, they started pretending that they were famous producers who were working with me to mix a song they had selected. Nigel pretended he was Robert Stigwood, and Armin pretended he was Michael Omartian. Stigwood and Omartian were two of the biggest producers in Los Angeles at that time.

They sat down with their coffees—essential after the three-beers they had downed—and they went into full dramatic mode. I figured out very quickly what they were trying to do. They wanted to see how well I could interpret vague instructions from clients.

We started rolling the tape and they listened attentively as I made adjustments on the console.

Armin started providing directions as Omartian.

"Yes, the mix is coming along," he said thoughtfully, and then he paused dramatically. "But you know, the guitar should be…more…*orange*…"

"Orange," I repeated. "Okay. So are you thinking the guitar needs to be warmer?"

"Yes! That's it," replied Armin. "But…what does warmer mean?"

"Well, warm is more down in these frequencies here."

I motioned to a couple of nobs on the mixing board.

"In this case, this guitar is a little heavy around 2k to 3k, which are somewhat harsh frequencies. They really bite and cut. The ones that hurt when you turn it up. They're very useful for certain things, but in this case we might want to reduce those frequencies a bit and add a little more in the 1k to 1800 cycles. And then maybe a little bit more at the top."

"Oh! That sounds logical. Well, let's try," said Nigel, chiming in.

"Oh yes! Let's try that," said Armin with mock enthusiasm.

So I would make the adjustments, and they would exude, "Yes! That's it! That's getting closer! Good. But now the bass…it needs to be…more purple!"

"Okay, purple," I replied cautiously. We discussed what purple meant, and I made adjustments.

"Okay, the guitar and the bass sound great, but I can't quite hear the vocal the way I would like to," interjected Nigel. "Now the guitar seems to be taking too much space. Can you make the voice stand out a little bit more?"

"Well, we could do a couple of things," I replied. "We could add some echo. That will make it stand on its own. We'll add a little bit of echo, and we'll work on the frequencies.

"It's not always just a volume thing. It's also how it sits within the track."

Another dramatic response. "Oh! It's how it sits within the track! What do you mean?"

"Well, the track is an entire body of work, and all of these instruments have different frequencies and harmonics. It's important to think about it in the context of the overall mix, so it's not just a volume thing."

"Ah! Okay, that makes sense," said Armin.

"So let's take the voice just a little higher," I said. "We'll bring the voice up." And I made the adjustments on the board.

"Oh! Now the bass drum…" Nigel sighed. "I'm not hearing the bass drum. Let's turn the bass drum up."

"Okay, sure, let's turn the bass drum up." And again, I dutifully turned up the bass drum.

I hadn't realized it yet, but they were deliberately boxing me into a corner. To understand what I mean, you need a little background in sound engineering.

When the recording engineer is working on a mixing console, there is a left and right output. In most North American consoles of the time, the outputs would be represented by two VU meters. This SSL console happened to have PPMs, or peak program meters, which were more common in Europe. They show the absolute peak of the outputs, whereas VU meters show more of an average, so they are regarded as being less accurate by some sound people.

Ideally, the volume of the PPM outputs is kept close to zero at all times. You want to keep the volumes near zero because the signal is outputting to a two-track tape that will represent the final master. If the amplitude of the output of the mixing console is too high, you will over-saturate the tape and produce distortion.

Additionally, you want your left and right master faders to be sitting right at the top of their range for optimal signal-to-noise ratio. If the combination of all of the tracks gets a bit too loud, you can just reduce your left and right outputs a little bit by pulling them down. A tiny bit is fine, but it's most efficient when the faders are set right at the top.

A problem arises when you continue to increase the guitar, the vocals, and all the rest. You end up having to pull that left and right master fader down more each time. And this is exactly what was happening to my mix. Nigel and Armin knew exactly what they were doing and had successfully managed to back me into a difficult spot.

Instead of turning up the vocal track or the guitar track to hear more of it, I should have been turning something else down. Sound engineering 101. It's not always a matter of increasing volume, but rather decreasing the volume of other elements that are taking up too much space in the track.

We got to the point where I was looking at the master fader, and I could see that we were still pinging the output levels. The PPM output meter was hammering the top of its range and the master fader was down about 20 percent from the top.

I suddenly realized I was in trouble. I knew I needed to pull everything down and get the left and right masters back to the top where they should be. I looked at Nigel and Armin.

"I'm sorry, but I'm going to have to trim my levels. It's going to take me about fifteen minutes."

The two of them groaned dramatically.

"What do you mean? We're so close with this mix!" said Nigel.

Armin held up his hands beseechingly, dramatically. "We're spending already 200 Deutsch marks per hour for the studio. Now you need another fifteen minutes? Why?"

"Well, what happened here is that we turned everything up," I explained. "Instead of more of this and more of that, we should have been turning certain things down. If something's getting in the way of the vocal, or of the bass is too loud, or if there are frequencies in the guitar that are interfering with other parts of the track, it's often better simply to adjust the volume of that instrument or reduce those frequencies. That way the vocal stands out without having to turn something else louder in the mix."

"Oh, I see," said Nigel thoughtfully, though he knew exactly what had happened. "Well, how do you suppose this happened?"

"I fucked up."

Those were my exact words. I didn't try to sweeten things or cover my tracks with excuses. They looked each other grimly, registering expressions of disappointment.

"Well, okay, fine," said Nigel. "Do what you have to do."

They left the room.

At that point, I figured I had either just blown the interview entirely, or they would come back, we would continue, and they would forgive me. There was nothing else for me to do but stay the course and hope for the best.

So I continued working, though I was so exhausted that I hardly knew whether I was coming or going.

A wave of disappointment and despair washed over me, and I started to feel overwhelmed. I felt like I might lose it, so I lit up another smoke. I had no choice but to focus and carry on. I trimmed my levels, and got the mix sounding even better than it had before. Nigel and Armin returned, and within twenty minutes we were able to produce a really nice mix.

They seemed happy, so we put it to tape.

"Okay, let's go outside for part B," said Nigel.

I was thinking, *you've got to be kidding—how many freaking parts are there to this interview?*

We went out onto the studio floor and they asked me to set up microphones for the different instruments.

"Here's a drum kit," said Armin. "How would you mic it?"

I took a look around, examined the different microphones that they had, and I asked a few questions. I was familiar with a few of them, but not others. With the unfamiliar ones, I asked them what kind of mic it was. Whether it was ribbon or a dynamic, how big a diaphragm it had, and so forth. Then I proceeded to mic the drum kit. I had a real affinity for recording drums so this was a fun exercise for me.

Then we talked about guitars, and we looked at the Hammond B3 organ that they had in the studio. They told me that it had belonged to one of the keyboard players from Santana, and it had toured for several years with the band. The moment Nigel turned it on and played a few notes, you could almost hear "Black Magic Woman". It was extremely cool. They asked me how I would mic it. We spent about 45 minutes altogether on that portion of the interview, and it went extremely well.

When we were finally done the interview, I apologized again for screwing up with my levels during the mix portion. Nigel and Armin had dropped their impersonations of Stigwood and Omartian by this point, and they reassured me that it wasn't a big deal. But I couldn't be sure if they were just being polite or not.

We said cordial goodbyes, they said they would get in touch with me, and I left.

I spent another couple of days in Frankfurt. I wasn't sightseeing much since I was pretty much out of money, but I had the opportunity to stay with the assistant manager of Hotline Studio, an English guy named Geoff Hall, and his wife Gitta. They were very nice people, and they basically gave me the opportunity to spend a couple of extra days to get to know the city.

I slept on a fold-up bed in their living room that looked like a caterpillar, but I couldn't go to bed until Geoff went to bed, which was usually about 4 a.m. Geoff was one of the most laid-back guys I have ever met. He smoked a serious amount of pot. He would roll a joint, smoke it, then light up a cigarette, smoke that, and then repeat. By 4 a.m. each night, I was cross-eyed with fatigue and my eyes looked like road maps from all the smoke.

Four weeks later, back in Canada and fully recovered from my marathon job interview, they sent me a letter to offer me the job.

Three weeks later, I was on a plane back to Frankfurt. The plan was to arrive ahead of Jane so I could find an apartment for us. Once she came over, we would rent out the house in Calgary.

I had a very difficult time finding an apartment while I was working full time at the studio. Norbert Friedl the studio manager—had told me that they would help me find an apartment, but their help ended up being less than I anticipated. It ended up consisting of Norbert telling me to pick up a copy of the Frankfurt newspaper to get the apartment listings.

"Okay, Mark, on Friday afternoon at one o'clock, the early edition of the Frankfurter Rundschau newspaper comes out," explained Norbert. "That's where all of the apartments are listed. So what you need to do is go downtown to the Rundshau, buy the first edition as soon as it comes out, and then run over to a phone booth and start calling."

I'd been in Germany for three weeks, so by now I was up to about twelve words in my German vocabulary. My only hope was that whoever answered would be able to speak English. Needless to say, I didn't find much success.

One Saturday, I actually succeeded in booking an appointment to go and see an apartment. It had a beautiful loft and I would have loved to rent it. I could imagine Jane and I living there, but there was a lineup twelve people deep. As well, several of the prospective renters were local German working professionals, so I hardly had a chance as a foreigner. I stood in line anyway.

About a half hour later, the victorious rental applicant emerged from the apartment. He was well dressed in a pair of wide wale dark blue corduroy pants, oxblood lace up shoes with thick soles, and a light blue collared shirt with a grey sweater vest and a dark grey blazer. Following directly behind him was the landlord who dismissively waved us off.

Someone in front of me, speaking in German, said he was an architect. I actually understood the word "architect" when he said it, as it sounded very close to the English word. I thought to myself, *I now know 13 words*. The afternoon was not in vain.

After five weeks in Frankfurt, I still hadn't found an apartment. I had stayed with Geoff Hall and his wife Gitta while I continued looking, sleeping on the caterpillar mattress on their living room floor. When Jane arrived from Calgary, she and I moved into the Hotel Bolivar on Echesheimer Landstrasse. It was just a simple room with a hot plate in one corner. We stayed there for about six weeks after Jane's arrival.

One day, Norbert told me he had been contacted by a friend who had an apartment that he would soon be vacating. Hallelujah! The clouds had parted and the sun was suddenly shining through. In short order, we were moving into his vacated flat at number 64 Stahlburg Strasse.

I remember arriving at our new apartment with all of our worldly possessions packed into four suitcases. We were greeted at the door by the building manager, Holgar Reimer. He was a heavyset guy with a red nose—perhaps the result of over consumption of alchoholic beverages—and a voice that sounded guttural and that of a heavy smoker. But had a gentle manner about him. When he opened up the door, we looked up and saw a bare light bulb burning brightly from a dangling socket connected to a double strand of wire.

"I didn't think you would have any lamps so I found this light for you," said Holgar.

As primitive and austere as it was, it was still a warm welcome. Gratitude is never wasted, and we were ecstatic to be out of our tiny room at the Hotel Bolivar.

Our bare-bones apartment was quite different from anything we had seen in Canada. At that time in the late 1970s, and perhaps still to this day, many German apartments didn't even have closets. Kitchens were generally bare rooms with a small counter top and some cupboards, where occupants had to supply their own fridge and stove. However, our place had a full kitchen. Bonus! We also managed to scrape together some basic furniture, and Norbert loaned us a black and white television. We only lacked a phone and a car.

It was an extremely rich time for us. Life was simple, and the daily rhythm in Germany was different. For one thing, the studio had later hours than those that I had worked in Calgary. At Sound West, I basically worked nine to five like anyone else. At Hotline, I worked every day from one o'clock in the afternoon until nine or ten at night, and I would get home late and sleep well into the morning. It's just the way they did things there. Definitely the rock and roll lifestyle.

And we seldom had to cook dinner. The studio maintained a supply of pre-made frozen dinners that they offered to clients to keep them from going out for lunch, where they would frequently over-indulge in German beer and thereby make a hash of the subsequent afternoon recording session.

The studio also encouraged the sound engineers to take them home whenever we wanted. So for the most part, I would take dinner home each night. We only lived six blocks from the studio, so I would heat up two meals and simply carry them with me down the street.

Hotline seemed to be a revolving door of talent, and I had the opportunity to work with many amazing artists. I remember one band from Stuttgart decided they wanted to bring in some outside talent for a couple of tracks on their album. Who did they hire? A couple members of the Scorpions. It was a trip for me to work with these guys as they were one of the first big metal bands to make it in North America, and I loved their music. I also worked with several studio musicians who were part the rhythm section of Boney M. They were a studio band, and this was particularly interesting to me at the time, as I hadn't realized until then that Boney M was basically made up of studio session musicians and singers. For example, the low-pitched lead vocals were actually those of their producer, Frank Farian.

It was cool to work with such internationally recognized artists. For the most part, all of the clients at Hotline were signed to a major label. For me, this was one of the big differences coming from Calgary where perhaps one in ten of the bands or artists might have been signed to a major label. At Hotline, every artist was signed to CBS, Warner Brothers or Capital/EMI. But they were mostly German artists and bands, and the studio seemed to have a reputation for recording rock and heavier stuff.

It was a big step up from what I had experienced in Canada, and it was really challenging me as an engineer. I was surrounded by some very talented technicians and engineers, and the artists I was recording were all signed and funded by major labels with big budgets, so the bar was very high. I was expected to produce a world-class sound. I felt I was a match for the task, but it was still a big step up from my days and nights at Sound West in Calgary.

Hotline consisted of two recording rooms: Studio A and Studio B. Studio A contained the main control room with the big SSL-Acorn console and the recording room itself. The recording room had a white Yamaha baby grand piano, and it also had this incredible Hammond B3 organ with a Leslie speaker that had toured with Santana. With it's very cool unmistakable signature growl that was so prominent on the classic Santana records of the 1970s.

Studio B was smaller. It had a small recording room and an Amek Console in the control room. It was used mostly for overdubbing vocals and single instruments, as well as some mixing.

Both recording rooms were very "dead" acoustically—the walls were extremely absorbent and designed not to reflect any sound. When you walked into either of the studios, you felt your ears almost pop. Since then, contemporary recording studios have become much more "live" or "reflective" in order to create a more natural sound.

There was also a small kitchen and lounge area which contained a few foosball tables. I became an expert foosball player as I was constantly being challenged by members of different bands to participate in round-robin tournaments. Sometimes I wonder how we actually got any recording done!

In December 1979, Norbert approached me about a client that had called from Zagreb, Yugoslavia—which is present-day Croatia. Yugoslavia was a pretty quirky place at the time. It was still an amalgam of several Balkan countries, and Field Marshall Tito was still the socialist head of state. Apparently the band had said that they wanted to record at Hotline, but they wanted an "American" engineer.

"Well, we have one engineer *from America*," replied Norbert, taking some liberties with geography. "His name is Mark, and we would be happy to assign him to your project. Would that be fine?"

"Yes, this will be acceptable."

A couple of weeks later, the entourage started to arrive from Zagreb. It was a rock band called Silverwings. At least that's how you would say it in English. In Croat it was *Srebrna Krila*.

Srebrna Krila was a cast of characters. There were about six guys in the band, but they had additional supervision. The musical director was a guy named Georg Novkovic. He was the musical director for the label, Jugoton, and he also composed a lot of the band's music. There was another guy named Branco who was an engineer from the Jugoton studios, and the label wanted him to come to learn recording techniques from me so he could take the knowledge back to Zagreb. True to promise, he watched what I did with great intensity and enthusiasm.

I had never seen more gear in my life. About two months earlier, they had all gone to Manny's Music, the famous instrument store in New York. They were like kids in a candy store. They each bought about fifteen guitars and all the most exotic amplifiers and accessories you could imagine. Instruments and equipment of this caliber simply weren't available to them in Yugoslavia, so they had taken full advantage of their opportunity. When they started loading their new gear into the studio at Hotline, I was immediately thinking, *Where are we going to put this stuff?*

They also ordered about forty rolls of tape for our recording sessions. That amount of tape was just unheard of. Usually in recording an album, you might use five or six rolls of two-inch tape. We actually needed two four-wheel handcarts to move the tapes in and out of the vault each day.

But these guys had big ambitions. This was their second album, and their first record had already sold seven million copies, between their home country and other eastern block countries. So they were huge. They were as big or maybe even bigger than the national soccer team of Yugoslavia. And that's saying something.

They exuded a lot of excitement and enthusiasm, and they asked a lot of questions. Meanwhile, I was just trying to get things set up and sort out the truckloads of equipment they had brought with them. I was trying to get the drum kit put together, get all the amps positioned, and get everything plugged in and turned on so I could start to get drum sounds. Then we could start to record our basic guitar, bass and drum tracks with a scratch vocal.

We were about three hours into the session, and we were still just getting everyone organized. I went back out into the lounge just as this other guy walked up the stairs and into the studio reception area. He had long dark hair and big sunglasses, and he was wearing black boots, black jeans, black t-shirt, and a full-length black sable coat draped over his shoulders. I can't imagine what it would have cost.

I thought: *Who is this cat?*

He obviously had to be with the band. I gave him a little wave of salutation.

"Hi, I'm Mark."

The guy didn't answer. He walked over to me, reached into his pocket, and pulled out a gold Dupont lighter. Dupont lighters have a very recognizable sound when you open and close them—it's a very distinctive clink that is kind of cool.

He opened his lighter, flicked it, and lit his cigarette. Then he put his lighter away. I can still hear the sound of the blond Virginia Marlborough crackling as he took a long drag. And then with more than a hint of cinematic drama, he took the cigarette out of his mouth, exhaled, and stretched out his hand:

"Vlado."

This was Srebryna Krila's lead singer.

Vlado turned out to be a great guy. Over the next several weeks of recording, I grew very fond of him, along with all of the other members of the band. He was larger than life. And he had this voice that sounded like gravel. If Marlon Brando had been a pop singer in Croatia, he would have sounded like Vlado.

And we had the most remarkable time recording that album. They were the most enthusiastic guys I had ever worked with. If you recorded a drum track and they liked it, they would jump up and down and then hug me.

"Oh Mark! The drums! I love the drums! Amazing! Turn it up!"

Between takes, I would want to stop the tape to conserve it, but they would insist that I keep it rolling. "You never know when something good is going to happen!" said Albert the producer.

And these guys loved to goof around. Sometimes they would make me say things in Croatian to the other guys. So if one of the guys was in the studio doing a guitar overdub, and all of the other guys were in the control room with me, they would come over and hold down the talk back button—which was how you communicated with whoever was in the studio recording at the time—and say, "Mark, say these words…".

So I would say the words, of course, and no doubt it was something unsavory or inappropriate. And they would all jump up and down and collapse in laughter.

About ten days before we finished the album, the band invited Jane and me to have brunch with them. The plan was to meet at about eleven in the morning to eat and then head to the studio around one o'clock. It sounded fine on paper, but when we got to the restaurant, the guys started ordering plate after plate of food. To this day, I don't think I have ever seen so much food consumed in one sitting, nor wine drunk.

By two o'clock, we were three sheets to the wind. And we still had to go to work.

We staggered collectively over to the studio, and of course, the band members were fine because half of them could just sleep on the sofa. But, man, did I ever struggle that day. I practically had to prop my eyelids open as I tried to focus on what I was doing at the console.

We were approaching Christmas, and time was running out to get the album finished. Albert and Georg asked Norbert if I would be able to work on the morning of Christmas Eve for five or six hours just to wrap things up.

"No, we're closed on Christmas Eve," Norbert replied simply. "Our engineer needs his rest."

The studio was very protective of the engineering staff. They limited us to five days per week and eight to nine hours per day. That was it. They wanted to prevent us from burning out.

There was a bit of back and forth. Finally, as a small concession, Norbert offered to ask me if I'd be willing to come in.

Vlado said, "Yes, please, and tell him we'll be willing to pay him extra for doing this."

When Norbert asked me, I said, "Yes! Of course!"

It wasn't a common request, and I was just as interested as the guys in getting the album done right and wrapped up. I agreed to come into the studio from 10 a.m. until about 3 p.m. on Christmas Eve.

We did the session, and afterwards Albert Neugebauer handed me an envelope.

"Thank you, Mark. This is for showing that we are appreciating very much the work you do for us."

The envelope contained fifteen hundred deutschmarks. That represented about one-thousand dollars cash. Today, that would be a nice bonus for anyone. In 1979, right before Christmas, it was like winning the lottery.

Vlado, Dusko, Dado, Muc and Adi—I won't forget them any time soon. And Albert Neugebauer, their Croatian producer who lived in Frankfurt. Jane and I still talk about the way those guys could eat, their camaraderie, their laughter, and their general enthusiasm for life.

That was one of the things that Jane and I regularly observed in Germany. There was a clear sense that Europeans worked to live, whereas North Americans tended to live to work. To this day, very few people in Germany and Europe own their own home. They rent, and they spend the rest of their money on restaurants and clothes and being social with their friends. This was one of the life facets that Jane and I enjoyed most about living in Germany. We were also amazed at how quickly we forged new friendships, and the openness and warmth that we encountered with so many people.

I remember one particular Saturday evening just after Jane had arrived, and we were in our room at the Hotel Bolivar wondering what to do with ourselves. Suddenly, the phone rang. Jane and I looked at each other quizzically. It seemed strange that someone would be calling because we knew so few people. I picked up the receiver tentatively.

"Hello?"

"Hello, Mark," a voice on the line said. "It is Mathias. Your remember me?"

Mathias was the bass player in a band called Garden, which was Geoff Hall's band—the assistant manager at Hotline. I had gone to one of their gigs a few weeks back and mixed the main PA system for them.

"Yes, Mathias, of course I remember you!"

"You know Rocky Horror Picture Show?"

I was only vaguely familiar with the movie, but I said, "Yes, of course!"

"You want to go?"

Within a few minutes, we were racing through the streets of Frankfurt in Mathias' Opal Europa 2 door sedan. The movie was utterly mind-bending for the time. Jane and I had certainly never seen anything like it. People dressed in drag, and the audience throwing rice during the wedding scene and slices of toast when there was a toast to the bride, plus spray bottles or water guns when it was raining.

Of course, Rocky Horror went on to become on of the biggest cult movies ever made. But this evening became the start of a wonderful and enduring friendship between Jane and me and our friends Hella and Mathias. Their zeal for life continues to inspire us.

I continued working at Hotline into April of 1980. Then one day I received a call from Calgary. It was my old band buddy, Neil McCallum.

He had an offer for me. He and I had previously talked about building a recording studio in Calgary—something state of the art that could really impact the landscape of music recording in western Canada—and while I had been in Germany, things had started to take shape. Now the project looked like it was becoming a reality, and I had the opportunity to be one of the founding partners.

I told Neil that I needed a couple of days to mull it over. I hung up the phone, and I told Jane the news.

Jane and I talked about it for a long while. In the end, we decided it was a special opportunity that was too good to miss. As hard as it was to leave the friends we had made in Frankfurt, and the job that I loved at Hotline, we figured that destiny was calling.

In late spring of 1980, we boarded the plane again. And suddenly we were on our way back to Calgary with a new mountain to conquer.

That summer, Srebryna Krila's second album was released. In the years since, whenever I have met just about anyone from the former Yugoslavia, and I tell them that I was the recording engineer on this album, they just about fall off their chairs. It sold over a million copies in Yugoslavia.

ELEVEN

Thunder Road

On my return to Canada, I felt like I had been away a lifetime. It was May 1980, and after being immersed in German culture and the very progressive Frankfurt music scene for the better part of a year, Canada seemed strangely foreign to me now.

It had been a difficult to leave Frankfurt, as we had felt very comfortable there. We had made a lot of great friendships, and we were very settled into the German lifestyle.

But I recognized that we had a special opportunity with the plan to build a new studio like nothing Calgary had ever seen. Prior to my leaving for Germany in 1979, my friend and fellow sax player Neil McCallum and I had spent hours discussing the possibilities. Together with his brother Ron, we had seen that the community was really lacking a world-class facility. In my absence, things had gradually taken shape as Neil and Ron had connected with a couple of prospective investors.

By May 1980, the dream was ready to become a reality. Now we had the chance to actually build the facility and create something special. I felt that we could make a significant contribution to the Canadian recording industry. Our hope was to build a facility so killer that it would become a destination studio for bands throughout North America, and even the world.

We would be starting from scratch, and that was a key selling point for me. I believed I knew what was required to create the ultimate studio and what made a studio work in terms of layout and design, so by starting from square one in concept and construction, I knew that we had the opportunity to create something that really hit all the key markers for design, layout and recording technology. But first we needed to find the right building.

We knew that we wanted the studio to be designed by a world-class architect. In our research, the name Tom Hidley kept surfacing. We quickly learned that getting Tom Hidley to design your studio was like getting Jack Nicklaus to design your golf course. During the 1970s, he had steadily built a reputation as one of the great founders of modern studio design. He had designed studios such as Strawberry North in the United Kingdom for the band 10CC and two studios for the Record Plants—one in New York and one in Los Angeles. Our research also introduced us to a company in Los Angeles called Lakeside Associates that had built several top-end studios designed by him.

Neil, Ron and I flew to Los Angeles to meet with Tom Hidley and Lakeside Associates, and we ended up hiring them. The first step was to help us with the initial site and building selection. One of their partners, Steve Fouce, flew up for an initial consultation. When we met at Neil's house, I felt an instant connection with Steve, and we ended up becoming close friends for years to follow. During his two-day stay, he helped us to establish the criteria for what kind of building and location we would need.

We spent the next four months looking at possible buildings for our studio. We looked at a couple of old Safeway stores and a bunch of different warehouses before we finally signed off on leasing space in a new commercial building that was going to be constructed near the airport.

We committed to taking just over 12,000 square feet. We planned to include a recording studio, a dubbing theatre for film sound postproduction, and a lab for processing 16 and 35-millimeter film. By now, it was 1981—long before "multimedia" became a buzzword—but we were already calling it a multimedia facility.

We figured if we were going to build something in Calgary, we had to make it really substantial, otherwise people wouldn't take it seriously. Looking back now, I don't think that Calgary was the right place to build a studio that was worth a million dollars, but that was our thinking at the time.

Steve and Lakeside provided blueprints from Tom Hidley and we were underway.

I ended up being intimately involved in every stage of the studio's construction. During my teens, I had worked every summer in construction, some of it as an apprentice carpenter, so I knew how to swing a hammer, shoot elevations, build concrete forms and all the rest. As we negotiated the lease of the building, Neil and I felt it would make sense for me to be part of the construction process. The property owner, Joe Sefel, was fine with the idea, so I was introduced to the superintendent of the project, a guy named Lou.

It was a great arrangement because I could help to make sure the building met some of our special requirements. Lou was a gruff character, so he was a bit hesitant to embrace the idea. He thought it was a bit weird that one of the owners was going to help him build the building. As well, this was "man's work" and I was a very tall lean artsy type. However, with a little pressure from the building owner, Lou agreed to hire me, and it ended up working out very well. We also probably got a bit of leverage from the building owner from having signed a five-year lease at $10,000 a month.

I showed up on the first day at 7:30 a.m. with by big metal carpenter's tool box. Lou looked me up and down, then he showed me the elevation drawings. We reviewed the building's footprint, and he asked me to build batter boards so we could string thick wire to mark the building foundation lines. I grabbed my tools and went to work without hesitation. When I completed the task without any help or coaching, I managed to win his respect. That set the tone for the rest of the project—and we would go on to become friends through the process of building the studio.

Being so closely involved in the construction of the building allowed us to ensure that certain special structural features were addressed. One feature included troughs in the floor slabs, so we could create cable runs between rooms. When you normally build a recording studio, you generally start with a building that is already built. If you want to run cable from one room to the next, you have go over the ceiling or you have to go around the walls. At best, it's always like an add-on. The most elegant solution is when you can actually put the cables right in the ground.

We reviewed the studio plans and the layout, and we made sure that the cable runs were formed into the floor when we poured the concrete slab. Afterwards, we created access panels with lift-off lids flush with the finished floor for all of the runs. It was a great feature, as we were able to run cables from all over the building without creating obstructions for people and equipment.

To oversee construction of the new studio within the new building, we hired Steve and his partner Carl Yanchar. They hired a guy from London named Paul to be the foreman. He was a trained carpenter *and* a specialist in building recording studios, so we got along very well. We built the studio together with three other trades guys that I had hired named Harold, Matt and Nube.

The studio was essentially designed to be a building within a building. That is, the walls of the actual studio did not touch the outside walls of the building structure. The outside walls were constructed of concrete cinder blocks, and these were in turn filled with kiln-dried sand. This made the walls very dense and soundproof.

The walls inside of the cinderblock walls were then constructed with two-by-six lumber. The outside of these walls was sheeted with donnaconna board, and the inside with three layers of gyproc and particle board. The gyproc and particleboard were then covered with a variety of finished surfaces such as hardwood, stone, mirror, or tree bark. Tree bark from Africa was a big thing in studios during the 1970s and 1980s because it had a great texture that helped the acoustics, and it also looked cool.

The interior walls sat on their own floating concrete slab, so the slab inside the studio never made physical contact with the slabs of the interior walls or the surrounding building beyond. From there, the studio floor was poured as two one-foot-thick concrete slabs, one lying on top of the other. Each of these slabs floated on a bed of inch-and-a-half insulation to prevent sound vibrations from travelling between them, and the top slab was further divided like a jigsaw puzzle into isolated room-sized slabs for drums, piano, string room, and main room.

We poured all of the isolated slabs first, stripped the forms, and then lined the edges of the slabs with half-inch rubber insulation before pouring the rest of the top floor slab around them. When we were done, you could stand on one slab and hit the slab next to you with a sledgehammer and you wouldn't feel any vibration. This meant that there would be no sound vibrations travelling through the floor from one area to the next during recording.

We also created an isolation room with similar aims. It was entirely glass across the front with huge glass sliding doors. On the inside, the ceiling sloped from a height of eighteen feet high at one end to about sixteen feet over a 20-foot distance. This avoided creating parallel surfaces between the floor and the ceiling, which could create the problem of standing sound waves.

While the studio construction was underway, Neil and I had set out and started to buy studio equipment. We were like kids on Christmas morning, reviewing different consoles, tape machines, microphones, and outboard equipment and effects devices such as compressors, digital delays and harmonizers. Our goal was to equip the studio with the best of the best in every aspect, starting with our Rupert Neve 8108 mixing desk (only the twelfth of its kind ever made) and an arsenal of handpicked microphones that were each chosen for particular characteristics and uses.

It took us about six months to complete the studio. In the end, I won Lou's respect as an able builder and we managed to construct an exceptional facility. The entire experience was thoroughly rewarding. For me, it represented the culmination of so many years both working as a musician and dreaming of making records, going all the way back to my grade five "band" where I first sang into the microphone of an old tape machine.

We needed a name for our new facility, and I dubbed it Thunder Road Studios. "Thunder" because we wanted to make some noise, and "road" because it would be a conduit through which great music and great art would flow.

Now it was time to get down to the business of drawing clients and actually making recordings. The studio's two main investors had been Helmut Hoffer and Neil's brother, Ron McCallum, and Neil and I were the minor investors. Nonetheless, I was a principal founder of the studio and its chief engineer. It was therefore my responsibility to manage the bookings for the studio, along with any other engineers who might work for us, and oversee the maintenance of the equipment. So I was very much at the heart of the daily operations of the new studio.

It wasn't long before we were busy. We didn't get a lot of big stars, but there were a lot of local artists, and a lot of people who came in for just a day or two.

One small job was funny. After the studio had been open for about a year, I got a call one day from an ad agency in Los Angeles. They told me that they had a U.S. client called Chief Auto, and they had just signed a deal with Don Adams, the star of the late-1960s television sitcom *Get Smart*. And I had loved *Get Smart* as a kid.

It turned out that Don Adams was in Calgary doing dinner theater, and they wanted him to record a bunch of voiceovers at our studio for some U.S. commercials. While we recorded, the ad agency would connect with us from Los Angeles by conference line so they could hear Don and provide direction. I would run the session, record everything, and then send the tape to Los Angeles.

"Sure, no problem," I said. We scheduled a recording session for the following Tuesday.

"By the way," said the guy from the agency. "It's his birthday next Tuesday. Can you organize a car for him?"

"For sure – I'll even pick him up myself!"

The following Tuesday I went to the Calgary Inn Hotel to pick up Don Adams in a chauffeured car. In the car coming back to the studio, we made chit chat. He was a bit aloof, but I told him that I was a huge fan, and we talked about some of the different episodes. He seemed to warm up once he saw that I really knew the show and the characters.

We arrived at the studio and started recording. The first thing that they wanted him to read was the word "sparkplug."

I don't know why he did it this way, but Don said it just the way anyone might say it in their normal voice. The agency guy on the phone line from Los Angeles said to me, "No, we need it in the Maxwell Smart voice."

So I looked at Don in the sound booth, and I said, "Don, they're kind of looking for something more like *sparkplug*!" And I said the word "sparkplug" in my well-practiced Maxwell Smart voice.

He looked at me and chuckled. "You get in here and do this!"

"Well, my rate is probably cheaper!"

Everybody laughed.

We ended up having a good time doing the session. In the car on the way back to the hotel, I said to him, "I have to tell you my favorite *Get Smart* episode."

"Which one was that?"

And I proceeded to reenact an entire 5-minute passage of dialogue between agent Maxwell Smart and his arch-nemesis Ludwig Von Zigfried of KAOS, perfectly replicating Smart's nasal-intonations and Ziegfried's exaggerated German accent.

He looked at me and his jaw dropped. He recognized the episode, and I had basically nailed the entire dialogue word for word. We laughed our heads off. That day remains one of my fondest memories of Thunder Road days.

But we eventually started to struggle. Another studio called Smooth

Rock was built in Calgary around the same time, and it was also a very good studio. So the city now had two world-class facilities when two years earlier it had none, and there just wasn't enough business in Calgary to sustain both. In 1985, the bank called our loan, and we had to sell off the equipment. It was a very sad time. Our partner Helmut Hoffer, who the bank went after first for repayment sued Neil and me. The lawsuit arrived at my house via bailiff at 4 p.m. on December 24, 1986. I am certain there was no coincidence in the timing of it's arrival. Merry Christmas!

Our intentions had been good, but ultimately the market just wasn't big enough. We had probably overestimated the need in Calgary, but sometimes you just don't know until you try. We gave it everything we had and I had turned myself inside out to make it a success. Nonetheless, I am still extremely proud of the studio that we built and the mark we left behind. We created some great recordings while we were there.

Taking time out for a bit of target practice after my newspaper deliveries. Winnipeg 1962.

My first selfie taken on Victoria Glacier, Lake Louise. Exhausted having just arrived at 9000 ft. The silence was deafening. October 1973.

Breathtaking beauty on Victoria Glacier. The tent was up. The universe was definitely conspiring to find me the only tree…well above the tree line. October 1973.

Early days...one of my first bands "Piebald Shark". Calgary 1974.

Saying goodbye. With Jane October 3, 1975 in Santa Cruz, Tenerrife, Canary Islands.

Recording Linda Curtis album—Sound West Studios, Calgary. Money was tight. The envelope in my pocket is an electrical bill that was going to be paid from what I earned playing the session. November 1978. Photo: Ivan Knowles

)la) 336	**65**	~~How How How~~ R. Chapman, G. Whitehorn, Chappell Instant (RCA) 60 61 · 7. Woche **Roger Chapman** ZB 69 103, Maxi: ZC 69 104	
ßt 717	**66**	**Geh nicht in die Stadt (heut nacht)** H. Steinhauer, M. Kunze, Mambo/Siegel Mambo (WEA) 69 59 · 14. Woche **Juliane Werding** 249 510-7	
)la) 086	**67**	**Only You** Clarke, Clarke, Gerig Virgin (Ariola) 72 44 · 19. Woche **The Flying Pickets** 106 103, Maxi: 601 135	
BS) 291	**68**	**We All Live Together – So Bad** Dunhill, M. Dash, J. Ellenson, Ed. Alice EMI (EMI Electrola) 54 54 · 7. Woche **Melissa** 1654 647	
)la) 637	**69**	**Talking In Your Sleep** Marinos, Palmar, Skill, Canler, Solley, F., D. & H. Epic (CBS) 68 67 · 12. Woche **The Romantics** EPC A 3861, Maxi: 12-3861	
)la) 182	**70**	**Ci sarà** D. Farina, M. Hofmann, C. Minellono, Gerig Baby (EMI Electrola) – 70 · 9. Woche **Al Bano & Romina Power** 2000 627	
dec 115	**71**	**Get Out Of Your Lazy Bed** M. Bianco, M. Bianco, Intro WEA 66 – · 2. Woche **Matt Bianco** 24.9532-7	
)la) 411	**72**	**Hold Me Now** T. Bailey, A. Currie, J. Leeway, Wintrup/Point Arista (Ariola) 62 60 · 17. Woche **Thompson Twins** 106 037, Maxi: 601 085	
)on 067	**73**	**Hypnotic Tango** Ginko, Tayx, Sugar Music Blow Up (Intercord) 55 33 · 18. Woche **My Mine** INT 110.543, Maxi: INT 125.522	
dor GG) 1-7	**74** NEU	**Rainy Day In London** M. Holden, M. Holden, Rüssl CBS **Boulevard** A 4277	
)la) 194	**75**	**Ballet Dancer** S. Dohrow, R. Schreinzer, Intro Hansa Int. (Ariola) 63 63 · 16. Woche **The Twins** 105 986, Maxi: 601 068	

First entry into the Billboard top 100 European charts, April 1984. We were in the presence of some good company, Rainy Day in London ultimately topped out in the low 40's but we were still very stoked! This chart entry would go on to change things for Boulevard and open a lot of doors for us back home. The clipping is framed and still hangs on the wall of my office.

Our house phone. A phone booth at the end of Stalburg Strasser, Frankfurt. December 1979.

Studio 2 at Hotline Studios, Frankfurt, Germany. Perhaps a late one the night before. November 1979.

With Carl Yanchar, Lakeside Associates—building Thunder Road. Looking toward what would be the isolation room, used to record strings and orchestral performances. Calgary 1981.

Setting up for our big day of recording half of the Calgary Philharmonic for the Charlene Prickett album at Thunder Road. Calgary 1983.

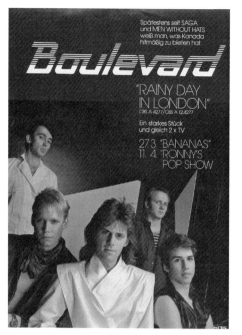

Our first release in Germany on CBS records. 1984.

Happier times with Randy Gould. Boulevard's first gig in Victoria before setting off on our cross-Canada tour with Glass Tiger. July 1988.

Signing our recording contract with MCA Records in Bruce Allen's office. Left-Right: Tuerino Barbero, MCA; Randy Burgess, Bass; Randy Gould, Guitar; Bruce Allen; Cliff Jones; John Alexander, Head of A&R MCA Records Canada; Andrew Johns, Keyboards. January 1988.

Backstage, Pacific Coliseum, Vancouver. Left-Right: Andrew Johns, Randall Stoll, Randy Gould, Bryan Adams, David Forbes. 1988.

Backstage with Boston. They were such amazingly generous guys to tour with, giving us access to use most of their lighting and PA system. Typically unheard of for an opening act. We felt like rock stars! Seattle Coliseum. December 1988.

Backstage with the All-Star Band at the Music Express Awards. Left-Right: Allan Frew, Glass Tiger; Mike Levine, Triumph; Lee Aaron; Sass Jordan; Kenny Maclean, Platinum Blonde; Dominic Troiano; Gil Moore, Triumph; Ian Thomas. February 1989.

On set with Joan Rivers. Vancouver, March 1994.

Three generations. April Point Lodge—First Catch. Campbell River. June 1996.

With Dan Lowe in Cannes, France on Ezone business. May 1996.

At the top of Lombard St. in San Francisco immediatly following our pitch to Comm Ventures to fund Hip Digital. May 2006. Left-Right: Peter Diemer, Vered Koren, Karim Mitha.

Back on my on my new Cervello time trial bike climbing Alpe D'huez. June 2008.

At Ironman Canada in 2009 racing to raise funds in support of my friend and fellow triathlete Frank Kurucz who we'd lost to leukemia a few years earlier.

Where it all started. My interpretation of the the Peace symbol. Acrylic on canvas. Vancouver 2011.

With Jane, sailing in the Adriatic. The island of Hvar, Croatia in the background. August 2010.

Peace, how big could I make it? August 2013.

Final touches…shooting our first PR campaign video with my beautiful model, my daughter, Ashley. Vancouver, August 2013.

How many people does it take to make peace. Four and a good photographer. Kits Beach, Vancouver 2013.

At Mark Holden Fashion "Design Central" with Don Bull. New shades from Paris.

Early morning in Union Square, New York City. A moment to reflect before the mayhem, as 65 Andie MacDowell "look-alike" models rode through the streets of Manhattan. June 2014.

With Andie MacDowell and the 65 model "Bike Brigade" ready to take to the streets of Manhattan to promote the hit series "Cedar Cove". June 2014.

Feeling the 47°C degree heat in Qatar at a trunk show for our collection. August 2014.

First few notes…our first rehearsal in 26 years. Left-Right: Dave Forbes, Andrew Johns. Vancouver, March 2014.

With Elliot and Ashley at our first Vancouver gig in 26 years at the Backstage Lounge—our final show proir to heading off to the UK for Firefest. October 2014.

Pre-show warm-up backstage at Rock City. Nottingham, England, October 2014.

Firefest 2014, Nottingham, England. Moments after our show. Left-Right: Randall Stoll, Andrew Johns, Thom Christiansen, David Forbes, Dave Corman. What a blast!

Recording backing tracks for the new album Boulevard IV at Abby Road Studios, Studio 2. London, October 2014.

At work on the new Boulevard album at Andrew's house in Vernon, Canada. Dave Corman, Guitar; Andrew, keyboards. June 2016.

Working on the book at my favorite work station. Like so many afternoon writing sessions, I would suddenly look up after being totally lost in the process and realize it was dark out. Vancouver 2015.

TWELVE

It Figures

During my time at Thunder Road, my reputation was growing. And from time to time, I was presented with opportunities that might not have come my way had I not been connected with the studio. It was all great fodder for the career and life ahead of me. Probably one of my best lessons came when I was asked to create some music for an exercise guru.

In 1982, I was approached by Charlene Prickett to write a theme song for her television exercise program. She had a successful show called *It Figures* that ran on one of the three local television channels in Calgary at that time, and it also ran on the Lifetime Network in the U.S. where it was very popular.

"No problem!" I told her. "I have a few ideas in mind. Why don't I write you something, and if you like it, we'll record it. You can use it and we'll figure out payment later."

Charlene was slim, fit, energetic and spoke with a bit of a twang from her native Arkansas. She nodded enthusiastically in agreement. "That sounds great!" she said.

So I went away and wrote a song that I thought would be a fit. When I came back and presented the recording to her a week later, she really liked it, so we discussed a modest price and she wrote me a cheque. I believe the amount we settled on was $300. She subsequently ended up using the music on every show for the opening and closing titles. Given what I would come to learn in the following years about the value of music for television and music rights in general, perhaps I had been a bit too generous. But this opened up a door that I felt could lead to bigger things. And it had all the potential to do just that.

A few months later, Charlene came back to me with another request.

"Mark, I've been approached by K-Tel," she explained. "They want to do an exercise record. Can you help me with it?"

At that time, Jane Fonda exercise videos were all the rage. Charlene's show was very similar and also very good, so the timing was perfect. She had a great following in the U.S. and Canada.

We sat together, and I asked her what they were offering her.

"They're saying that they'll give me 30 cents per record," said Charlene. "I don't know what's good and what's bad."

"Do you want some advice?"

"Absolutely!" she replied.

"Well, that's not a phenomenally high royalty rate," I said. In fact, it was very low compared to market standards. "But there are other options as well."

"What would those be?"

"Well, you can form your own label, and do it yourself," I said.

"But I wouldn't know where to start!" she replied.

"Well, I might be interested in doing it with you as a partnership. We can form a label, and I will raise money to make the record."

"How would that work?" The tone of her reply was an odd mixture of curiosity, suspicion, and a hint of condescension. I would later come to learn that my instincts based on this single question and her tone would be closer to the truth than I could possibly have imagined.

"Well, I can track down some investors who are likely to be interested in this kind of project, and we can offer to pay them back at a rate twice their principal. The deal will be the same for any investor that comes in. I can also cut deals with the musicians, and with the studio as well."

As one of the owners, I knew I could do that. We went through the numbers together and discussed what it could look like.

"You can take a small royalty on the K-Tel record and you will probably do okay," I said. "They will probably sell a lot of records because they've got a great advertising budget. But your royalty is very low, and you won't get to control anything. They may say 30 cents, but there may be all kinds of clever accounting that you don't know about. So when it comes time to actually get paid, what you think you're going to get and what you actually see may not be the same thing."

I wasn't saying anything out of school. That was just classic record industry practice at the time.

She mulled over what I had said, and she decided that she would like to make her own record with me.

So we got started. We began by selecting the music. One of the tracks that I had written, the opening music for her television program, was expanded into a full blown song called "Got What it Takes?" That was the first track we chose. We also decided to do a cover of the Queen song, "Another One Bites the Dust."

We discussed how Charlene really liked the series of records called Hooked on Classics. It was really big in the early 1980s. The producers would take classical music by composers such as Beethoven and Mozart and record it with a disco beat. Charlene liked the idea of doing something similar, so we set our sights on doing some classical recordings in the same style with local symphony musicians.

On the business end, we needed a label to produce our record, so I formed a record company called Rubicon Records. To cover production costs and manufacturing, I approached a few potential investors and managed to raise $25,000 from five of them with the agreement that we would pay them double their money within twelve months.

The Hooked on Classics approach meant that we needed an orchestra. I went to my friend Cenek Vrba, who was the concertmaster of the Calgary Philharmonic. I had worked with Cenek numerous times in the past on various session recordings.

I told Cenek that we wanted these recordings to sound huge, so I figured we probably needed a majority of the Philharmonic to pull it off. That was going to be costly.

So I asked him, "If I offer to pay the musicians double their normal scale for a three-hour session, do you think they would be willing to defer their payment until I had sold enough records to pay them back?"

Cenek said, "Well, let me try."

He talked to his group, and they agreed. Most of them knew me from doing sessions at Thunder Road, so I had already built a relationship of trust with most of them.

We ended up having a very large collection of musicians and instruments, including a harp, six violins, four violas, three cellos, a double bass and two percussionists. It was a meaningful cross section of strings. I made up a little contract and each one of them signed it as they arrived at the studio. We had some other musicians as well, including a guitar player, a bass player, and a singer. It was a great selection of musicians, and the energy in the sessions was excellent.

With the studio filled with about two thirds of the Calgary Philharmonic, I found myself thinking a few times that afternoon as we were recording, "Wow! I can't believe I pulled this off! Now all we have to do is sell enough records to pay for this lavish collection of highly accomplished musicians!"

My euphoria was quickly replaced by a slight lump in my throat as the reality set in. As I moved forward as an entrepreneur in the years that followed, this was a feeling that would become abundantly familiar and pretty much commonplace for me.

We made the record, we pressed the albums, and we manufactured the cassettes. Now we had to sell some records.

I sat down with Charlene, and I suggested the approach we should take. I told her we should place a 10-second tag the end of every one of her shows along the lines of "For your copy of Charlene Pricket Does Floors, call 1-800." We would flash the picture of the album cover, which featured Charlene sitting on the floor with her legs up in the air in an athletic posture.

She agreed that this was a good idea. We would have a 1-800 number that people could call and order a copy of the album, and they would send their cheque or money order in. This was long before the days of VISA online payments and PayPal.

So we made a little 10-second tag at the end of every show, which we would send to all of the different TV stations that were running her program in Canada and the U.S. I did the voice-over myself to save money on having to hire voice talent. But first I had to go and cut the deal with the Lifetime Network, which was owned by ABC-Hearst-Viacom in New York.

I went to New York with a copy of the tag and met with a member of their staff, Andrea Ingram, in the Time-Life Building on the Avenue of the Americas. I flew down on my own nickel, paid for my own hotel, met with the ABC-Viacom Network people, and reached an agreement whereby they would run our advertisement and we would give them a dollar for every album we sold with no cash advance from us. (These types of deals typically required some sort of advance from the producer up front that would cover set-up costs and go against orders as they came in.)

In addition, we would use their 1-800 call center in Atlanta and pay the cost of an additional $1.50 per call. It was a win for them and a big win for us.

I flew back to Calgary and told Charlene that we were good to go. She was excited, and I was too. We had the records, and we had cassettes—now we just needed to fulfill the orders as they arrived.

It's a bit heart warming for me to remember how we did it. Every time I think about it, I get a bit emotional. Because it was a testament to my wife Jane's wonderful "get-right-in-there" attitude and her complete willingness to support me in all of my entrepreneurial ventures before and since.

We started tagging the program with our advertisement, and almost immediately we were receiving thirty or forty orders per day from all over the U.S. and Canada. I bought cardboard mailers, I bought packing tape, I bought tape guns for taping up the packages, and I bought a business postage machine with a scale. Suddenly the basement of our small home in Calgary was a fulfillment house.

My workday took on an entirely new shape. I would work all day at the studio, then come home for dinner, and then Jane and I would work from seven o'clock until about midnight packing up records and cassettes. We would label them and attach the right postage, and then I would deliver them to the post office the next morning on my way to the studio.

We did this for several weeks until we were seeing double with fatigue, and our hands were cut to ribbons from paper cuts.

But Jane never once complained. She stayed right in there.

Several weeks into this process, I met with Charlene. She said, "Mark, I don't mind saying you look dreadful!"

I told her what we had been doing.

"You're kidding!" she said. "That's crazy! I know a woman who works at the post office, and she has a little back room where she does fulfillment for things just like this, and she does it all."

This was a massive relief. We talked with Charlene's friend, Tuck Taylor, and I went out and bought my first computer—an Apple IIe—so she could make the labels. We got her set up, and she took over the mailing.

We ended up selling close to 30,000 albums. And at that time, 50,000 in sales was a gold record in Canada. We were more than half way there, so those were substantial numbers.

All of the investors were paid double their investment, and every musician was paid double scale. The studio was paid at a premium, and it was a profitable venture for everybody involved.

And all of it basically happened out of the basement of our home. If you want to talk about taking something from concept to final product on a shoestring and delivering serious sales, this was a stunning success.

As far as I was concerned, this was just the beginning. I saw much of our work to that point as being simply the initial investment for something bigger. We were laying the groundwork for more projects. Establishing the label, establishing the mailing system, establishing all of the deals I had done with the investors, and with ABC-Hearst-Viacom. This was just the first phase of a much bigger vision. With all of the start-up costs paid, we would really start to make profit on the second and subsequent albums. It was exciting to imagine where we could take things.

Unfortunately, Charlene would soon take a different view.

When I went to New York and did all of the leg work with Lifetime Networks, it had been a big undertaking and a huge risk for me. But my hope and expectation, of course, was that Charlene and I would go on and do albums number two, three and four together. But when it came time to discuss album number two, Charlene had other thoughts.

"But Mark," she said in the exact same simple, matter-of-fact tone she had used when we first met, "Why would I do this with you, when I can just do it by myself?"

I was nearly dumbstruck. "Well, you certainly can," I replied, trying to get the lump in my throat to settle and the saliva to return to my mouth. "But I thought we both understood that we were doing it together. You know as well as I do that the first program or product that you create is always the most expensive, and it takes the most effort and time.

"Everything from organizing the cardboard mailers to the printing plant back east at Quality Records, negotiating a deal with them, and negotiating their pressing and duplication rates, negotiating publishing deals and rights clearances without an entertainment lawyer representing us. All of the groundwork to produce and market the record— I did all of that."

Charlene more or less just shrugged. So we parted ways without any clear commitment one way or another.

We never did do a second record. She ended up making a lot of money marketing her own videos, so she simply continued on that track. And that was the end of our venture together.

That's life, right? Things happen. But I gained a couple of valuable business insights through the experience.

The number one takeaway for me was that it was possible to take something from concept to market and do well. The key was determination and thorough planning, and the willingness to work your ass off.

The other takeaway was to learn more about contract law and partnership agreements.

Whatever happened to a handshake?

THIRTEEN

Boulevard

Long before moving to Germany to work at Hotline, I had carried a burning desire to write my own music. It had been burning ever since I first heard Bob Dylan and Neil Young when I was in grade school. To me it was the ultimate form of expression. Yet even though I had now been immersed in the music business for several years, I had only ever dabbled in song writing. I had scored my first co-writer credit on a song called "Something Good" for a Linda Curtis in 1978, when I played sax on her album, but I had never quite found the time and the discipline to make it happen on a bigger scale. I still hadn't truly delivered on my childhood dream to write a significant body of my own work. This started to change after Jane and I moved to Germany.

Living and working in Frankfurt as a recording engineer was inspirational and transformational for me. I was surrounded by talented musicians and singers who were creating art and making money while they did it. Encouraged and inspired by their example, I finally started writing in earnest at every possible opportunity.

Whenever I came up with ideas for melody lines and themes, I would just throw down a whole bunch of ideas together and then leave it for a day or two, or even a week, and then I would come back and revisit it. When ideas came to mind, I was often scrambling to find a piece of paper to write down a lyric or reaching for a small portable cassette recorder to hum or whistle a melody. Obviously, this was long before cell phones and voice memo apps were available. This ultimately became my creative process through the duration of my career and it still is.

When I came back to my notes, sometimes my ideas would surprise me by being better than I had remembered, but sometimes they were outright horrible. Often I might find myself whistling something, so I would write it down before I forgot it. Other times I might get an idea in the middle of the night, so I would run down to the piano and very quietly play the melody and get it on a tape recorder so I didn't lose it. More than once I would wake up the next morning and listen to it, and I would wince: *Good grief—what was I thinking?* But very often, I would find a beautiful surprise, and that provided so much of the pleasure of creating.

While this process of writing continued in Germany—jotting down different lyrical ideas, capturing fragments of melodies, and so on—I didn't have the opportunity to record them even though I was working full time at Hotline. I didn't have access to the studio to record my own ideas. But I continued writing nonetheless, and I was slowly accumulating an audio "sketchbook" of ideas.

At the time, I was very inspired by Alan Parsons. He was a brilliant songwriter and engineer who had worked his way up from an assistant engineer position at Abbey Road Studios. In addition to his own Alan Parsons Project albums, he may be best known for engineering and producing the epic Pink Floyd album, "Dark Side of the Moon". I was a huge fan of his work, and I drew a tremendous amount of inspiration from his music and his production techniques.

By the time I had settled back in Canada in 1980, my craft had been well-honed from my time working in Germany with a number of international albums to my credit, and I had logged some serious hours of studio time. Now I dropped back into the Canadian music scene, and I was primed and ready to finally create some music of my own.

Once the studio was built and running, I began to record my ideas at Thunder Road in my spare time. By now it was 1982, and I was excited to try to create my own project album in line with what Alan Parsons had done.

I managed to pull together enough funds from an outside investor, and I joined together with my good friend Dan Lowe, who was a talented musician-producer. Dan and I rooted through hours of my cassette tapes and sheets of lyrics, and we went through the process of selecting the best from what we found. Next, we began to pull together the various pieces, different sounds, melodies and effects that we thought would weave together a solid body of work. I ended up writing and recording a complete album's worth of material that I called "Modern Minds".

One of the songs I wrote was called "Rainy Day in London", and I was especially pleased with how it turned out. It was a really mellow ballad that had a distinctive Pink Floyd influence.

I was very excited about the Modern Minds project, and I started to shop it around to different labels and agents in the hopes of attracting interest. Almost on a whim, or perhaps even on a wing and a prayer, I sent a copy of the tape to a friend of mine in Germany, Rudi Rockenschaub.

Rudi was a very talented backup singer whom I had met during many recording sessions at the studio in Frankfurt. Different bands would hire her to do vocals, and she would come down from Hamburg to record with them at Hotline Studios. She was a phenomenal talent, and a colorful character, and she became a very dear friend.

I sent her a copy of three or four of the songs , and I asked her to tell me what she thought of it. I told her that if she liked it, I could send her more copies and we could perhaps send it to a few labels in Germany.

After all, I really liked the music scene in Germany, and I had a feeling that my music might have an opportunity there. The German music scene at that time was very progressive and self-sufficient. If you were signed in Germany, especially if you were a German band, you could sell half a million records very easily, which meant you could survive and make a living with German sales alone.

I mailed my demo tape to Rudi, and I continued shopping the demo to different labels in Canada. However, I couldn't get anyone at any one of the record companies to return phone calls or respond in any way. My efforts to get any label attention seemed to fall on completely deaf ears. In the music industry at that time, the expression for this complete lack of interest was "I couldn't get arrested".

I did get one rejection letter from EMI's head of A&R—artist and repertoire—Deane Cameron. But he was the only guy who ever wrote back. He basically said, sorry, we're not going to sign your band, but thank you for submitting your tape.

I didn't know it yet, but we were destined to meet again in the not-so-distant future as Deane and I would go on to work together in a very different capacity and become friends. However, for the time being, my demo was essentially getting no interest from anyone, and I couldn't help but start to feel discouraged. To make matters worse, my budget for blank cassettes and postage was running very thin.

Then, in the autumn of 1983, I was suddenly awoken in the middle of the night by a phone call.

I looked at the clock radio, and it was four o'clock in the morning. I was completely disoriented. Who could be calling at that hour? The first thing I thought was that someone had died.

I picked up the phone and braced myself for bad news.

It was Rudi calling from Germany.

"Mark! You got a deal!" she said excitedly. "You got a deal!"

"Wha…What? What do you mean?" I stammered in my daze.

"Hans took your tape to CBS and they want to sign the band!"

"Hans who?"

It turned out that Rudi had loved the demo, and she had in turn taken it to her friend Hans Kruger, who was a music publisher and a partner at a publishing company in Hamburg called Russell Music. He was a very connected guy and took our tape to CBS in Germany.

"My friend Hans loves 'Rainy Day in London' and he has you a deal with CBS!" Rudi went on.

Within a few days I was on the phone with Hans, and contracts were being drawn up. CBS liked the music, and they especially liked the "Rainy Day in London" track, but they didn't like the name Modern Minds, so they said they wanted to change the name of the band.

For the most part, the tracks had basically been recorded by studio musicians, with the exception of Andrew Johns who was our keyboard player and lead singer at the time. I quickly began to assemble the rest of the band, and I had some back and forth discussion with Hans over a band name. In the end, I think I simply said, "Well, how about Boulevard?" He ran it by CBS and they liked it.

Our band's first line up was Andrew Johns on keyboards and lead vocals, Randall Stoll on drums, Hans Sahlen on bass, Randy Gould on guitar, and me on sax.

Before we knew it, CBS was flying us over to Frankfurt to shoot our first music video for "Rainy Day in London." We arrived in Frankfurt around 10:30 a.m. and we were taken immediately to the video studio for an 18-hour day of shooting. We were wiped out with fatigue by the time we made it back to the hotel.

I was also very ill with a bad cold that I had contracted on the flight from Canada. At the time, our son Elliot was 8 weeks old and as he was not a sleep-through-the-night kind of guy. He was up all night every night, so I had not had more than a few hours sleep per night for weeks. Classic parenting with babies. So my immune system was pretty much non-existent when we made the trip to Germany.

Our song was released on three different compilation albums in Germany, and we made a few television appearances. One of them was called Ronnie's Pop Show, which was shot weekly in Cologne and hosted by a chimpanzee named Ronnie. We also appeared on a national television program called Bananas. Prior to the show, I found myself sitting in a make-up chair and looking over at Tracey Ullman sitting beside me. She was also getting prepped to appear on the show.

When we were all in our wardrobe and made-up with tons of hair product to give us all that famous 80s "big hair" look, we were ushered into the studio for taping.

All of us were totally gob-smacked when we walked onto this massive sound stage with a 20-meter ceiling. They had built a set that was basically London after a nuclear meltdown. Buildings were burning, smoke was rising from the debris, and lying among the wreckage were beautiful models in black body suits covered in cobwebs. The set was absolutely mind-blowing, and I think we suddenly realized that our record company's commitment to making the band a success was much greater than any of us had imagined.

There we stood, feeling more than a little intimidated, when a large set of double doors opened and in strolled no less than 20 photographers from all the major magazines and music publications in Europe. They proceeded to jostle for position in a line just in front of us, and we were told that they had three minutes to shoot photos of us. We all tried to look at the one who would call out trying to get us to look their way. This was a real eye-opener for a bunch of guys who had only been humble session musicians up to that point.

A few weeks later, "Rainy Day in London" entered the *Billboard* charts in Germany, Switzerland and Austria. One of my favorite bits of memorabilia from our band's history is a little magazine clipping that I have framed in my office at home. It's a copy of our entry into that week's Top 100 *Billboard* chart.

It was a *huge* moment. It was just so incredibly exciting to actually have a chart position on *Billboard*. (We ultimately reached number 45.)

And we were a band from Calgary, Canada.

At that time, the odds of a band from Calgary—or for that matter, any new band without management or some form or representation— ending up with a Billboard charted single position in Germany were probably slim-to-none, but as I always use to say, "Hey—why not us?" And I still say it.

As a result of our success in Germany, there was suddenly a lot of interest back in Canada from some of the major labels. And from there, things started happening pretty quickly.

We continued writing and recording demos of our songs. The next single was called "Far From Over" and it was co-written by a writer from Germany named Moonique and me. It had been sent to us as a possible follow up to "Rainy Day in London". I didn't feel it was quite there at first, so we made some changes to the lyrics and added a bridge.

Both songs made it onto compilation albums in Germany where our name appeared alongside artists that I could only have dreamed of being associated with. One compilation actually had Alan Parsons on it, which was incredibly ironic considering that he had been one of my biggest inspirations. We also appeared alongside groups like Wham! and the Pointer Sisters, and I think one of the compilations even had a Michael Jackson song on it. It was just an incredible time for us as a band, and the ultimate satisfaction for me as a songwriter.

By this point, I was starting to write with Randy Gould, the new guitar player in our band. I had been introduced to Randy by a guy named Dennis Marcenko who had played bass on the original Modern Minds demos. Dennis was an incredible player, and I had previously worked with him on a bunch of different records in Calgary, so he was the natural choice when it came time to record Modern Minds. At the time, I had told him that we were looking for a guitar player, and he told me that I should talk with this guy named Randy Gould. It happened that Randy was a young guy who had just moved to Calgary from Winnipeg, and he was looking for a band. Although he had only been in one or two groups, I saw a great energy in him, and I thought his playing was really inventive. We decided to collaborate on songwriting, and we soon started to hit it off.

Actually, my friend Dennis actually had already had a near-miss with rock n'roll fame himself. We met in 1978 while I was working at Sound West, when both of us were gigging around Calgary. We played together sometimes and bumped into each other a lot. He called me one day in

June of 1979, after I had just finished recording the very first demos for a new band called Loverboy one month prior.

Dennis asked me, "Do you know Paul Dean?"

Paul Dean was the lead guitarist for Loverboy.

"Yes," I replied.

"You recorded those tracks for Loverboy, didn't you?"

"Yes."

"What do you think of those guys?"

"They're great," I said. "Paul played guitar for Streetheart, so he's definitely got the chops, and Mike Reno the singer is awesome. Great voice and great presence. I have a feeling they could get signed and make some noise."

I knew they were also managed by Lou Blair. He was an influential guy who managed a club in downtown Calgary called the Refinery, and it was one of the fixtures in the Calgary nightclub scene in the late 70s and early 80s. Just about any band that came through town had played there, including Loverboy.

"Why do you ask?" I said finally.

"Well, Paul called me and asked if I was interested in joining Loverboy."

"Wow! That's Great!" I said.

Dennis wasn't so sure. He explained that he had just finished his investment securities course to become a stockbroker. Like a lot of musicians I knew at the time, he was trying to secure a good day job so he could make a living while he continued to play music at night.

He said, "What would you do?"

I thought for a moment. "Well, if it were me, I would take him up on his offer, because I do think they have a real shot. I just have a feeling about these guys."

"Besides, it's kind of like you don't have anything to lose. As far as stockbroking goes, brokerage firms are a dime a dozen. You're a good-looking guy, and you're smart and outgoing—you can pretty much write your own ticket if the band doesn't work out."

He didn't take my advice. He became a stockbroker instead.

Jane and I moved to Germany shortly after our conversation, and it was the following spring of 1980 when the first Loverboy album came out. Their single "Turn Me Loose" rocketed up the charts—one of the best rock songs by any Canadian band ever—and I suddenly remembered Dennis. It occurred to me that he had probably made a mistake.

Winding the clock forward to 1982, having completed his short-lived career as a stockbroker, Dennis ended up playing bass on the Modern Minds project, and he had introduced me to Randy Gould. It was interesting how our lives had more or less come full circle.

But back to the story of Boulevard.

By early 1983, "Far From Over" and "Rainy Day in London" were riding the charts in Germany, and we were ready to go back to the Canadian labels with a demo for a new song that Randy and I had written, "Never Give Up".

The band had a bit of momentum now, and that helped us to get the attention of John Alexander, the new head of A&R for MCA in Toronto.

This was a big opportunity. If the A&R guys liked you, they would solicit the support the president, the marketing and promotion department, and the sales department. And if all of them bought in, you were one step closer to fulfilling the dream of getting signed.

John was in, so he started working to get everyone at MCA excited about us as well. This took about a year, during which time we continued to write more songs, one of which became our biggest hit, "Never Give Up". Eventually our discussions started to get serious. Finally, John decided to fly out to Calgary to meet with me in person in December 1984.

He arrived in Calgary one night when the temperature was about 30 degrees below zero. I picked him up at the airport and I drove him to the studio, and we listened to the songs in the control room, including "Never Give Up" at body-massage-volume. I watched as he listened with his eyes closed, letting the sound move through him.

He looked serene as he leaned back in his chair, and I could tell that he really liked what he heard.

After listening to the demos, we jumped into my 1969 Volkswagen Beetle and I drove him to his hotel downtown.

It was about a 25-minute drive, and the heater in my car had again stopped working. It was a gas heater, the type that required a glow plug, and it tended to be a bit temperamental. Sometimes it worked, sometimes it didn't. So we were rolling down the highway in my Beetle with no heat. By then, the mercury had fallen well below minus 20 degrees outside.

We could see our breath with every word that we spoke. All the while, I tried to keep up the conversation so as to draw attention away from the fact that we were bloody freezing.

Meanwhile, John still hadn't said anything about the demos, although I was pretty sure he liked what he heard, he hadn't provided any clear indication of how we were going to move forward in our negotiations. But I could tell that he was excited about our band.

We were about halfway to downtown, and I had just scraped the inside of the windshield with my driver's license for the fifth time to remove the frozen condensation. John suddenly turned to me: "Look, Mark, I'll tell you what. I'll sign your band. Just turn the heat on!"

I was completely caught off guard.

"John, I'm really sorry," I said, "but I honestly don't have any heat. The gas heater has just stopped working."

"But will you still sign us?" I added nervously.

Months later, we would still be laughing about that night when we almost froze to death in my car.

Despite the certainty of John's offer, we continued to go back and forth for weeks as we ironed out the details. We didn't have management at the time, so it made negotiations much more complicated. And one of the things that MCA really wanted was strong management for the band.

I understand why. As a label, you want to deal with a band that has sound management. If the management is flakey or non-existent, the business affairs of the band are not handled properly and mayhem typically ensues. Band guys are good on the creative side, but they're generally not very good with handling the business details, so management becomes critically important to the success of any group.

A good manager is like the extra member of the band, even though they may not have a musical bone in their body. Their instrument is their ability to negotiate, operate a calculator, create spreadsheets, and pay fierce attention to the details. They also have to be part-time psychologists.

Sometimes you might find guys within a band who actually have a sense for business, and I think I probably did, but it didn't matter. The labels still want to have that layer of management between the artists and themselves.

This is why record labels like to deal with band managers who are real business people. Most musicians would prefer to leave the business stuff to someone else anyways. It means that they can focus on their real purpose and craft: creating and playing music.

In January 1986, still recovering from the demise of Thunder Road, Jane and I decided to relocate to Vancouver in the hopes of new opportunities and finding a manager. I took a job mixing film sound at a post-production facility called Alpha Cine so I could keep paying bills. I didn't have a lot of experience as a film mixer, but I had learned enough on a couple of television projects in Calgary to get started. So with our two-year-old son Elliot, Jane and I packed up and moved to the west coast.

A few weeks after we arrived, I made an appointment to see Lou Blair who had taken up residence at Bruce Allen Talent. Again, I already knew Lou because he owned the Calgary nightclub called The Refinery where I had played a few times. Loverboy had started there, and he had helped to manage them to international stardom. Lou in turn knew Bruce Allen who had managed Bachman-Turner Overdrive and Bryan Adams, among others. I wanted to be introduced to Bruce because I knew that if he took us on, we might finally get signed and committed to the MCA deal.

Especially with big American labels, it was critical that you had a manager who was not only good at managing the band members and their affairs, but was also connected in the industry. These types of managers travelled in the highest circles, and Bruce and Lou fit the bill. This meant they could use their connections to get us onto the right tour or the right TV show, and have us played on the right radio stations,

So I went down to the offices at Bruce Allen Talent in the Gastown district to meet with Lou. Their offices were located on Water Street on the third floor of a funky old brick building built at the turn of the last century. All of the floors creaked and it had the musty smell of an old warehouse. The décor was minimal and eclectic. Nothing flashy. The walls were exposed red brick, the old wood frame windows had decades of paint on them, and the support beams were hewn of ancient Douglas Fir. Each one would have been a giant tree in the days where lumber was cheap and plentiful in western Canada. The walls were covered with gold records and the whole place was just a revolving door of rock and roll bands and big hair.

Sandy was the receptionist. She always answered the phone with a sharp, slightly-nasal tone: "Bruce Allen Talent!" Just a hint of the classic New York City secretary that you see in the movies.

Bruce and Lou had the two big offices at the back, and I think there was a small boardroom for meetings. Kim Blake, the woman who handled public relations, had her desk right in front of Bruce's office. She was the person who phoned the Tonight Show or David Letterman whenever they were booking Bryan Adams or any of the other artists in their roster. She was awesome to us.

Lou greeted me, and then he took me into Bruce's office to introduce us. I had dropped of a demo tape of our songs a week earlier and both of them liked our stuff. Bruce was interested in the band, and he told me to let him know how the contract negotiations went with the label.

Outwardly I was positive but I remember thinking, *I wish Bruce would commit now so we can negotiate a killer deal*. I felt very much like David against Goliath. Regardless, I remember walking up to Georgia Street to catch my bus home with a bit more bounce in my step despite the dark and damp of that January night. We were getting close. I could feel it.

I called John the next day to let him know that I had met with Bruce and Lou.

"That's really good news," he replied. "Here's what I think we should do. We could sign with the Canadian label right now, but I think we should hold off and get signed to the U.S. label out of Los Angeles."

He said our record deal would still be worked through Toronto, and MCA Canada would be directly involved in everything. However, if the band could be signed out of the head offices in Los Angeles, it meant that our record was sure to get distribution in the United States. It was potentially huge for us, so he recommended that we hold off on signing the contract.

It was a tough call. If we had a record deal in Canada, at least it would be a start. But if we waited too long for the U.S. deal, and it didn't come through, we ran the risk of the trail going cold with MCA Canada.

I talked with the guys, and they agreed with John's suggestion. We decided to take the risk and try to sign with the U.S. label.

I remember thinking to myself: *I hope we're not kissing a record deal goodbye.*

We had to exploit every possible avenue to make the deal happen. I didn't want this chance to slip away. I could feel that we were very close, but something wasn't quite clicking. And it dawned on me what it was.

I told John, "I have a feeling we can get Bruce Allen to manage the band if we've got a U.S. deal."

John relayed the message to his superiors, and the label came back with the answer: "Okay, here's the deal. We'll sign you out of the U.S. if Bruce Allen will manage."

I was stoked. I set up a meeting with Bruce, and the next day I was sitting in his office ready to press for the deal.

As I sat across the desk from him, I was confronted by a massive painting on the wall behind him. It was a huge painting—probably about eight feet by eight feet square. In fine detail, it depicted a giant face of a boxer traced by a large bead of sweat. Its placement behind his desk was clearly intended to intimidate.

I thought it was a cool piece of art. I liked it, and I liked what it had to say. I sat there with this giant face staring at me, and I simply said, "Look Bruce, L.A. will sign the band if you manage us, and if you manage us, they'll sign the band."

"Okay," he said. "I'll manage the band if you're signed out of the U.S."

So I set up a call with John and Bruce for the following day back at Bruce's office. Once again, I sat across the desk from him with this giant face staring at me. I was on the phone with John on the other end of the line. I turned to Bruce and basically reenacted our conversation from the previous day for John's benefit.

"Bruce, L.A. will sign the band if you take us on, and if you manage us, they'll sign the band," I said, "so will you take us on?"

And he said yes.

"Okay," said John. "We're done".

And that was it. True story. I'm not making this up.

The paper started to flow back and forth, and we were finally signed in January 1988. Four years after signing our first deal with CBS in Germany, we sat in the boardroom of Bruce's office and signed a seven album deal. It was an epic moment for us. Not all of the members could be at the signing, but the photo of that moment is hilarious. We all looked like kids.

We recorded the first Boulevard album, and there was a great buzz around the band. Our producer was a guy from Montreal named Pierre Bazinet, who was best known at the time for producing the Montreal singer Luba. We liked his work, and we liked him. He ended up doing a great job on our first record. We recorded some of the tracks at Ocean Sound in Kitsilano and the rest at Little Mountain Sound in Vancouver.

During our time at Little Mountain, Aerosmith were recording overdubs for their album Pump in Studio B next to us. Over the course of the following weeks, we hung out with them a lot.

One afternoon I was sitting in the control room recording keyboard overdubs when Randy burst in holding a beautiful ovation guitar.

"Joe Perry just lent me this to play on our track!"

One of rock's greatest guitar icons lending you his guitar: it hardly gets better than that.

John Alexander came out and spent the better part of two months in Vancouver while we recorded the album. He was staying at the Meridian Hotel where Aerosmith was also staying. I went to work out with John in the gym of the hotel before going into the studio most mornings. We would often see Joe Perry and Steven Tyler working out as well. I remember looking over at the treadmill next to me and thinking, *This is cool—I'm on a treadmill next to Steven Tyler, and Joe Perry is over there on the rowing machine.*

Later that month, Aerosmith rolled out and another rock icon rolled in. Randy went into the kitchen one day and found Bon Jovi in there making a snack. He blew back into the control room and could hardly speak.

"You won't believe who I just met in the coffee room—Jon Bon Jovi!"

It was a very magical time. Looking back, this was still the peak of the recording industry, the likes of which we would never see again. Massive budgets and—at the time—no end in sight.

A lot of famous bands recorded at Little Mountain because they wanted to work with Bob Rock, the top engineer there at the time.

Mike Fraser was the guy who was engineering our tracks along with Bob. He had been Bob's assistant for years. He also assisted on the tracks that Bob mixed. He has since gone on to work with some huge bands. He was a great guy, and very soft spoken.

Our album also received a bit of attention from a very respected engineer named Umberto Gattica in Los Angeles. He had recorded and mixed Michael Jackson, Julio Iglesias, and some other real giants. He was something of a superstar engineer in Los Angeles, and so MCA hired him to mix "Far From Over". I was a big fan of his work and I was honored that he was into working with us.

In May of 1988, we went to Seattle to do a photo shoot for the album cover with a photographer named Jim Cunningham. MCA sent up props that had been made at Universal Studios, including a balsa wood telephone pole and a foam-core sign that said "Boulevard". To capture the gritty feeling of the street, we went into an alley about a block from Pike Place Market that Jim had scouted earlier.

Once the album was released, everything became a rollercoaster ride. I was sent on a three-week press tour with David Forbes our lead singer across the country. We did a ton of radio and television interviews, including an appearance on MuchMusic in Toronto. The fact that I was a saxophone player drew a lot of attention. People seemed to find it a bit unusual to have a sax player as the leader of the band. It's almost always the lead singer, or at very least, one of the guitarists. So we were a bit atypical. This point would often get brought up when we were being interviewed.

The head of national promotion at MCA was Peter Diemer. Peter was like the Tasmanian Devil in shoes. We had originally met in college when we both attended the Southern Alberta Institute of Technology, and we had become good friends. I remember finding out that he was going to be picking up me and David at the Toronto airport and then chauffeuring us to all of our various radio and TV interviews.

That was cool. My friend, now the head of national promotion, was personally throwing all of his efforts into our first release. He worked his ass off and managed to get our first two singles into the top ten in Canada.

That summer, we were scheduled to tour across Canada with Glass Tiger. Our first gig leading into the tour was in Victoria. We played one night in a downtown club just so we could perform our set one more time live before we launched into our countrywide tour.

We went back to Vancouver the next day and immediately flew to Toronto to play our first major show as a headliner in Windsor. It was a wild experience. Our first large-scale concert on our own. We had a road manager, and someone mixing our monitors, and someone else mixing our mains out front. And we were on the road. We were thinking: *Wow. We have arrived.*

We played on an outdoor stage in a park overlooking the Detroit River with the towers of downtown Detroit across from us. There were a few thousand people there, and none of us had ever played to a crowd of that size in our lives. We played our set, which was only about sixty minutes long, but we saved "Never Give Up" for last.

It was the single from our album, and the video had been given heavy rotation on MuchMusic, Canada's big music channel at the time. When we played the opening bars, the crowd suddenly surged forward towards the stage.

I'll never forget that feeling as long as I live. The energy and the atmosphere completely changed in one explosive instant. Everyone was suddenly on their feet and pressing forward, until there were several thousand people standing right in front of us, jostling each other and singing along with the lyrics.

Up to that moment, everyone in the audience had been more or less subdued. Some had been sitting, some had been standing, and everyone appeared to be enjoying the music, but it was pretty polite and calm. Suddenly I was thinking, *Holy crap! These people have actually heard this song!* And they must like it.

And of course they had heard it. The radio had been playing "Never Give Up" to death for several weeks, and we had become minor rock stars in the meantime without really knowing it.

After the Windsor concert, we joined Glass Tiger in some place like Thunder Bay for our first show with them. We toured with them for about six weeks, working our way eastwards to St. John's, Newfoundland, and then all the way westwards across the prairies to the west coast. Our last concert was at the Memorial Arena back in Victoria, where we had played almost two months previously in a downtown club for our warm-up gig.

We had departed Victoria, wide eyed, full of nervous excitement, wondering what lay ahead. We rolled back into town, feeling like seasoned veterans with more stories than the Empire State Building.

Shortly after arriving in Victoria, I went down to the ocean and touched my hand to the water. I had previously dipped my hand in the Atlantic at Cape Spear in Newfoundland, the furthest eastern point of North America, and I wanted to complete the symbolic journey.

People are actually warned not to go down to the water at Cape Spear because of rogue waves and strong currents. Many people have drowned there, and there are warning signs everywhere. But of course I went down there with Randy, and it was a symbolic moment.

The St. John's concert was the first time we actually had difficulty getting to our tour bus. We had already built some popularity before we arrived in St. John's, and the concert energy was amazing. By the end, when we exited the arena door to get to the bus, each one of us had to be grabbed by a security guard. We were being completely swarmed by the crowd waiting outside. I remember I had my tenor sax case in my hand, and the security guy grabbed the handle and said, "Hang on." That was another first for me, and a first for all of us. We made it onto the bus and we just collapsed into our seats.

Again, all I could think was: Wow. I can only imagine what bands like the Beatles or the Rolling Stones must have experienced on tour.

Later that same year, we landed a tour opening up for Boston. Our last show with them was in Seattle, but most of the tour was actually in Canada. They were an incredible bunch of guys. Total pros with nothing to prove. This was evidenced by them letting us use four out of six follow spotlights and two-thirds of the lights for our set. This was somewhat unheard of. Typically, the headliner would restrict the lighting for the opening act.

Despite our touring and promotion efforts, we never really established a big following in the United States. We received decent radio play in a few spotted markets, and album sales reflected it. We had a situation where "Never Give Up" had done really well in Canada. It was in the top ten and getting heavy rotation on radio. But in the United States, it was getting limited airplay and muted market response. It was sort of normal. The Eagle in Dallas loved us—they were a huge rock station. And Sacramento and Buffalo were also good markets for us. However, on the whole, we didn't experience nearly the same success that we had experienced across Canada. In that regard, a lot of our Canadian success had to be credited to the tireless work of Peter Diemer and the incredible staff at MCA/Universal.

Bruce Allen saw the lack of success in the U.S. market, and he wasn't happy. So one day he picked up the phone and called Irving Azoff in Los Angeles.

At the time, Azoff was the chairman and CEO of MCA. He was basically chief of the music world. Meanwhile, Bruce was a pretty brash guy and he didn't pull any punches. Apparently, it was a pretty short conversation.

I'm told Bruce said to Azoff:

"Okay, 'Never Give Up' has been top ten for the past three weeks in Canada. We're just shy of gold. You fucked this one up. What have you got up your sleeve for the next single?"

I heard this from Cliff Jones, who was part of the management team at Bruce Allen Talent. He phoned me at my house to tell me, and I remember him using his "here-at-Bruce-Allen-we-don't-fuck-around" tone of voice. Whenever I heard him speak in that tone, I would brace myself for some form of unsavory or aggressive remark.

I was stunned and breathless—like someone had just punched me in the stomach. When I managed to gather myself and process the full meaning of what I had just heard, I replied in a quivering voice:

"Cliff, Bruce didn't really do that, did he?"

"You're fuckin' right he did."

I broke into a cold sweat. "We're fucked," I said.

I found out later that Bruce's call indeed marked the beginning of the end for us. Apparently Azoff had responded to Bruce's call by saying, "No one talks to me like that. I don't give a shit who this guy is." And that was pretty much the end of the band in America.

It was a complete heartbreaker. It had practically taken me a lifetime to arrive at that point. The equivalent of crawling through broken glass on your hands and knees for a decade. All the crap, the back and the forth, and the rejections, and the ups and the downs, and the sacrifices, and the doing-without to try to scrape together enough money to do another set of demos and finally get signed. To arrive at that point—and basically have years of sacrifice and sweat undone with a single short phone call—it was horrible.

I called John Alexander to express my profound sense of loss.

John was equally dismayed. "Bruce didn't really make that call did he"?

"Apparently, yes," I responded.

The line fell silent for what seemed to be an eternity. "Hmmm. I'm disappointed," said John.

We still recorded a second album for MCA, which was released in Canada and the United States, but there was no real push to promote it in the U.S. It did okay, but not great.

By this time, we were facing other troubles as well. Personal differences within the band had been simmering for a while, and now they were coming to a hard boil.

The band had split more or less into two groups. There was the Randy Gould camp, and there was the Mark Holden camp. As the band had started to achieve more success, Randy showed that he wanted to lead the band and take it in a strongly guitar-based direction. In the process, he was also being encouraged by management who felt that we should become more of an "arena" rock band.

My position was that we were who and what we were, and the success we were experiencing was as a result of a lot of people out there liking our music. I was confident that we would become an "arena" band when we start filling arenas, and that was going to happen by us writing what was true to what we were as a band. We would start filling arenas when we had attracted enough of a following and sold enough records.

You don't just decide to create music that "works in an arena"—the thought was ridiculous to me.

I had originally thought that the issue was really between Randy and myself, and that the rest of the guys were somewhat apathetic. It became very difficult for me to know who had my back and who would jump into Randy's camp on any given day. I began to feel very alienated, that if I turned around to see who was supporting me in a decision or some other piece of band business, I would just see a barren landscape vacant of anyone—just the sound of the wind to greet me.

I would find out years later that there was a serious amount of influence peddling and bullying going on between Randy and the other members of the band. If I had known this, I would have fired his ass.

Although I can't be certain, I believe part of the conflict between Randy and myself originated with something that had happened when we were making the first album.

At the time, Randy and the rest of the guys were still back in Calgary and I had gone out to Vancouver ahead of them essentially to set up camp. Shortly after I arrived, Bruce Allen and Lou Blair put me together with a Vancouver songwriter named John Dexter who was also managed by Bruce Allen's office. They thought it would be a really good idea if John wrote a song with Boulevard because if he could get a track on our album, and if we sold a couple of hundred thousand copies, John would also benefit. As a songwriter, you always want to write with artists who have record deals because it means that your song will get released and hopefully sell a lot. As they were John's management, they were also looking out for his interest as well.

I said, sure, cool, no problem. And we ended up getting together and writing a song called "Dream On". It was never released as a single, but it was a pretty decent song and it made it onto our first album.

I would find out later that as far as Randy was concerned, this represented some sort of betrayal to him as we had written most of the balance of the first album together. Meanwhile, John Dexter wasn't part of the band, so Randy felt that he shouldn't have been allowed to write a song on our album. From there, things really started to unravel between us.

If I had known sooner how Randy felt, I might have been able to mend the relationship. But by the time I understood the feelings involved, it seemed like our relationship was completely irreparable. And I liked Randy a lot. When he moved to Vancouver, we wrote a ton of music together, and for a while he even lived with me, Jane, and our children in our house. He was almost part of the family, so it was a bit of a heartbreak to have this happen.

With the band, it seemed now battle lines being drawn behind the scenes. I would bring an idea for a song for the next record and it would almost be sabotaged during rehearsal. And if there was any way Randy could rally support against it, then that would happen. This division ran very deep. By the time we recorded the second record, there was so much tension between Randy and me that it made the entire process very uncomfortable. And ironically, it was me who had asked him to join the band after we had secured the first deal in Germany.

In hindsight, I might have glimpsed his true colors when we were making the first album. Something odd happened during that period, and it came to have more significance for me later.

We were doing another photo shoot for the first album, this time in Vancouver, and they had given Randy hair extensions to give him long hair. And it changed him. He suddenly developed this edge. It was almost like he felt that he had to act a certain way to be a rocker and rock out. Now that his hair was long, he was obligated to take on a certain cocky, belligerent persona. I wasn't alone in noticing this. I just remember finding it strange and thinking: *This dude is taking the rock star thing way too seriously—he's being an asshole.*

That energy would continue right through the making of the second record. Things would grow so strained that by the time we shot the second album cover, I was completely disenchanted and disengaged with the entire process. I had really worked tirelessly to that point, but now I wasn't enjoying the band experience at all.

Behind all of this, there were growing philosophical differences about our musical direction. Randy was working hard to get us to become more of a guitar band like a Bon Jovi. Unfortunately for me, I think management supported that view.

Meanwhile, I saw Boulevard more as a melodic band like Phil Collins, Roxy Music, or INXS. Our first album had that sort of sensitivity and tone about it. I did not see us as a big-hair guitar band such as a Bon Jovi or Def Leppard, even though I would have loved to have had their success.

At one point, I approached Randy and tried to mend things.

"Randy, you know, I'm not sure how to repair this," I said. "But it means so much to both of us to make this work, and we'll never have another opportunity like this again."

I didn't realize just how dead-on the money I was. Getting that sort of record deal signed out of Los Angeles—with big recording budgets of several hundred thousand dollars, and $150,000 per video—those days are long gone. They are so long gone that they're just a speck in the rearview mirror now.

But I knew what we had was special. The support from John, the support from the Canadian label, and all of the work we'd done to earn it. I knew we had established a great foundation for the band and we had an opportunity to make a real impact.

Around that time, one of the honors that was bestowed on us was a nomination for a West Coast Music Award. I think that was the spring of 1989. Our song "Never Give Up" was nominated alongside Sarah

Maclachlan's first single. Sarah Maclachlan won that night, but we were one of the bands that had been nominated, and that was prestige enough.

We were also nominated for a Music Express Award. Music Express magazine was the Canadian *Rolling Stone*. It was a great magazine for promoting the Canadian recording industry and Canadian artists, and it was kind of like the Bible of pop music in Canada. They hosted an awards show every year, and we were nominated to win Best New Canadian Group. Previous nominees had been the Tragically Hip, Blue Rodeo, Pursuit of Happiness, and Sarah Maclachlan. This year, about six bands were nominated.

They flew Randy and me to Toronto for the awards, and that gave me the feeling that we had won. The awards were being hosted at a huge club in Mississauga that seated about 5,000 people, and the atmosphere was spectacular. At the end of the night, we were named the winners and we felt on top of the world. We ended up winning by 63 percent of the popular vote, and the remaining 37 percent was split between the other nominees. Given the list of nominees, it was an almost unimaginable margin.

But there was one snag that night that didn't do anything to enhance my relationship with Randy. I was asked to play in an all-star band, and he wasn't. And I think it really bugged him.

Regardless, I made sure I enjoyed the experience while it lasted. After all, it was a seriously cool band. There were about fifteen of us on stage, including Ian Thomas, Dominique Troiano, Sass Jordan, a few guys from Platinum Blonde, and Mike Levine and Gil Moore from Triumph. Long John Baldry was also there, lending his energy in the rehearsal room before we went on stage.

The entire evening event was being used as a fundraiser for a young burn victim named Joey Fillian who had rescued his little sister from a house fire. He saved her life, but he was badly burned in the process.

After the awards, we went back to Mike Levine's house. He, John Alexander, Randy and I sat up until seven the next morning, and that's where I first learned the details about what went on with senior executives at MCA in Los Angeles after the conversation had taken place between Bruce Allen and Irving Azoff.

A few months later, in the late autumn of 1988, the exposure that Boulevard had achieved at the Music Express Awards was brought into stark contrast with another Canadian awards event: the Junos. The nominations came out for the Juno Awards—the most prestigious of Canadian music award events—and Boulevard didn't get a single nomination.

It was a bit of a shocker. At least it was initially. Then the picture started to become clear.

It turned out that the Juno Awards committee that year was made up of journalists and music business hipsters who were really into the indie music scene, I guess. Maybe they had decided that we had sold out as a band because we were managed by a music establishment icon like Bruce Allen. So they simply didn't like us on principle.

It was bizarre in light of what had happened at the Music Express Awards and our success on radio and MuchMusic. It turned out just about every one of the other bands who had made up the other 37 percent at the Music Express Awards a few months previously had been nominated.

It was a bit disappointing for the band, but I was particularly disappointed for everyone at MCA who had worked tirelessly in support of us, and promoting our record.

Ross Reynolds, the president of MCA in Toronto, later wrote a letter to the Juno Awards committee. Ross sent me a copy. He basically said: shame on you. This band has sold just shy of gold in Canada, they've done two major tours with Boston and Glass Tiger across the country, they've had two top ten singles, they've been top ten on MuchMusic for ten weeks running, they won 63 percent of the popular vote at the Music Express People's Choice Awards, and yet you won't give them a nomination for a Juno. What the fuck?

.MCA RECORDS CANADA
A DIVISION OF MCA CANADA LTD.

ROSS B. REYNOLDS
Executive Vice-President
and General Manager.

February 10, 1989

Mr. Gerry Lacoursiere
President
A&M Records of Canada Ltd.
939 Warden Ave.
Scarborough, Ontario.
M1L 4C5

Dear Gerry,

I am extremely disappointed that the CARAS nominating procedures prevented BLVD. from being nominated for Most Promising Group. When you consider the following, it is almost inconceivable that they have been excluded.

- Third in sales in this category;
- Voted by the readers of Music Express as their <u>first</u> choice as Most Promising new Act. Of the 65,234 votes, 63% were for BLVD.;
- Three national hit singles;
- Two major Canadian tours, one with Glass Tiger and one with Boston, plus many other major dates;
- International releases.

I can only assume that BLVD. was not considered "hip" enough by the media panel that influenced the nominations. As a Founding Director of CARAS, I have been under the assumption that one of the primary functions of CARAS was to promote the commercial success of Canadian artists without apology. To include music critics, who notoriously dislike commercially successful mainstream acts, in the nominating procedures is blatantly inconsistent with what should be a continuing goal of CARAS. The music buying public has clearly indicated they prefer BLVD. over some of the acts that were nominated. Why should CARAS defer to the questionable opinions of a group of writers who have very little influence on record sales?

Unfortunately, the damage has been done to BLVD. Hopefully, the nominating procedures will be changed to be more consistant with the objectives of CARAS. Please consider reverting to sales as the sole nominating criteria. This is the clearest expression of public interest.

Sincerely,

Ross B. Reynolds

RBR*ce

2450 Victoria Park Avenue, Willowdale, Ontario M2J 4A2   (416) 491-3000   Telex: 06-966876   Fax: (416) 491-2857

Ross Reynolds' letter to CARAS President, February 1989.

By the time we were putting together the second album in 1989, I knew that my remaining days with Boulevard were numbered. At one point we were taking photos for the second album cover, and I just wasn't feeling it. The photographer, James O'Mara, looked at me and said, "Mark, you're not giving me anything."

And it hit me. "You know, what? Because I don't have anything to give. I'm done."

I didn't want to be at that photo shoot. I was there simply out of obligation. Someone looking at the album cover probably wouldn't see it. But maybe they would if they knew me personally. They might think: *Hey—Mark looks kind of pissed off!*

I realized it was the beginning of the end. I finally left Boulevard in the early summer of 1990. From there, Randy more or less realized his ambitions and became the leader of the band. In my absence, he was recognized as "the guy" and started to exert his vision for the direction of the group. He had finally arrived.

And I thought: *Hey guys, good luck with this asshole.*

Meanwhile, I was devastated. Honestly, it took me years to get over it.

The band went on to do a few tours, a few little concerts, mini tours and so on, but the wheels started to come off the bus within a few months. It was about year later when I received an official letter from MCA saying that we had been dropped from their label. It was actually a very polite and respectful letter. Still, my heart sank with the finality of it.

In the ensuing months, I had to process a lot of grief. But I wasn't just grieving the loss of the band and my place in it. There were relationships that were lost.

During Boulevard's journey, we had forged special friendships with so many brilliant people—Peter Diemer, and Lesley Soldad, and Stephen Tennant, and Ross Reynolds, and John Alexander—and Randy Lennox, who was for years the head of Universal Music Canada, and now head of Bell Media. They had put so much incredible work and enthusiasm into making us a success and allowing us to enjoy it.

When the end finally came, I felt like I was letting them down. This amazing team of people that had embraced us and allowed us to experience something that very few people will ever even glimpse. The 80s was the peak of the glory days in the music industry. With the advent of the internet, the flight to free music and growing disregard for copyright, and the rest, it's unlikely that we will ever see something like it again. We were simply very fortunate to have been a part of it while it lasted.

FOURTEEN

Microsoft and the New Sound

Tom Taylor and I were sitting in a small, sterile meeting room across the table from three Microsoft executives in Redmond, Washington in November 1990, and we both felt stupefied. After months of due diligence and racking up the highway miles between Vancouver and Redmond, one of the executives whom both of us had come to know very well just looked at us and said:

"Okay, guys. What is it that you really have in your sound card technology?"

Tom and I looked at each other. The question had come completely out of the blue, and for a moment, neither of us knew what to say.

"We have the answer to a giant void in the delivery of quality sound in personal computing," I said.

Another of the executives spoke.

"Okay. I tell you what. How would you and Tom like to come and develop the product here at Microsoft?"

H ope springs eternal, and in my different career and artistic ventures, including Boulevard, entrepreneurialism has always been one of my hallmarks. I love being part of the process of creating something new, especially if it has the potential to move people in a big way, and I have always been excited by new technologies.

Following the demise of Boulevard, this helped to set the stage for my next life venture: joining M-Sound, a small technology startup in Vancouver, in early 1990.

By the end of 1989, it had become clear that the writing was on the wall with regards to my relationship with our guitar player, Randy Gould. Mentally, I had been exiting the band for weeks, awash in a torrent of emotions that left my insides knotted.

The whole process had left me thinking:

Wow, outside of friends and family, my entire focus for the last several years had been Boulevard. What's next?

It was precisely as I was contemplating my exit from the band that I received an unexpected call from Steve Fouce, my friend and previous business associate who had helped to build Thunder Road in Calgary. He wanted to know if I would be willing to join him in a new venture.

Steve had invested in a tiny Vancouver company called M-Sound that had been started by a young inventor named Tom Taylor. Tom apparently had a special new technology that promised to have a huge impact on sound for personal computers. Steve figured I would make a good addition to the team.

Tom was an extremely bright guy, and a real technical whiz. There was an apocryphal story about him taking apart his mother's microwave when he was ten years old and trying to reconfigure the parts to create some sort of other device. I don't think it was his intention to create a bomb, but in the end he blew the door off of his mother's microwave. He was that kind of guy.

But Steve hadn't invested in Tom's company to produce exploding microwaves. It turned out that Tom had invented the first digital sound card for personal computers. He had started M-Sound to develop the technology, manufacture it, and market it.

Steve wanted me to help manage the company because he knew my background in sound production, music and the entertainment business. Tom had invented a great technology, and the prototype was working beautifully, but he would need help taking it to market. Like so many inventors, Tom's main interest and expertise was in refining and improving the technology, and he wouldn't be able to market it effectively while he was focused on development.

M-Sound's competitors at that time were a Canadian company called Adlib and SoundBlaster by Creative Labs in California. Both of them used a licensed FM synthesizer chip from Yamaha, so their sound cards relied purely on synthesized sound. Basically, sound files generated by what sounded like one of the early Moog keyboard synthesizers, evoking the sound stylings of an old 1960s sci-fi film.

Tom's card didn't produce synthesized sound. It delivered real sounds in the form of digital audio samples.

"I've already taken the liberty of calling Tom and told him that you would be giving him a ring," said Steve. He was evidently confident that I would find the company and the product intriguing enough to come on board.

I went to meet with Tom. He was set up in a couple of small, funky offices strung together on West Fourth Avenue in Vancouver. At that time, West Fourth still showed signs of a hangover from the sixties and seventies. There were a couple of hippie tie-die shops near the office that sold records, second hand clothes, and leather belts, as well as hookah pipes and other paraphernalia related to psychedelic drug culture.

Upon arrival, I was immediately struck by Tom's appearance. With his glasses, beard, and slightly long, frizzy hair, he looked like a young version of the nutty professor. He was wearing a pair of white tennis shoes, jeans, a white tennis shirt and a blazer. I would come to know this attire more or less as his work uniform. He also looked a bit like Steve Jobs, but slightly nuttier. If you took Steve Jobs and put his finger in a light socket, you might get something like Tom's appearance.

Tom and I hit it off like a house on fire. He was very bright and he had a great sense of humor. He also demonstrated a commanding knowledge of technology that was matched by his ability to speak about it in layman's terms.

Tom showed me what he had developed, and I immediately recognized that he had developed something very significant. I didn't need any further convincing—I agreed to join the company.

I took on a management and marketing role where I was responsible for developing business with all of the independent software vendors (ISVs). Tom and Steve trusted me in that role because I had a couple of different touch points that made me a good fit. Firstly, Steve and I had a track record from working together building and operating Thunder Road Studios, so I was a known quantity. Secondly, and perhaps more importantly, I understood and was passionate about quality sound and the importance of it to the big picture.

At the time when I originally met Tom, I was working part-time as the second unit sound mixer on a couple of television shows, including MacGyver. Even during the Boulevard days, I had continued mixing sound for television and film because Boulevard didn't provide a steady paycheque to take care of my family.

Since M-Sound aimed to help complete a cinematic sound experience for the personal computer user, and especially video game players, my experience as a music engineer and my background in audio postproduction for film and television would be invaluable. I also had the proven ability to communicate effectively and develop strong relationships. Building relationships was something that came very easy to me. I could walk into a room and within 10 minutes make everyone feel comfortable with me and each other.

I started putting together strategies for developing our business in earnest. Tom hadn't yet developed a real business plan, so we spent a lot of time early on looking at the various markets and identifying the low hanging fruit. It became very obvious to me that the market with the greatest need—and the least awareness of their own need—was the video game industry.

They didn't know it, but they were missing something big. *Real sound.*

The more I thought about it, the more excited I became. This was a classic case of opportunity creation—where I would be able to go and tell a company what they were missing, and that we had the solution. Our sound card would add real sampled sound to video games to provide a startlingly realistic experience for the user. Today, that might not seem special, but in 1989, it was completely revolutionary.

So we started lobbying software developers in the video game industry. We were soon knocking on the doors of companies such as Electronic Arts, Sierra, Maxis, Lucas Arts, and other major game developers.

Tom and I would go into meetings with these big developers, and they would bring in their CTOs and the brightest technical minds that they had. They would examine how the new sound card worked, make sure that it was properly vetted, and generally do their due diligence on our technology. They would frequently shoot significant technical questions at Tom. He was always able to answer them very succinctly and clearly, and that helped our meetings immensely. It was obvious that we knew what we were talking about and that we had something behind our technology.

The first trade show that we attended was the CES trade show in Las Vegas. For a week prior to leaving to Las Vegas, we worked like madmen to get all of our presentation and display materials together. It was typical of everything I've ever experienced since around trade shows. You prep for it, but something goes wrong at the printer, and you finally receive your materials about two hours before you have to get on the plane, and then you're quickly stuffing brochures so you don't miss your flight.

On this occasion, I think we pulled an all-nighter to get everything ready prior to our flight the next morning. We had to make sure that the brochures and printed materials were ready, and that the demos that we would play at the booth were working. I think we managed to grab about two hours of sleep before our seven o'clock flight down to Las Vegas.

We ran into grief at U.S. Customs, because we didn't have the proper forms for our computers and our boxes of brochures, so we had to explain that we were exhibiting at a trade show. We got through Customs eventually, but it was an eye-opener for me. In subsequent trips, we made sure that we had the proper processes and protocols in place whenever we travelled with equipment and materials.

We finally arrived at the trade show convention center in Las Vegas, and we started setting up our game demos in our booth.

I looked around the floor and tried to process the frenetic activity surrounding me.

I had been around music business and film business people, but this was my first real exposure to the tech world. I was blown away by the difference in people's personal presentation and general conduct. There was a certain crispness and youthfulness to everyone. The world of personal computers and software for mass consumption was still very new, and most of the people in the industry were themselves very young. It made a big impression on me as I stood in our booth surrounded by all of the big software developers and hardware manufacturers.

This was my first time ever participating in a trade show, and I quickly discovered how exhausting it could be to stand there for eight hours just talking to people. But we were drawing great crowds. People would walk by, and they would immediately stop when they saw someone playing a flight simulator game or a tank simulator with this amazing ambient, cinematic sound.

During the CES trade show, I also started to gain a new self-awareness about what made me tick as a person, as a creator, as a business person. Music and technology. Right brain and left brain. I saw clearly, perhaps for the first time in my life, that I had always oscillated between creativity on one side and technology and business on the other. This was a big strength for me, along with my sensitivity to people and my ability to build meaningful relationships.

As creative as I was, there was clearly a side of me that was fascinated by how things work. I think what I brought to M-Sound was my very practical approach and my ability to peel back the layers of the technology to understand how it really worked and what it could deliver. I was then able to apply that understanding to optimize the market appeal of our M-Sound card.

By the end of the CES show, we had made a lot of important connections with different companies. I went back to Vancouver with a real sense that we were poised on the edge of something very big. I knew that we were developing something that would not only increase the quality of the gaming experience but the entire listening experience on a computer. That was going to make the M-Sound sound card a red-hot product.

One of the companies that took a keen interest in M-Sound was Advanced Gravis. They had the world's bestselling joystick for computer games—considered the best joystick in the gaming market. Gravis had a very close partnership with Logitech, One of the giants in the computer peripheral's industry. They ended up investing in M-Sound and they agreed to help us with product sales through their existing distribution networks. Sound cards and joysticks were a good marriage, so it made sense as a business decision.

But the Las Vegas show paled in comparison to what came next.

About two months after Las Vegas, I was contacted by the organizers of the Software Publishers Association conference that was to be held in Cannes in June 1990. They wanted me to present on the future of sound for personal computers and introduce our sound card.

When the invite came, everyone at our M-Sound offices paused and drew a breath. The possibilities. This was huge. We would definitely be seen at this event by all of IT's biggest players. The question was, were we ready? What was I going to present?

Of course there was no way we could pass it up. I confirmed that I would present at the conference, and I started to develop my presentation.

I wasn't sure what to do beyond showing the demo that I had taken to Las Vegas, which was more or less the same demo that I typically showed to software developers in our regular meetings. The presentation in Cannes was going to be of an entirely different magnitude. I would be on stage in front of hundreds of the top IT executives in the world. Would my existing presentation be enough?

My presentation involved a game demo that had been prepared by members of our team at M-Sound. Basically, we had chosen a couple of video games that were currently popular and well known, and we had created a sound track using digital samples that matched the action in the games. But we felt that we needed to take things to the next level.

The plan for the presentation in Cannes was actually to hack into a game and create "hooks" within the action that invited the use of particular sound effects.

And ours were killer. Explosions, jet engines, rockets being fired, that sort of thing. And when we couldn't find a real sound sample to fill the requirement, we created it ourselves. The more spectacular the effect, the better.

This process took a bit of trial and error, but we eventually succeeded. The effect ended up being incredibly flattering to the games and the developers. One of our demos used a flight simulator game made by Microsoft. The game featured an F-18 fighter jet idling on the runway. We had it rigged with this incredibly realistic ambient sound of the jet engine, and it really created the feeling that you were there in the cockpit.

Each time I had presented the game demo at meetings with developers, I would start by playing the original game with its stock sound, just as it came out of the box. There was basically no sound because the sound that came with the game was pretty much non-existent. As I played, their game programmers and designers in the room would typically look at each other smugly as if to say, "Why is this guy wasting our time? Doesn't he know we have code to write and lattes to drink in our black t-shirts back in our office cubicles?"

But then I would switch over to our sound card and play the same game again with the full sound track. The effect was always immediate and complete: they would practically fall off their chairs.

So I decided to go to the SPA show in Cannes and do the same thing.

I went to Cannes with Tom's brother, Rob Taylor. I would deliver the presentation and the demo, and he would rig the equipment and provide technical support. On the day of our presentation, the plan was to meet at 8:30 a.m. and then wheel all of our equipment down to the Palais des Festivals where the conference was taking place. The Palais is the enormous hall where they host the big screenings for the Cannes Film Festival. I started to grow anxious just thinking about how small I was going to feel on that stage in those grand surroundings.

On the morning of the presentation, I found myself sweating even more as I stood on the street outside the Martinez Hotel waiting for Rob to show up. It was June, it was the south of France, I was wearing a suit and tie, and Rob was nowhere to be seen.

I was pacing back and forth on the sidewalk and just about to give up on him when I saw him coming down the street to meet me. He wasn't looking good. He had been out until about six in the morning, and he basically hadn't slept. I was seriously miffed.

I was already very nervous and worked up about the show, and now I was drenched and full of anxiety from waiting for Rob to show up. But I had to brush it off. Deep breath. I had to get into the right mindset because I knew that this was a huge opportunity.

We ended up making it to the Palais on time, and we were able to load all of the gear into the hall before the presentations began.

I felt very intimidated as I sat offstage waiting for my turn to present. The presenters before me all had these incredibly elaborate slide shows with graphs and charts and research. They all worked for big publishing or video game companies, and they had all kinds of elaborate presentation materials and accessories. I remember one guy from London presenting just before me who was with Gage Publishing or somebody of similar magnitude. I thought: *Damn. This is going to be a hard act to follow.*

Suddenly it was my turn. They were announcing M-Sound and Mark Holden. Rob and I walked out onto the stage amidst the customary polite applause, and we took a couple of minutes to set up. Then I turned to face the audience as Rob took his place at the side of the stage.

"Hi, I'm Mark Holden, and I'm with M-Sound. We're a Canadian company, and we've developed the world's first digital sound card for the PC computer, and this is how it works."

I was sweating bullets. Here I was on a stage the size of Carnegie Hall, and I've set up a little table with a Compaq 386, a monitor, and two little speakers from RadioShack. But I also had a subwoofer underneath. Our secret weapon!

I started playing this flight simulator game without any sound, and everyone in the audience kind of looked at each other—as they always did—with perplexed expressions. Some people were holding their programs over their mouths, whispering to the guy next to them and shrugging. If cell phones had been around at that time, many of them would probably have been reaching for them.

These were scientists, software developers and high-powered executives in suits. I imagine they were probably saying to each other, "Who is this Canadian guy?"

I loved it when they did that, because I knew what was coming, but they didn't.

I played the game for 30 seconds, and then I turned to them again.

"And to demonstrate that sound is at least half the picture, I'd like to play this game again from the beginning, but I'm going to make just one small addition."

I turned on the amplifier and I rebooted the game. And then I started to play again.

The game was a flight simulator developed by a company called Velocity that was very popular around 1990. With the sound card activated and the speakers cranked, I started to rev the engines and I took off. We had rigged it with an incredibly realistic jet engine sound, and it really created the feeling that you were there in the cockpit. I think I also fired a few rockets for added effect.

After having just played the game with the standard PC sound, this new experience was spectacular. It was like going from watching a silent movie to watching *Star Wars*.

The reaction in the room was immediate: the crowd was buzzing. After about 15 seconds, I stopped playing and turned to my audience again. I began to talk about the technology, how it was being employed, and why we thought it was important. I talked about sound in movies, and I spoke about the process of post-production and how I felt that this would soon become a very large part of computer game development. I even suggested that game developers would soon need to have recording studios that were as sophisticated as music industry recording studios or dubbing theatres where film sound is mixed, as well as post-production studios for sound editing, effects layering, and all the rest.

No one was whispering behind their conference programs now. Instead, I saw a lot of thoughtful nodding and focused attention as I spoke.

I finished my presentation, and because it was the last one of the day, the moderator made a closing address. I stayed on stage as he spoke, and when he finished a few people came up and started asking me questions about the sound card and M-Sound.

And there was one guy who was standing apart from everyone. He seemed to be hanging back and waiting to speak with me alone. He wore glasses and a white polo shirt, and he actually looked a bit like Bill Gates. He had a name badge, but from a distance, I couldn't see what was written on it. He waited patiently behind all of these other people, and then he approached me after everyone else was finished.

"Hi Mark, my name is Jeff Raikes," he said. "I'm with Microsoft, and I just wanted to say that I really enjoyed your presentation.

"I really think you're on to something. We would be very interested in talking with you and your company."

He asked me if we would be able to meet with him and other Microsoft staff the next week in Redmond.

I paused for a moment, then I replied, "Yes, I think we could make that happen."

Of course, I was exploding with excitement just thinking about the possibilities, but I didn't want to show it then. A very senior executive from Microsoft had come up and complimented me on my presentation. And I would later learn that Jeff Raikes had been the number six guy at Microsoft.

We had delivered a dynamite presentation, and now we breathed a huge sigh of relief. We had opened the door to having discussions with Microsoft, and there was no predicting where that might take us. Maybe it would go nowhere, but certainly the door was open. Rob and I flew back to Vancouver and told everyone at M-Sound the news.

One week later, Tom and I were on our way to Redmond in his 4x4 for a meeting with Microsoft. It was a three-hour drive from Vancouver, so it gave us time to discuss what we might be getting ourselves into.

We arrived at the Microsoft campus, my first thought was: *wow, this is really austere.* There were new buildings and new asphalt everywhere, and you could tell that everything from the sidewalks and lamp posts to the trees and shrubs were laid out with fastidious care and attention. Everything looked efficient, clean, tidy and purposeful. Kind of like Pleasantville.

It wasn't necessarily attractive or inviting, but it definitely made the impression of being organized crisp and new.

Jeff greeted us at the front reception desk and he led us into a boardroom. A guy named Raleigh Roarke was heading the meeting. He was one of the guys that ran the hardware division of Microsoft, and he took a minute to introduce everyone.

At some point, he mentioned that one of the signs of status at Microsoft was where you parked your car each morning. There were no assigned parking stalls. You could park wherever you wanted. But it meant that the earlier you arrived at work, the closer you could park to the front door.

It created renewed bragging rights every day. If you came to work at five o'clock in the morning and managed to park in the second stall, then everyone would be able to look out their window and see that you were one of the first into the office that morning. This would also keep staff from leaving the campus for lunch because it meant that you would have to park at back of the lot when you returned.

I just remember thinking how that wouldn't have worked for me. I'm simply not an early riser. I also didn't think it was necessarily a good metric for deciding who was making the biggest contribution to the company. But it was clearly important to their organization's culture to be seen as a keen over-achiever.

During our meeting, it became clear that Microsoft was interested in creating a sound card, and they wanted to talk to us about developing M-Sound's technology. Initially, we discussed the possibilities of whether it would involve joint development or acquisition, but as we got further along, the discussions definitely turned more towards the idea of acquisition.

There was a lot of back and forth meetings and phone calls in the days and weeks that ensued, but the net outcome was that we agreed to provide a couple of M-Sound engineers to work alongside the Microsoft engineers in Redmond. The idea was to develop something jointly that we imagined would eventually become a Microsoft product.

Our engineers were there for about nine months, and Tom and I made a lot of trips back and forth between Vancouver and Redmond to attend meetings. There was constant talk of something new called "multimedia". It was a fancy new word at the time, and Microsoft had a new multimedia group. Microsoft had big plans for their hardware division as they moved into this new area, and the development of the sound card was a key part of their plans.

All the while, there was always the sense that we were David dealing with Goliath. We always wondered about how much we should say in meetings, or what we put up on a white board, or what we disclosed about our technology. The reality is that all of the non-disclosure agreements in the world can't completely protect you or your intellectual property.

We continued driving back and forth to Redmond, and we were burning about $200,000 a month in operating costs. We had around 15 engineers in an office in Vancouver, so it didn't take us long to expend 1.3 million dollars in capital. And we weren't cash flow positive yet.

At the end of nine months, Tom and I attended our umpteenth meeting with Microsoft management in Redmond. This time there was a distinctly different tone and feel to the discussion. I can't remember who it was who finally said it, but one of the Microsoft people just looked at us and said:

"What do you really have?"

Of course, our response was that we had a great technology, but we didn't have cash flow yet.

And then they posed the question. They offered to buy M-Sound, and they also offered to hire Tom and me as employees. Their offer was $120,000 per year for each of us, which was a substantial salary in 1990, plus something like 75,000 share options in Microsoft.

I knew this was a significant offer, and I was breathless as I sat there in my chair.

We told them that we would have to take a bit of time to consider the offer.

We got in the car, and I think Tom said, "Can you believe what just happened?"

He paused and reflected. "Do you want to work for Microsoft?" It was a serious question.

We knew that they were making a play. If you want to acquire a company, one of the best strategies is to offer jobs to the executives of that company as a sweetener. There was no question, they had definitely made both of our compensation packages look very appealing, and both Tom and I had to give it some serious thought. But of course, only history would be able to eventually tell us whether or not the stock options would amount to anything.

We went home to Vancouver, and I called Steve to tell him about the Microsoft offer. I never learned what the actual cash offer was for the company, but at that time Microsoft was trading on the NASDAQ exchange, and I remember Steve wasn't interested in NASDAQ stock. If we were going to sell M-Sound, he said he wanted to be bought by somebody that was trading on the NYSE or similar. Steve had very strong opinions about how things should happen, and he didn't think this was the right move.

So we didn't sell the company to Microsoft and we didn't become Microsoft employees. And I remember thinking that we were all missing an opportunity.

I had started to realize that selling the company was probably the smartest thing at that point. To launch our sound card properly, it was still going to take a lot of capital. More than Steve was prepared to invest or even had available to invest.

On the other hand, if we had the power and weight of Microsoft as our partner, we weren't likely to lose. And ultimately I would rather own 10% of *something* than 100% of nothing. In my previous dealings in the music industry, I had often used that strategy when I was negotiating with record labels. It was about giving up part of what we had in order to become part of something bigger.

I think I stayed with M-Sound for about another six months. Ironically, it was not that long thereafter Steve was running out of funds for the project and decided we should look aggressively for a buyer. Sierra Semiconductor made a successful bid for the company. I didn't feel this was a good fit, so I didn't make the move.

I was thinking: *Steve, with all due respect, less than a year ago, we brought you an offer from Microsoft which was probably the best thing we could have done, and now we are accepting a lowball offer from a company who manufacturers semiconductors.*

Culturally, Sierra was light years away from knowing what to do with a sound card. Its primary application was to enhance the entertainment experience of computer users. The only "entertaining" these guys did was to entertain the idea of reducing the costs per thousand with their integrated circuits production in China. A couple of our engineers joined them, but that was it.

It turned out Sierra weren't very successful with marketing the sound card. They really were all about semiconductors and manufacturing, and their skill set was not in marketing to software developers. The product floundered and before too long other manufacturers started marketing similar sound cards and the early opportunity was gone. I think Microsoft also came out with a sound card around that time, but I don't remember it having a very big impact in the market.

The whole experience was a bit of a heartbreak for sure.

A couple of years later, I had lunch with Dick Brown, one of the guys that owned SoundBlaster, the main competitor to M-Sound back in 1990. I was in Palo Alto doing fundraising for another project, and we managed to touch base and arrange to have a social lunch. SoundBlaster had also been acquired by a bigger group by this time, and he and his partner had done very well. Both of them were now worth many millions of dollars.

Dick looked at me: "Mark, the day you guys went away, I got down on my knees and thanked God."

He had known that M-Sound had a far superior product to theirs. We had been a force to be reckoned with, and we seemed to be everywhere. It had to have been a big concern for him.

Now SoundBlaster were now the *de facto* standard in the world of sound cards. They were being integrated into computers that were being shipped directly from factories. That had been our next big goal: seeing the M-Sound card built right into new systems. There wouldn't be a separate sound card anymore, and you could put a decal on the computer similar to the "Intel inside" sticker.

Much later, around 2012, Tom and I got together over a glass of wine and we talked about our M-Sound days. As we were reminiscing, we started speculating on what our 75,000 shares would have been worth today if we had taken the Microsoft offer. After all of the stock splits and market growth since 1990, we figured the value would probably be in the ballpark of $30 million each.

It sort of pains me to think about it, so I do my best to forget.

FIFTEEN

Big Screens and Big Finance

With the sale of M-Sound, I was back in the hunt. My experience with M-Sound had given me a serious taste for entertainment technology, and I was convinced that I wanted to continue working in that sector. I needed money while I looked for new opportunities, so I went back to mixing sound for film and television so I could support the family in the meantime.

It was now 1992, and I started working on a series that was shooting in Vancouver called *The Highlander*. Over the next couple of years I would also be part of the production crew for a number of additional television series, television movies and feature films, including a brief but very memorable few days on the 1993 film *This Boy's Life* with Robert De Niro and Leonardo DiCaprio.

The film and television industry had always been good for me because it allowed me to work on a show for three or four months, make a bag of money, and then take three or four months to develop passion projects like Boulevard and M-Sound.

But the Film industry was very hard on personal health and relationships. Mostly because of the hours. A short day would be 12 hours, and many were 14 hours or more.

To compound things, a lot of the actors had a 12-hour turnaround. This meant that if we wrapped at nine o'clock in the evening one day, we weren't able to have them back on the set until nine o'clock the next morning. As a consequence, production would start progressively later on every day of the week. If you started at seven o'clock in the morning on Monday, your start would be nine o'clock on Tuesday, and then eleven o'clock on Wednesday, and then one o'clock in the afternoon on Thursday. On Friday, production might start as late as three or four o'clock in the afternoon.

For this reason, they would typically schedule all of the exterior night shots for Friday. We might start inside the studio at four o'clock on Friday afternoon and film until nine o'clock, and then we'd often go outside and shoot the night exteriors until the sun came up.

Saturday morning would often find me driving home at eight o'clock. And since I had been missing Jane and the kids from a week of being mostly absent, I would only allow myself to sleep until about noon, and then wake up and try to pretend that I had some semblance of a family life and a weekend.

This would go on for months and months. I was lucky if I had one night to see people socially, including my family, and then I would be back at it on Monday at seven a.m. We were always fine as a family and we never had any issues—other than the fact that I felt like a zombie half of the time—but it was easy to imagine how some people would burn out.

One of my strategies for staying sane and healthy was to run. During different productions, I became known as the soundman who ran at lunch every day. Running had been a big part of my life for some time. I had already run the New York Marathon in 1989, and I competed in my first triathlon in 1991. So when they called lunch, I would quickly change and hit the road.

By my calculations, I knew I had about 45-minutes from the moment they called lunch to the time the last crew made it through the lunch line. So wherever we were filming, I would set out on my run and continue in one direction for about twenty-two minutes, and then I would turn around and run back. Then I would quickly grab a salad from the catering truck, and I would eat it during pauses in filming over the next two hours.

Film sound wasn't something that I saw myself doing for the rest of my life. If you had asked me as a kid if I wanted to go into the film business as a sound mixer, I would have said no. Absolutely not. I would have chosen to be a writer or a director. But I could make a living doing sound, and it allowed me to get my other projects off the ground because it paid so well. But if you did a 22-episode series, you were stuck in this routine for about nine months, and it was tough slogging.

During this period, I became involved with a company called Rainmaker, previously known as Gastown Post and Transfer. In addition to film processing and transferring film to video, they had started working in digital imaging. Their digital effects department was now growing quickly as many of the big studios started to hire them for visual and special effects. They had licensed a video compression technology from Phillips in the Netherlands, and they approached me to help them build that side of the business and develop Rainmaker Interactive. This was the early nineties and the term "interactive" was all the rage.

After M-Sound, working with Rainmaker was a very natural step for me on the digital media path. It was clear to me that digital technology was the future of things in media and entertainment. I got it and I wanted to be part of it.

Once I started working with Rainmaker, I stepped away from mixing film sound. I remember occasionally running into my old workmates from film and television on the street, and they would say, "You escaped."

A lot of people in the industry talked about "escaping" because most of them felt trapped. They were making great money, and they could afford to feed their families, pay their mortgages, and buy really nice cars. But they couldn't break away from the seductive power of the money. Consequently, they felt trapped, and they expressed some envy when they saw me.

In January 1995, I went down to the annual Consumer Electronics Show in Las Vegas as I had done for the previous four years. From my days at M-Sound, I had maintained a habit of attending CES in Vegas so I could keep abreast of developments in the industry. CES always provided a preview of the latest technologies, what were the hot new items, who was doing what, which new games were selling, what their platforms were, and all the rest.

While I was preparing to head down to Las Vegas, I learned that my old friend from Calgary, Danny Lowe, was going to the show as well. We made plans to get together for dinner.

Danny and I met for dinner at a restaurant in the Forum Shops at Caesar's Palace, and we had a very inspired evening. We caught up on family and everything else, but soon we started to talk about what we had seen at the first day of the CES show.

Both of us had been very impressed by the new flat screen television technology. We talked about how they opened up possibilities for deployment just about anywhere. As we shared ideas on the fly, we started to get excited. We agreed that there was potential for something very profitable here.

We discussed how the new screens would more than likely see increased use in restaurants, bars, airports, supermarkets, and health clubs.

I was very familiar with the lack of entertainment while working out at the gym. As we talked about it, one of us finally said, "What if we started putting these screens in exercise clubs?"

The light bulb came on.

We wouldn't just put up the screens. We would control the content as well. We would create and broadcast targeted content that included advertising for specific demographics of men and women as they worked out. It could mean *serious* dollars in advertising revenues.

Today, the concept of targeted digital content and personalized entertainment systems is a basic requirement in most exercise clubs. In 1995, it was essentially unknown.

And we would add a twist. We figured it was the Holy Grail. What if we created the world's first Hi-def 3D head-mounted display as part of the experience? We knew that the technology for 3D visors was being developed, so we started to imagine a visor that would allow the health club user to experience their workouts as part of a virtual world. Imagine running through the streets of New York in 3D as part of a group of runners, or cycling through Central Park as part of the peloton!

This could be *amazing*.

Dan had already spent a bit of time looking at the market and exploring the possibilities for a 3D head-mounted display system with Dr. Todd Simpson, a very bright guy who could take an idea from the back of a napkin and create a product that worked. Todd apparently believed a new 3D head mounted display system was very doable. So we knew something about the technology and we knew someone who could potentially partner with us to make the venture successful.

I went back to my hotel room after dinner, and I was so excited that I hardly slept.

I was staying at the Bellagio Hotel and Danny was staying down the strip at the Luxor. We had agreed to meet for breakfast at 8 a.m. at the Luxor, so when I woke up the next morning, I went down to the lobby to hail a taxi.

I discovered that there would be a one-hour wait, which was typical during big trade shows. I knew right away that this wasn't going to work. I was wearing jeans, dress shoes and a blazer, and I had my briefcase on a strap slung over my shoulder. I decided I would simply jog from the Bellagio to the Luxor.

And I just started running down the Las Vegas strip.

I was totally pumped about the giant sea of opportunity that I could see in the future, and I wasn't going to let a taxi ride get in my way. My feet hardly touched the pavement as I made my way down the oversized sidewalk, which later in the day would be jammed with all order of humanity strolling out of casinos and staggering along with oversized drinks.

As I moved along, I overtook another jogger in runners and shorts. The guy looked at me as I went past him.

"Hey! You're making me look real bad!" he laughed.

Anyone driving their commute that morning was probably wondering what the hell I was doing.

I arrived at the Luxor, took off my coat to air myself out, and I wiped the sweat off my brow with my handkerchief. For me, it wasn't a hard run, so I hadn't actually broken much of a sweat. And now I was at the Luxor in time for breakfast!

Danny and I continued to develop our business concept during our breakfast meeting and in the weeks that followed. Within two months, we found ourselves establishing E-Zone Networks Inc. together with Lee Guthrie and Todd Simpson.

Lee was another entrepreneur whom Dan had also crossed paths with. He had been a pioneer in the fitness industry back in the 1970s with Nautilus and Life Fitness. Lee would tell us stories of the early days where he and the former chairman and CEO of Life Fitness, Augie Nieto, would deliver Nautilus machines to clubs in California out of the back of a station wagon. Lee was—and still is—a larger-than-life guy who could sell anything to anyone.

The plan was basically to create our own cable network. We would put head-mounted displays into health clubs and connect them to the cardio equipment, which would in turn be connected with a central server in each club.

To demonstrate this immersive 3D experience for potential investors and customers, Dan and I decided to create a series of short 3D videos. We would shoot a couple of different ones from the perspective of the person walking through the rain forest, running through city streets, or cycling in a peloton.

One of the demo videos ended up being a beautiful seven-minute reel that was shot in Santa Monica, Malibu and Vancouver. We put a lot of effort into the production, and the result was stunning. I knew it was effective because everyone who watched it would always ask to see it again the moment it ended. A good sign!

We had high hopes as we made arrangements to pitch our new entertainment system to the fitness industry. To start, Lee set up a meeting with the executives at 24 Hour Fitness in San Francisco. At the time, this was the biggest chain of health clubs in California with over 120 locations. If we could land this account, we would basically be validating our business model, and our fundraising worries would be over. Up to this point, we had been self-funded. I had personally written a cheque for a hundred thousand dollars, which represented approximately 25 percent of my net worth after M-Sound, because I truly believed that we were going to take this to the moon.

We made our presentation to a very receptive audience. However, as one of the 24 Hour executives, Mike Feeney, took the visor off his head, he looked at me, Dan and Lee.

"This is a lovely piece, very impressive," he said, "but give us television. People go to the gym to work out and watch other people. If you strap one of these onto your head, you effectively cut yourself off from the other people and become antisocial."

Dan, Lee and I looked at each other. In 10 seconds, our business plan changed.

From there, we continued to develop and refine the plan. We finally arrived at the idea of delivering a mix of regular television and custom content that was gender and age specific. Fitness club members would enter their own personal six-digit pin code, and the system would turn on and recognize them. It would play four ads tailored to their demographic, which was determined by four simple categories. They had to indicate whether they were male or female, and whether they were over or under 35 years old.

If we could show advertisers how reliably we could deliver their ads to specific demographics, we would be able to charge premium advertising rates. For example, using our system, we could verify that each person was on that treadmill for a particular time period required to see the ads. We had a captive audience, and we could prove it. It wasn't like conventional television advertising where advertisers never really know how many people bolted for the fridge during their spot.

Again, this kind of targeted advertising might not sound especially innovative in the age of internet advertising, but this was back in 1995. There was no such thing as Google ads or the like, and very few exercise clubs even had televisions. We were very far ahead of the times – so far ahead that it was crazy.

E-Zone quickly became a pretty hot commodity. Over the next four years, we raised over $110 million dollars, and our partners came to include the Ontario Teachers Pension Fund and Scotia Capital. We ended up with a 17-person board of directors and eventually deployed over 12,000 television screens in health clubs across the United States, and acquired an Australian company called Cardio Theatre.

Part of our strategy was also to develop a channel called E-Zone radio that would also deliver targeted, custom content and advertising. To help us pull it together, we engaged my good friend and seasoned Canadian broadcaster Jesse Dylan. At one point, we went looking for a host personality for the channel, and one of our radio consultants, Randy Lane, introduced us to a young guy in Los Angeles named Ryan Seacrest.

We met with Ryan over breakfast at the Beverly Hilton in Los Angeles, and we immediately liked him. We talked with about him becoming the host of E-Zone radio, but we soon determined that we couldn't afford him. He was a great guy though, and you could tell he was destined for big things. Which he indeed was.

Even though we didn't land Ryan Seacrest, everything was still looking great for the company. We weren't cash-positive yet, but we seemed poised to become a smash homerun. Then events beyond anyone's imagining conspired to stop us in our tracks.

I had been concerned for some time about the rate at which we were burning capital. I knew that if we were unable to raise more investment, we would be in a very difficult position where even a small a correction in the stock market could impact our ability to raise more capital. And this is exactly what happened.

In late 1999, we decided to arrange a very big round of new financing. By early March of 2000, we had a team of our executives and E-Zone finance people preparing to go into meetings with TD Bank, Scotia Capital and the Ontario Teachers' Pension Fund in Toronto. When they got out of bed on the morning of March 13th they discovered that the markets were tanking. One of our finance people in Toronto that morning, Bob Mackenzie, called to tell us that the banks had cancelled all meetings and all new financing was frozen.

We had negotiated something in the area of $100 million in new financing, and suddenly it was gone.

The market crash hit us at a critical juncture. E-Zone had become a massive cash-burning machine by this point, and we were in the process of expanding aggressively. We had offices in several U.S. cities and we had around 450 employees. Suffice it to say, our burn rate was very high with a lot of monthly bills to pay.

But we weren't able to fund E-Zone any further. And without new financing, the company quickly started to choke. Within a few months, we were cutting operations, laying off employees, and selling assets.

By the time E-Zone ceased operations, we were by far the world's largest private network. The next closest was Blockbuster video, who had about 4,500 screens networked between their video stores.

To be fair, it wasn't just financing that led to E-Zone's collapse. Management issues had also contributed. As the company had grown, the board had also ballooned. With every $10 million invested, it seemed someone else came onto the board to represent their stake. Eventually, it became nearly impossible for the board to build consensus on anything. Too many chefs in the kitchen—and some strong egos among them.

The fall of E-Zone was a heartbreak for those of us who had started the company. I think the company was really ahead of its time, and it had the potential to become much bigger. Maybe even global in scope.

But sometimes things happen that sink even the best business ideas. In this case, we couldn't control the financial markets, and we ultimately couldn't control our own board.

To make matters worse, Jane was diagnosed with colon cancer that spring, and we were struggling with a costly renovation to our Vancouver home that threatened to destroy us financially.

Blue skies seemed to be darkening and storm clouds were rolling in. I know that in everyone's life there will always be a bit of rain, but this was a fucking thunderstorm.

SIXTEEN

Back to the (Sound) Board

E-Zone was finished, and a new reality began to set in. Jane and I were faced with her cancer diagnosis, and we were also dealing with a home renovation that had spiraled out of control. I wasn't seeing a silver lining anywhere.

I had been with E-Zone for nearly five years, and during that time my life had been a blur of airplanes, trade shows, and constant travel to raise money and develop the company. Now I had to figure out what I was going to do to keep our household together.

First and foremost, I needed to generate cash flow. I was working very hard to get something else going, but given the state of the financial markets in 2000, any good idea that I generated fell on deaf ears. Most investors had just taken a big hit to their net worth, and they were not in a mood to expose themselves to any further risk. Regardless of how good the idea might be, they weren't interested in anything that didn't promise a guaranteed return.

Only one thing seemed to be doing well in Vancouver. The film industry. So as much as it vexed me, I eventually decided to return to mixing film sound.

I put out the word out and it wasn't long before small jobs, or day calls as they are referred to in the business, started coming up. One of them was a one-day stint on a new television series called *Smallville*. A friend of mine named Patrick Ramsey was the production sound mixer, and he needed me to fill in for him for one day.

It was September 12, 2001. I will always remember that day for a number of reasons, but for one reason especially. Halfway through the shooting day, we stopped and the entire cast and crew participated in a minute of silence with candles lit in memory of those who had perished the previous day.

Despite the somberness of that date, my one day on *Smallville* went well, and a couple of weeks later, I had another call from Patrick.

"Mark, I'm going to leave the show at Christmas," he said. "Do you want to take over and do the last eleven episodes starting in January?"

I thought long and hard about this as I knew what I would be in for. But I needed money, so of course I said yes. And in January 2002, I took over the show from Patrick and went back to working full time as a production sound mixer.

I'll never forget it. That dark January morning, Jane was standing on the deck of the house as I started to pull away. I was driving Patrick's rusty old GMC van that he had loaned me for the next few months of shooting. The shocks were blown, and it was loaded to the gunnels with sound gear. This was one of the last things I wanted to be doing but given our dismal financial state, it would solve a problem for us and get things back on track.

I rolled the window down and I looked up at Jane, a knot forming in my stomach. Trying to put on my bravest comedic voice on for her, I simply said, "Living the dream, honey." And I drove away.

It was hard. I get choked up just thinking about it. Because I knew what it meant. I knew what the workdays were like, and how isolated I would be from my family because of the long hours. It also didn't help that I had just undergone abdominal surgery for a hernia in mid-December. So I was challenged to get in and out of the car.

It was Monday, January 7, and we were shooting in downtown Vancouver in an office tower on Georgia Street. I was acutely aware that I had old friends and associates with offices in the building, and I had been in a number of them wearing a suit as a partner with E-Zone. Now I was turning up as a member of a film crew at seven o'clock in the morning in the pouring rain, wearing a pair of jeans and running shoes and a wool beret. A true exercise in humility.

It was very hard for me mentally and emotionally. It was a combination of feeling that we had failed—or more especially that I had failed—at E-Zone, and then feeling frustrated beyond belief because I had actually seen things coming undone well ahead of time and felt helpless about being able to do anything about it. And here I was back on the set as a consequence.

There had been one other time when I had the exact same feeling. It was in Calgary after Thunder Road closed in 1985. Again, I had needed money, so I started this cover band called The Edge. Our first gig was at the Penguin Pub below the old Grand Theater. As we were unloading our gear off a half-ton truck in the alley off First Street, I had that same feeling: *I'm going to see someone I know, and I'm loading band equipment into a dingy little pub.*

After I had been a respected studio owner and chief engineer at Thunder Road for five years, it was very humbling.

In the first week of shooting on *Smallville*, we had one day where we worked for 19 hours, and then I had a one-hour drive home afterward. I drove home so fatigued that I was literally going cross-eyed. I think I had underestimated the toll the recent surgery had taken on me. I was afraid that I would fall asleep at the wheel, so I rolled down the windows and cranked the radio so loud that the sound distorted.

But there was no denying the fact that I was adept as a sound mixer. So I figured that I could take some pride in that fact.

One of my first entries into film sound had been in 1986 when I first moved to Vancouver from Calgary in my quest to secure a record deal for Boulevard. To make ends meet, I took a job as a post-production sound mixer at Alpha Cine Labs. This was the final stop for the soundtrack of a film once it had been edited and pieced together. As a mixer, my job was to take all of the tracks that the sound editor had created, including the dialogue, and mix the level of the dialogue sound effects and music relative to the picture while watching the film.

For example, if there were two cowboys sitting around a campfire, each of their voices would be on separate faders so the level of their voices could be adjusted independently. Then there might be the sound of crickets in the background, the crackling fire, and maybe a bit of wind. Each of those elements were separate tracks that had to be mixed to provide a consistent ambient background while the actors talked.

When it came time for me to mix sound on location as a production mixer, I was able to lean on all of my previous experience in post-production sound. It meant that I had a lot of knowledge and sensitivity for what was required in the final mix and a clear understanding of what the editor and post-production mixer would be looking for. .

The process of capturing on-set sound would involve watching the rehearsal with the actors, and then determining the best approach to capturing the dialogue or effects. For example, knowing where to put all of the microphones. Sometimes the boom operator was able to suspend the microphone in front of the actors just out of the camera shot, and if we were in a quiet location, he could move it back and forth between the actors without causing shadows.

Other times, however, when we were outside in a noisy location, and we had two or more actors doing what is called a walk-and-talk as they walked down the street, the boom mic was not practical because it picked up the sound of the footsteps of the actors and the three-to-five crew such as the cameraman, focus puller, often a dolly grip, and a few more walking just in front of them. In an instance like this, I needed to hide radio microphones under the clothing of each actor.

Those were tricky shots. The biggest challenge was getting the microphone positioned so it wasn't visible and it didn't cause a rustling sound when the actor moved, You wouldn't believe the sound produced by a microphone inside a silk tie when an actor is walking. It sounds like sandpaper. My job was to make sure that didn't happen and the sound was warm and natural.

I was grateful for the healthy film industry in Vancouver which had allowed me to fall back on something I knew how to do, so I could take film sound jobs while I was getting a new idea off the ground or trying to launch Boulevard.

Although mixing film sound was not topping the list of what I would have chosen to do as a career, it did have a very Zen quality to it that I enjoyed. During the times when I had to be laser-focused for long durations while the camera was rolling, it was very stimulating while being almost meditative. These short bursts of extreme focus would be followed by followed by hours of waiting around for the set up of the next shot.

The other thing about my years in the business were the incredible people I worked with. Since a typical week on a film or television series was 70 to 80 hours, all of us on the crew spent much more time together than we did with our immediate family and friends. The result of this was a real sense of "family" amongst us. To this day, I am very grateful for some of the lifelong friendships that I forged during these years.

I was also very fortunate to have worked with some of the most gifted actors who brought their unique energy to the set every day. During those years, I had the chance to work with the likes of Kevin Spacey, Kevin Bacon, Robert De Niro, John Voight, Joan Rivers and Paul Glaser.

Since that time, I have run into some of these different actors in the most random places all over the world. Once I was walking through a pedestrian tunnel in the Mayfair district of London which provides safe passage from one side of the very busy Bayswater Road into Hyde Park across the street. I was making my way to a meeting near Harrods in Knightsbridge, and as I entered the tunnel, I could see it was empty except for one couple walking toward me. They were backlit by the light at the far end of the tunnel, so they approached me in silhouette. As they passed by me, I realized it was Kevin Bacon and his wife Kyra Sedgewick.

I quickly turned and said, "Kevin."

Perhaps my voice resonating against the white tiles had startled him because he turned abruptly and seemed to assume a defensive posture.

"Yes?" he said, in a tone that suggested, *and who is asking?*

Recognizing that he was a bit taken aback, I immediately said, "It's Mark Holden—we worked together in Vancouver with Michael Glazer on *The Air Up There*. I stretched out my hand.

He dropped his shoulders and suddenly smiled. "Of course, Mark! Nice to see you again. This is Kyra."

I shook her hand as if I didn't know who she was, and the three of us chatted briefly before going our separate ways.

It took me a while to sort out why I wasn't all that excited about mixing sound, but I finally figured out why I was not feeling fulfilled in my work. I realized that it simply wasn't my destiny. Other than taking pride in providing a solid soundtrack for the editors to fold into the final film, which of course was the job at hand, deep down I really didn't feel that I was making enough of a contribution or doing something meaningful with my life.

As much as I have a tremendous respect for quality sound and the entire production process, and the talented technicians and artisans that are part of it, I realized that I needed to be *creating* the content or ideas that would move and inspire people. Content that would make them want to become better, happier, fulfilled. Instead, I felt I was just a very small spoke in the wheel of the film business behemoth.

I have learned that some of the most significant people and meaningful things in our lives often have obscure beginnings. And I have come to believe that everything we do leads to something, but often only history will dictate what it means in the grand scheme of things. How many times have I looked back on a rough patch in my life and said, "You know, it was during that time that I met so-and-so," or I did something that led me to be introduced to someone who would come to have great meaning in my life. It's all part of the journey, and it's nearly impossible to imagine trying to predict how these things will eventually shape our lives.

Within two years, the clouds had passed. Jane recovered from her cancer, and I dodged the Grim Reaper by a whisper with a near-fatal bowel obstruction. We finally finished the renovation, and we sold the house.

And I found myself looking forward with optimism to new business opportunities in digital media.

SEVENTEEN

My Father

Our lives are shaped in large part by our careers and the crazy things that happen us along the way. But it's easy to forget the influence of our childhoods. Especially as we get older and our upbringing becomes more distant. In my case, I can't deny the profound impact that my father has had on my world view—for better or for worse.

To understand what I mean, you need to know a bit about my early life with my dad.

When I was a kid, we were basically poor. Certainly by today's lifestyle standards, we weren't affluent. Take haircuts, for example.

As was often the case for struggling young families in the 1960s, my parents didn't have money to pay for haircuts for their kids. So every three or four weeks after dinner, it was time for me and my brother Shane to get cropped by my dad at home. And while my dad had a few talents, cutting hair was not one of them.

With bath towels draped over our shoulders, we would sit on a chair in the middle of the kitchen in grim anticipation, our shoulders hunched up to our ears like dogs waiting to be bathed against their will. My dad would plug in the black Wahl hair clippers, power them up with a loud *clack* sound, and begin the dastardly deed.

As he carved away at our thick heads of blond hair, we would feel the clippers vibrate violently as the electric motor labored under the strain. He always insisted in tapering the hair at the back of our heads up to within an inch of the crown, and it generally resulted in a cowlick reminiscent of Dennis the Menace. The hairstyle was generally called a bowl cut because it looked someone had put a bowl on your head and cut around the bottom of it.

Once my father had finished, my brother and I would immediately run to the bathroom to check out the damage. We would then find ourselves borrowing our mother's Dippity Doo hair product to try to glue the protruding hair down. I am certain that one of the reasons I was so driven to earn my own money at an early age was the ability to pay for my own haircuts.

I loved my father very much, but sadly, the first words that come to mind when I think of him are "troubled soul." On the surface of things, he lived a full and complete life. He married my mother, June—a wonderful woman—and he raised a healthy family while building a successful career as an architect. But fundamentally, he was always troubled in spirit.

My dad was extremely sensitive, and I'm sure that I inherited much of my own sensitivity from him. His feelings were easily hurt if someone said something uncomfortable or confrontational to him, and if he ever felt that he had hurt someone else's feelings, it weighed very heavily on him.

My father was born in 1935, and as soon as he graduated high school, he married his high school sweetheart, my mom. He went to study architecture at the University of Manitoba, where he struggled until he graduated to balance his demanding studies with the challenges of raising a young family. He began working as a professional architect with the Edmonton School Board, and he left the school board to start his own practice when I was 10 years old.

He was a good architect and he did very well in his independent practice. He was the type of person who obsessed about details, which of course is what you need in order to be successful as an architect. His specification books for projects were extraordinary in scope, typically itemizing everything down to the last box of three-and-a-quarter-inch phosphate-coated nails required to build an entire hospital.

He was brilliant in that sense, but he clearly paid a price for his obsessiveness. If he had seventeen jobs on the go, he wouldn't know how to delegate any of the work, so he would end up doing everything himself. Consequently, he was constantly burned out. He wouldn't sleep well at night, and then he would get up early the next morning and go straight back to work while never being able to stop obsessing about every detail of every job.

Naturally this type of mental anguish took its toll.

Growing up with him was difficult. Money had been very tight while he was studying architecture, and it continued to be sparse in our household for the first few years as he was establishing himself in his profession. When I was small, he and my mother would often argue, and I'm sure their arguments had a lot to do with money. There was often a strong undercurrent of deep discontent.

I hated listening to them, and I remember feeling anxious and distraught in my room when I heard them down the hall. It was very upsetting. I never really discussed the arguments with my brother or sisters. I do remember being concerned that my sisters, Erica and Brenley, who were both younger than me, would hear things and get upset.

Occasionally, the phone would ring while they were arguing, and they would stop to answer it. It would be a business colleague or a friend of the family, so my dad would be forced to change his tone. I was always grateful when that happened. I would think about the person who had called, and I would think, *thank you.* After my dad hung up the phone, even if they went back to arguing, my dad was never as angry as he had been before the phone rang. It was my definition of divine intervention.

In reality, my dad wasn't an angry or argumentative man. He was a very caring and sensitive man. He simply carried a lot of anxiety, and it was beyond my ken to understand it.

Looking back now, I'm certain he could have benefited from some counseling and medication to help him cope with his discontent. But this was back in the 1960s, and people simply didn't have the understanding and acceptance of mental illness that we have today.

He improved over the years, and the arguments with my mom became fewer and fewer, but he remained a fundamentally discontented man. It was sad for me to witness, and it was hard to tolerate at times.

Eventually, as I got older, I became aware of some of his issues. First and foremost was his apparent belief that he was completely inadequate. Despite his success in his work and the beautiful, healthy family that he had, he seemed convinced that he was bound for failure.

Eventually, I started trying to coach him.

We once drove down to Scottsdale, Arizona together when I was 12 years old. He was attending a conference there, and it was my turn to go on a "solo trip with Mom and Dad" as the only sibling. My parents had decided that it would be good for each one of the four kids to go on one of these mini vacations separately when opportunities arose. I was very excited about going on this trip as I had never been to Arizona, and it was January in Calgary with temperatures hovering in the -20 to 40 Fahrenheit range.

I ended up spending the entire trip coaching and counseling my dad. I swear to God, we had several conversations on the balcony of the Royal Inn in Tempe, Arizona where we talked for hours as I coached him through whatever was troubling him at the time.

"It will all work out, I'm sure," I remember saying to him as encouragement.

"Try to look at it this way," I would say.

"Maybe it just wasn't meant to be."

"This may be a bit of a rough patch."

"Yes, that person is a real jerk for treating you that way."

I didn't understand the term "silver lining" yet, but I reminded him frequently that there was one.

I was 12 years old at the time. Looking back, it does seem a bit unusual, given that I hadn't even entered my teen years yet.

As the months passed, I continued to coach him and reassure him.

Eventually, I began to realize that he was relying on me for constant support. He would look for it.

When he expressed a lack of faith in himself, I would say to him, "You're a great architect."

And he would respond, "Really?"

I'd say, "You can do great things, and you are doing great things."

And he would say, "Really?"

And if I didn't think I was having enough impact, I would often add, "And just look at all you have to be grateful for—your wonderful family, four great kids, and mom…"

Rationally, I'm sure he knew that he was a great architect. But he would never say, "I know I'm a great architect, and I do great work." Those words never came out of his mouth. He just didn't seem capable of giving himself that recognition. It was strange to me. Why the extreme lack of self-esteem?

What was also strange was that he never reciprocated with me by offering me coaching or support through my activities and difficulties. I would talk to him about what was happening in my life, and he wouldn't hear 95 percent of it. He was completely vacant, and often so totally wrapped up in whatever it was that he was obsessing about, that my words fell on deaf ears.

I could have said, "Hey dad, I just broke my leg in five places, and I'll have to get a cast, and I'll be on crutches for six weeks."

His likely response would have been something like, "Oh, really? Well, okay then. That's good. Great to hear it." He was so completely absorbed with himself.

If I said to him, "I've got a challenge here, and I wonder if I could run something by you," he would invariably give me an absent-minded response. He would come back with something like, "Yeah…well…a guy just needs to…to kind of…to get himself fixed up. But you know, the price of gas…*I just can't believe the price of gas…*"

And he would go right back to a conversation we had about an hour earlier or a day earlier that was more interesting to him. Like the price of gas or something else he was holding on to. And I would just shake my head.

Eventually, I learned to stop telling him anything about my life, my interests, my difficulties. I limited myself to asking him what he was doing, and then he would tell me, and I would expand on what he had said, giving him an outlet to express whatever was on his mind. This was often a slippery slope, but it was my way of maintaining a connection with him, as tenuous as it was.

My father was always thinking about something that had happened in the past or something that might happen in the future. And if it was something in the future, it was almost always bad.

Money was always an issue and a source of anxiety. With money and material things, he wasn't miserly or covetous, but he was very determined not to waste anything or throw anything out. He would say to us, "Well, you never know when we might have to go through hard times."

His father had used this expression during the Great Depression, and so had his father before him. To this day, I occasionally use the line with my kids as a joke. Jane once found some old t-shirts that I hadn't worn for a while, and she said we should get rid of them. I stopped her. "Wait a minute—not so fast! You never know when we might go through hard times!" And everyone laughed.

Of course, my dad's obsession with money sometimes manifested in him being very reluctant to enjoy the money he earned even during the good times. As an adult, I remember going out for dinner with him and my mom. When it came time to order, he would say, "I'll just have a small side salad and a glass of water." And of course the rest of the family would feel conflicted. No one else wanted to order anything more than a salad.

As much as I loved him, that part of his character really drove me nuts. I often wondered if he had any idea how his conduct impacted the rest of us.

In those situations, I would often say, "Look dad, I'll pay for dinner. Don't worry about it."

He would then softly insist that he wanted to buy dinner, but I would tell him that I would take care of the bill. I don't think he ever intended to do this consciously, but these dinners became less and less frequent as they just started to become too stressful for me. I think for the most part, deep down, I just wanted him to get the idea that his behavior was making most of us feel very uncomfortable.

I had always assumed my dad's attitudes and issues stemmed simply from his personality. Like it was part of his genetic makeup from birth. After he died in 2008, I learned something that changed my view entirely.

After the funeral, my Uncle Glen told a story that I had never heard before. When my dad was 12 years old, he was in a serious accident.

My dad's family was living in Vancouver at that time, and he had a paper route. One morning while he was delivering newspapers, he was hit by a car at the corner of Hastings and Cassiar.

The handlebars of his bicycle were driven into his abdomen. They went right through him.

Practically disemboweled, he was rushed to Vancouver General Hospital and admitted to surgery. The doctors ended up replacing part of his innards with goat intestines in order to piece him back together. He shouldn't have lived, but he did. He stayed a few months in hospital while he recovered.

The accident would have been enough to scar anyone for life. But what happened next was, I can only imagine, extremely upsetting.

My dad's mother came to visit him in hospital. She went to his bedside after the surgery, and she looked at him with visible disappointment and disdain.

"Look what you've done," she said.

He was lying in a hospital bed, just about dead, and these were her words of comfort. As I came to learn later in life, she had always been a bit strange.

In light of this, my dad's subsequent behavior might not seem too surprising.

"When your dad came home from the hospital, he wasn't the same guy," said Uncle Glen.

The story left me feeling very sad for my father. And it gave me a completely different understanding of who he had been. I wished someone had told me while he was still alive because it really explained a lot. He had never talked about this early episode of his life. He loved his mom, and he always spoke highly of her. He took the high road.

Meanwhile, I had a very strong connection with my grandfather when I was growing up. He was a remarkable individual. He had been the past president of the Wawanesa Insurance Company, and he had a long list of business and philanthropic accomplishments. He loved his grandkids and he would beam with pride whenever we showed him a piece of art that one of us had created. And he loved it when one or all of us would put on a mini music recital for him. Sometimes we would have my mother on the piano, my brother Shane and my Dad on the trumpet, my sister Erica on the violin, me on my clarinet, and my youngest sister Brenley singing or doing a dance routine.

Unfortunately, as much as my grandfather loved my dad, his focus was on his business and helping others while my dad was growing up. He was very absent as a father. I am certain that this contributed to my father not feeling loved.

How many millions of people in the world have family histories and issues like my father? And how many of their family and loved ones might take a different approach to them if they only knew what their brothers, sisters, fathers and mothers had been through?

Most people try to imagine having done things differently with their family. You tend to second-guess yourself. *I should have done this, and I could have done more of that*, and so on.

I don't know if my dad's mother ever forgave him, or if they never spoke of his accident again. But if I had known the story, I would have said to my dad, "Look, we're going to go and sit down with your mother, and we're going to get this straight, because it's not right what she did." I can think of so many options that would have been at his disposal had we been able to get this out into the open and treat it.

But that never happened. The upshot was that my father lived his entire life feeling tremendously insecure and devalued, and it impacted everything he did.

My mother was no doubt the brightest part of his life. When my dad married her at age 18, he won the lottery. She was completely selfless and infinitely giving, and she nurtured his fragile sense of self throughout their marriage.

It may have even been excessive at times. I remember being a kid, staying home sick from school, and having my mother fuss over me. She would make tea for me and get me extra blankets, and just generally dote on me. It was a wonderful feeling when I was sick. But when I got better, the doting naturally stopped. I would back to school and pick myself up again.

With my father, she never seemed to stop. Her constant attention was like an endless IV drip to him. I think he became addicted to the attention, and I think my mom became addicted to fussing over him. In that sense, despite of her best intentions, I think my mother may have been fanning the embers.

Knowing what I know now about my dad's childhood and his accident, I can see that his hunger for attention was no doubt a response to the neglect he experienced as a child, and perhaps even a direct reaction to that moment with his mother in the hospital. He was finally getting his needs fulfilled.

As strange and difficult as my dad was at times, I still enjoyed some special times with him.

One such moment happened when I was 17 years old as I was preparing to fly to Winnipeg to start a series of gigs with a band that had hired me for a few weeks. It was early in the morning, and I was still in bed in a state of semi-conscious sleep. I could hear my parents discussing something in the kitchen, which was directly above my room. I could tell from my mother's tone and a few words that I caught that she was telling my dad, "John, you better go downstairs and say goodbye to Mark because he will be gone when you get home from work."

My dad really struggled with expressions of emotion towards his kids. It wasn't that he didn't care deeply for all of us, but he could hardly look you in the eye if he paid a compliment or wanted to tell you that he loved you. Again, I knew this stemmed from his deep insecurity. I had always understood this was one of his characteristics and I would generally try to ease his discomfort by enthusiastically responding to any efforts he made to communicate.

There was a knock on my door.

I heard my father faintly on the other side, "Mark, can I come in?" His voice was timid.

I stumbled out of bed to open the door, and my dad entered. He was rubbing his hands nervously and shifting his weight from one foot to another.

"Good luck on the road Mark," he said very softly, "I am going to miss you."

He hugged me, and tears began to roll down my face. I think it was one of the most tender moments we ever shared. He started to cry as well. I think he was suddenly realizing that I could be gone for a long time, and he was overcome by a rush of remorse for having been so absent from my life.

My father was a great lover of the outdoors, and he seemed to be his best self when he was in nature. When he got away from his work, away from the city, and even away from my mom, he seemed to find a peace of mind that was otherwise never present.

When I was growing up in Calgary, he and I occasionally drove to Banff together, and we did a number of memorable hikes in the mountains over the years. Cirque Lake was one place we went, and another was

Taylor Lake. Cirque Lake was above the tree line in a bowl surrounded by the mountains, and the water was so cold that it had no algae. It was as clear as glass, and it was stunning to stand and simply stare into the depths in silence.

We also hiked to Moraine Lake a couple of times—the lake that used to be pictured on the back of the old Canadian twenty dollar bill. Located in a basin in the valley of the ten peaks close to Lake Louise, this lake is extraordinarily beautiful and spiritual. You can sit looking out at the lake amidst astonishing silence, and you can just feel the energy of the Rocky Mountains.

We also did a lot of canoeing, and my dad took tremendous pleasure in it. On one occasion, we canoed down the Spray Lakes above the town of Canmore. On another occasion when I was 12 years old, we were coming back from a family summer holiday in Penticton, British Columbia, and we canoed Shuswap Lake together.

That was an adventure and a half. On that occasion, we loaded the canoe with our tent, sleeping bags and food, and we left my mother and my sisters in the town of Sicamous. We set out in clear weather one afternoon, and we ended up canoeing a huge distance up the lake. We paddled for about five hours until we arrived at an inlet where there were no other people, only an old hermit who kept strictly to himself.

My dad was fascinated with this old hermit's prospector's tent. He had neatly stacked perfectly cut firewood on the inside walls of the tent making ready for a long winter ahead. I think my father had a secret fantasy to be that guy, living simply in this perfect pristine world.

I remember giggling silently to myself and thinking: *Okay, dad, we have had a good look at this hermit's cozy campsite, but perhaps we should go around to the next bay and let him have his space.*

He was a hermit, after all, and maybe there was a reason that he was miles and miles up this desolate lake by himself. Still, my dad made the decision to pitch our tent 200 feet down the beach from him.

We set up our tent for the night and we built a blazing fire out of driftwood. My dad tinkered with the fire for the entire evening, stoking it and nurturing the flames. We also cooked our dinner on it which gave my dad immeasurable pleasure.

We slept well that night. However, when we awoke the next morning and began to prepare for our paddle back down the lake, a storm started blowing and it began to pelt rain. It was a bit scary. Shuswap Lake is very big, and there were three-foot waves and whitecaps on the water. We were faced with paddling through it back to Sicamous.

My dad and I had actually done a lot of whitewater river canoeing previously, so we were reasonably confident about crossing the lake. As we headed out into the wind, with the canoe bobbing and rolling with the waves, I remember thinking that most people probably wouldn't have attempted to paddle in those conditions. It was a bit frightening, but it was also a great bonding experience for my father and me.

Many years later, knowing how much my father loved the outdoors, and wanting to rekindle some of the excitement and adventure that we had shared when I was younger, I found an opportunity to give him another memorable outdoor experience very late in his life.

In July 1996, my mom and dad announced that they were coming to Vancouver to visit us. They were driving from Utah where they had moved after my father became semi-retired. I had just helped to start E-Zone, and I was making a good salary. As long as I could remember, he had always wanted to go salmon fishing at one of the private fishing lodges on the coast. I remember him often saying, "Wouldn't it be neat to go salmon fishing to one of those fancy lodges one day?" He loved to fish, and he loved being on the water. So I booked a trip for him, myself, and my nine-year-old son Elliot to April Point Lodge on Quadra Island.

I surprised my dad with the plans when he arrived in Vancouver.

"We're going salmon fishing for three days," I told him. "Just the guys—the three generations."

He was practically speechless. He immediately asked me about the cost and started to fuss about whether or not I could really afford it, but I reassured him that it was all taken care of.

The day after my parents arrived in Vancouver, the three of us caught the ferry to Vancouver Island and drove up to Campbell River.

Once again, my dad became a completely different guy. He never once complained or fixated on anything negative, and we had the first real conversations that I could remember in a long time. He didn't obsess about the price of gasoline or the government, and he wasn't anxiously repeating his thoughts like he normally did.

We arrived at the lodge and checked in, and I became immediately aware that my father had never enjoyed a nice hotel. He gushed about the main building and the lobby. He pointed to the nice furnishings and artwork, and he was effusive about being able to smell the remnants of the fire in the grand fireplace from the night before.

One of the first things he noticed in the lobby was a photograph on the table beside the registration desk. It was a picture of U.S. General Norman Schwarzkopf who had led Operation Desert Storm in the first Persian Gulf War. He had been there two weeks earlier, and my father thought this was amazing.

"Stormin' Norman Schwarzkopf was here fishing? Just two weeks ago? That's incredible!"

He was really excited about this, and I was happy that he was excited. He was like a child again.

The reception desk was in the main building, and the resort accommodations were housed in adjacent buildings built in rustic west coast style. All of the buildings sat on a slightly elevated bluff overlooking the docks below where all of the boats were moored. From the main building, we looked down at the boats lined up and rigged with nets and fishing gear, and we watched other boats arriving from their day of fishing.

We had arrived around four o'clock in the afternoon, and you could smell that the tide was out. That unmistakable smell of ocean, salt, and shellfish with the slightest undertone of sulfur. The seagulls were swirling in the crisp blue sky, and there was some activity on the docks as the boats arrived.

We dropped our bags in our room, and I said to my dad, "Do you want to go down and check out the boats?"

His eyes grew big. "Sure! That sounds like a great idea!"

We walked down to the dock, and there was all kinds of wildlife in evidence. Looking into the water, we saw brightly colored starfish and muscles and oysters, along with minnows and herring darting about. We also saw dogfish, and there were a couple of seals lingering to eat any scraps of fish that might be discarded from the boats as the catch was cleaned.

The entire food chain was represented in this tiny bay. My father was practically coming out of his skin. "My god! Look at the seal!"

As we stood there, another boat arrived. My dad immediately approached the fishermen. "Hey fellas, do you happen to have any leftovers?" He was excited to feed their scraps to the seal.

He was so enthralled by the life in the water, that he eventually got down on his stomach so he could peer over the edge of the dock into the depths below. He used his hand to shield his eyes from the reflection off the water and he stayed there for nearly a half hour, providing a running commentary of what he was seeing.

He was blissfully happy, and we hadn't even gone fishing yet.

The next day, we got up early for breakfast, and we were down at the dock just after eight o'clock. The water in the bay was as smooth as glass, and the entire world seemed still. The air was fragrant with a blend of last night's fire, the scent of the salt chuck, the creosote on the dock pilings, and a trace of gasoline fumes from the idling engines of the boats. The stuff of high romance for anyone who loves fishing and being on the water, or remembers the smell of a four-stroke outboard engine from childhood.

I was dressed in a t-shirt and jeans with an old pair of runners, and my dad was wearing his brown Hushpuppies and polyester-cotton work pants with suspenders. This was standard dress code for him. He would buy his pants at either K-Mart or some work wear store, and he invariably had the waist riding somewhere between his navel and his Adam's apple.

My brother once joked, "You know, dad, if you could get your waist-band just a little higher, you could just skip wearing a shirt—all you would need to do is cut holes in your pockets and stick your arms out!"

Our boat might as well been the space shuttle. It was decked out with all of the latest in fishing gear and electronics, and our guide had the cool look and manner of the seasoned professional, complete with sunglasses, baseball cap and gum chewing.

The current was running very quickly, as was typical of the narrow waters between Campbell River and Quadra Island whenever the tide was changing. The guide fired up the engine, and we roared out across the water. He took the boat out the edge of some kelp beds, and we soon had our lines in the water.

My dad was awestruck. He was in a charter boat with a personal fishing guide. He couldn't believe it. He almost had to pinch himself.

Then we started catching these beautiful Coho salmon. Again, my dad was exploding with excitement, and I was delighted to watch him. We had a cooler full of drinks and snacks, and we were just living the good life.

At the end of the day, when we returned to the docks, we took a picture of the three of us weighing our catch. I still have the picture. The three Holden generations. Irreplaceable memories.

That evening, we sat in the main lodge enjoying dinner and drinks. The fireplace was crackling with a good blaze, and our noses caught the sweet scent of the burning wood. As I watched my dad enjoying himself and joking with my son, I felt a deep sense of gratitude to life.

We had three beautiful days together at April Point, and then we returned to Vancouver for another few days of visiting as a family before my parents returned to Utah.

That would be essentially the end of the story, except something curious happened three weeks later. I was walking past an art gallery in West Vancouver, and a painting in the front window stopped me in my tracks.

West Vancouver was hosting the Harmony Arts Festival, and there were artworks from all over British Columbia and the Pacific Northwest. This painting depicted three salmon swimming upstream to spawn. As was typical during spawning, their heads had turned red and their noses had become hooked. There was a small card below the painting with the name of the work: "Work in Progress." The artist's name was Fry.

The same painting had been in our room at April Point Lodge. Not a print of the same image—the same actual painting. It had been displayed in our room at April Point as part of the resort's efforts to promote works by local artists.

As I studied the image again, I thought to myself: *What are the odds?*

I regret now that I didn't buy it and give it to my dad. It felt like a sign somehow.

The fishing trip to April Point had been a slice of heaven for my dad. In fact, it might have been one of the best memories of his life. At the end of the day, it would have hardly mattered whether or not we caught any fish. He probably would have been equally ecstatic just riding in the boat or feeding breadcrumbs to the fish from the dock.

Following our trip to April Point, I established what would become a tradition of routinely scheduled calls on Sunday evenings. In late 2008, I had a conversation with my dad that would later prove remarkable, though I didn't realize it then.

From the moment my dad picked up the phone, I could tell by his quiet and timid tone that this call was going to be particularly tough. He was obviously feeling depressed. I asked him the usual questions as I tried to pull him out from the lonely place where he seemed to be, trying to breathe some positive energy into him. About twenty minutes into the call, I started to feel a bit desperate, as nothing I said seemed to be helping. Then I recalled a conversation with my good friend Allan Hobson a couple years before.

It had been the day that Jane received her cancer diagnosis. I had dropped her off at home following our meeting with the oncologist, and I was driving to the pharmacy to pick up a prescription for her. Suddenly I became overwhelmed by the feeling that I was completely alone. It felt like everyone around me had a better life. Distressed, I parked the car and tried to collect myself. Then I thought of Allan.

In addition to being the eleventh Canadian to summit Mount Everest, Allan himself was a cancer survivor. He was definitely not short on mental strength and determination. He had been there and back. I decided to call him, sensing that he could provide insight.

When he answered, I told him the news about Jane, and he listened carefully and quietly. When I finished, he spoke in a soft but purposeful tone.

"Mark, I'm going to share something with you that I think will help you and Jane to get through this," he said slowly. "It is something that has given me great strength as I continue to face my battle with cancer. Listen carefully."

I nodded as if he could see me, and I prepared to absorb every word. When he spoke, he offered a paraphrase of the famous American cartoonist, Bil Keane.

"Yesterday is history, tomorrow is a mystery, today is a gift," he said. "That's why they call it the present."

The words stopped me in my tracks. I seemed to fall into a momentary state of suspended reality.

"Take time to focus on where you are or what you are feeling or observing right now, right in this moment," Allan continued. "You will suddenly realize that for that moment, you completely forgot about what happened yesterday and what might happen tomorrow. When you start to feel overwhelmed, practice being present and enjoying the now. This simple practice will pull you through the dark and frightening times."

As I spoke with my father that Sunday night, what Allan had said returned to me. I decided to offer it to my dad, like an archer pulling what I felt was one of the last arrows in my quiver.

"Dad, I want to share something with you that my friend Allan told me." And in my most compassionate and heartfelt tone, I repeated the words.

My dad began to speak, then stopped himself. "Wow," he said almost breathlessly. "Can you say that again?"

I could hear him partially cover the phone receiver as he called out to my mom: "June! Pick up the other phone! You have to listen to this." I heard my mom make her way to the other phone, and when she picked up, my dad said, "Hey Mark, say that again! June, listen to this."

Again I repeated the words. My mom was similarly impressed. The three of us talked a while longer, and then we said goodnight and I hardly ever thought about it again.

A few months later, my father passed away. Jane and I travelled down to Utah to assist my mother in getting his affairs in order.

When I entered my parents' home that December afternoon, I was greeted with an extraordinary silence that seemed to wrap its arms around me. As I made my way up the stairs from the front door, I noticed a yellow sticky note placed conspicuously in the center of a large mirror in the front foyer, though I didn't pay much attention to it.

As I walked into the kitchen, I noticed another yellow sticky note on the door of the fridge. This time I decided to stop and read it. Written in my father's near-perfect architect's printing were the words I had shared with him a couple of months prior:

Yesterday is history, tomorrow is a mystery, today is a gift—that's why they call it the present.

I was immediately transported back to our conversation. And as I continued through the rest of the house, I discovered more yellow sticky notes with the same message just about everywhere I looked: on his bed side table, on the mirror above the vanity, above the kitchen sink, above the television, on the door leading into the garage, and even on the dashboard of his car.

A warm feeling came over me. I realized this had been a huge victory for him. He had taken the words to heart and tried to become more present, living and enjoying every moment. These words had become his mantra, and these notes were his reminders. After all the years of coaching and endless conversations, I had somehow managed to break through. It gave me great comfort. It was like a parting gift from him.

I have since spent a great deal of time wondering: what was it about my Dad's behavior that was so extraordinarily challenging for me to come to terms with? Was it that I saw parts of myself in him? The natural likeness that I glimpsed from time to time, which sometimes made me proud, but sometimes made me ashamed because I may have been repeating one of his negative behaviors, and thereby doing something that I had sworn I would never do when I grew up?

Or was it because I knew that I had to break the chain between how he was with us as his kids, and how I would be with mine and others around me?

As the years have gone by, and particularly since his passing, I now find myself able to enjoy my memories of him and the best of who he was: a funny, caring, and sensitive human being who was simply doing the best he could under the circumstances.

EIGHTEEN

An Industry Transformed, An Opportunity Realized

The 1990s were turbulent years for the music industry. With the advent of the Internet and digital file sharing, the music business was in full crisis mode. There was a lot of money at stake, a lot of careers, and quite simply, a lot of power and control. As an invested member of the music community, I took special interest when Napster introduced a shift of epic proportions.

I remember being in my home office in November 1999 with our "computer guy" Earl, who was there to service one of several computers we had in our house. As antiviral software had not yet become widespread, our computers seemed to be in constant need of technical support, so he showed up almost weekly to do maintenance.

Earl had just got my machine defragged and running again, and he looked at me.

"Hey—want to see something cool?"

I said, "Yeah, sure, as long as it's not adult content," I chuckled.

"Ever heard of Napster?"

"No—what is it?"

"Pick a song," said Earl. "Any song."

I thought for a moment, and then I suggested something that I thought was fairly obscure.

"Okay, how about 'Classical Gas' by Mason Williams?"

I had seen him on the Glen Campbell show when I was a kid and I loved that song.

Earl typed the song in and voilà, up popped several versions of it and various options for download. Earl clicked one and within seconds, I was flung back to my youth as I listened to that epic song.

Once I fully absorbed what Napster was, I immediately felt very conflicted about instant and free access to different artists' music. And knowing as much as I already knew about the massive shift the internet was going to cause, I recognized that it was the beginning of the end for the music business as we knew it. It was at once both exciting and frightening.

In the months that followed, as more and more music began to be shared via the internet, record sales and profits quickly began to plummet. It was terrifying for the record companies, and it was discouraging for the artists who already had enough trouble making a living through their music.

I certainly had mixed feelings about what was happening. On one hand, I didn't like to see artists losing their livelihood, but on the other hand, I could see massive opportunities being created in the music industry as a result of this giant digital pipeline to the world. It was a case where "the internet giveth and the internet taketh away."

As far as I was concerned, this monumental shift in music delivery would change everything and the record companies were in for a big correction. And to be clear, it was an industry where the business model had grown out of balance. The guys in the suits seemed to have most artists completely baffled and bamboozled, with the artists often having absolutely no idea how much they had recouped against monies that had been advanced by the labels to make and promote the records and the original budget. By the time Napster and other file sharing sites came along, the music industry was already bloated and top-heavy.

Much of the bloat was due to the "bubble" that was created by the carrier shift to music compact disks in the 1980s. The "carrier shift" was the change in the physical medium by which music recordings are sold and distributed. Up until the 1980s, you would record an album or a song, and you would release it on vinyl or cassette. Those were the two prevailing forms of carriers. Millions of records were sold, and there was no such thing as piracy beyond someone making a compilation cassette for a friend.

With the arrival of the music CD in the 1980s, the record companies suddenly experienced a spectacular windfall of new profits. With the hype and the consumer excitement around music CDs, the record labels had the opportunity to re-release every album in their catalogue. Every Beatles album, every Elvis Presley song, every Deutsche Grammophon symphony recording. Many people, myself included, rushed out and bought CDs for every album that they already owned on vinyl. And why wouldn't you? The new CDs were small, they fit into the dashboard of your car, they fit into your Sony Discman, and they purportedly had the best sound money could buy.

In an instant, the record labels were making billions, and executives from Los Angeles to London were looking for places to spend money. The industry was enjoying some very heady times—and at the same time, a false sense of reality.

Against this backdrop, it was inevitable, sooner or later, that there would be a crash. People wouldn't buy replacement albums on CD forever. And when Napster made music free, it just made the landing harder for the labels as the downward spiral in CD sales began.

If you took away the jump in record sales due to the introduction of CDs, and if you imagined that we had just stayed with vinyl and cassettes into the 1990s, the record industry would never have seen such ludicrous profits, and there wouldn't have been such a sudden and steep decline in record profits from 1999 onwards.

Again, I watched with interest as it all unfolded. I had already suffered my own personal loss and disappointment in the business with Boulevard, and now I watched artists who were used to getting cheques for $100,000 being paid one tenth of that amount just ten years later. It wasn't a happy sight.

When Apple released iTunes in 2001, it legitimized the downloading of digital music files. And it quickly proved itself immensely popular with consumers. New generations of listeners didn't seem to miss the liner notes and poster art that had been the hallmarks of vinyl albums. They embraced the easy use of MP3 files, and suddenly there was no turning back.

As I watched the new medium steadily take hold, I knew that it might present some big opportunities.

One day in 2005, I was drinking coffee at Delaney's coffee shop in Dundarave Village in West Vancouver and thinking, *what could be some new ways for artists to monetize their music with this technology?*

The light went on. What about connecting free music downloads to product and brand promotions? What if there was an online company that could help brands to offer song downloads as part of their marketing and advertising campaigns? I grabbed a napkin, pulled a pen out of my jacket, and I quickly started to scribble notes and a basic system schematic.

I sketched a series of boxes, circles and arrows representing a basic concept for the system architecture. I was really excited. What I envisioned could create a win-win for everyone involved. It would provide more income for the actual artists, and it would still give the labels a share of the pie.

I envisioned building something that worked like iTunes, but it was actually for the business-to-business market. The company I envisioned would create its own iTunes-style platform, and then use it to build customized music download sites for corporations or companies that wanted to sell music but didn't have the budget, know-how, or ability to license content from the record companies on their own. I could see specifically targeting businesses outside of the music world that wanted to promote their products and services by offering free music file downloads in their rewards programs.

I had no desire to try to build a consumer site that would compete against iTunes, because I knew it wasn't possible to compete against them. But if we could have a thousand online music stores selling music under their own brands, all accessing our backend server, we might have a business. Of course, the labels would also make money in the process, but the main connection would be between the artists' music and the promotional programs of the big brands.

I had to test my idea. Was it feasible to imagine doing this? Or did I have to be Apple?

The first person I called was Karim Mitha, my friend from our days together at M-Sound. He had been one of our key technical guys, and I knew he could offer some immediate insights.

We talked, and he thought the idea was brilliant.

He provided some thoughts on how the technology would work, and he suggested some possible timelines and costs to get started.

Next, I called my friend Warren Foster. He and his wife Wendy had done a lot of angel investing with startups already, and I felt they might grasp the concept.

I told Warren the idea and he liked it immediately. Soon we were meeting in person to discuss the startup financing.

Would we try to get other investors at this point? We decided we would wait. We agreed that he, Wendy and I would fund the company during our startup until we had something substantial to show to larger investors.

We discussed names for our new company, and soon we had one: Hip Digital. And by early 2006, we had the company registered.

Karim came on board as our CTO and we started working in earnest. Before any code was written or any servers were connected, we spent about nine months on a whiteboard to determine what the business model and backend architecture should look like. We wanted it to be robust, and we wanted it to be right.

Hip Digital's first staff hire was a young woman named Vered Koren.

She had been working for Canada's answer to iTunes, a Toronto company called PureTracks.

I had been introduced to Vered by a good friend who was a senior executive with EMI Records Canada. I had called Rob to tell him what I was doing, and he suggested that Vered would be a great addition. As fate would have it, Vered had just left PureTracks. I had phone a call with her, and then she came out to Vancouver to meet in person. I picked her up at the airport, and by the time we got downtown, she was Hip Digital's vice-president of licensing.

Vered was incredibly energetic, organized and determined in her approach to business. She quickly became a vital part of getting Hip Digital off the ground, and she became our lead in all of our licensing negotiations with the major labels and Indie label aggregators in the U.S., the U.K., and Canada.

Licensing music is a complicated business. To build an online music store and sell content from the major labels, we would have to go to each and every one of those labels and negotiate separate licenses for their content.

It wasn't easy. We would walk into the offices of labels like Warner Brothers in New York, and we would tell them that we wanted to license their content. They would respond slowly, calmly, and with no small hint of sarcasm: "And you are?"

Once we convinced them that we were worth five minutes of their time, they would start to ask us the hard questions: "What kind of money do you have behind you? What does your backend look like? We will need our technical team to review things."

We had to jump through dozens of hoops to get licensing, but we eventually started to make progress. I have to give special thanks to Deane Cameron, a guy who has since become a very dear friend. He was the president of EMI Music Canada, and together with Rob Brooks, he gave us our first license in Canada.

The first EMI license required a very small advance. I think it was about $10,000 and getting it was massive for us. When we received that agreement, it was high-fives all around. We had signed a licensing agreement with our first major label!

It may have been a modest start, but it meant Hip Digital was now in business for real.

At that point, Hip Digital had existed for almost one year. As yet, we hadn't signed any promotional deals with business customers, but we were getting close. We decided the time was right to go after capital, so I called another good friend of mine, Keyur Patel, who was the chairman of a venture capital company called Comm Ventures in Palo Alto, California. Jane and I flew to San Francisco that weekend, and Keyur and I met for breakfast. He agreed to put us in front of his board. He couldn't provide any guarantees, but we would have our shot at a $3 million pitch.

In February 2006, the Hip Digital management team flew to California to present our company in person. In addition to myself, the team included Vered, Karim, and my old friend Peter Diemer from MCA and the Boulevard days. By this point, Peter had joined Hip Digital as VP Business Development.

We went to the meeting well prepared. We had worked into the early morning hours in the lobby of the St. Regis Hotel in San Francisco— gathered in the corner with our laptops, going over the pitch one last time before our presentation. We really felt this was a giant shot for us. If we were successful, we would have lift off.

We arrived at the Comm Ventures offices in Palo Alto, and we took our seats in the boardroom. Karim, Vered, Peter and myself sat on one side of the table, and eleven senior partners and staff from Comm Ventures sat on the other. The head of their human resources department—a woman named Kathleen—was sitting directly across from me.

I thought to myself: *Wow, human resources? They must have big plans for us!*

I made my pitch, they listened attentively, and then they fired some very hard questions at us.

"What kind of data do you have to support these numbers?"

"What historical numbers do you have that we can measure against?"

Several times, I could only provide general answers.

"We don't really have any historical data," I was forced to explain. "No one has ever really done this before to any great degree."

We couldn't point to six companies that had already tried this idea and made X million dollars in revenue. We couldn't say here's where it worked and here's where it didn't work. There were no previous case studies to examine, so I had to struggle to find answers for some of their questions. It was a real test.

At the same time, we weren't especially concerned that we didn't have numbers for everything. The plain fact was that there was uncertainty in the opportunity. That was part of what made it interesting for investment. It was a hope certificate—an opportunity to be one of the first into the space. As with any truly innovative venture, risk was an intrinsic part of the deal.

We finished the meeting, exchanged goodbyes, and promised to talk again in the next couple of days.

I remember shaking the hands of all of the partners—taking one more opportunity to inject a final dose of positivity into our pitch. For those "weak sisters" or fence sitters, this last bit of eye contact might be enough to sway their vote in our favor.

As we headed out the door into the hot California sun and walked to our rented minivan, Keyur Patel walked with me and then motioned for me to hold back for a minute. The team got into the minivan and waited for me while we stood talking.

Keyur told me that they loved the story of our company. They loved our business concept, and they really liked the team that we had assembled. But there was a concern. And it had come from Kathleen.

She was uncertain about me.

Apparently, during the meeting, her sole job had been to read the body language of our executives. Especially me. This was why she had sat directly across from me.

According to Keyur, she wasn't convinced that I could be an effective CEO. Maybe because I wasn't able to provide answers quickly enough. Perhaps I had paused too often before I spoke, so she figured that I was unsure of myself?

I was devastated when Keyur told me this. My heart sank. A lump like a grapefruit formed in my throat and the inside of my mouth went dry.

That's it. We're not going to get funded.

Keyur reassured me that the overall presentation had been good, but he just left the question hanging with regards to my role as CEO. He told me again that we would hear from them in the next couple of days. I put on my best "okay, I'm cool" face, and we said goodbye.

I got into the van, and I was completely bummed as we drove away.

I reflected on how we had been up until three o'clock in the morning the night before preparing for the presentation. We had looked at the funding numbers from back to front and front to back, and we had reviewed everything we were going to do and why we were doing it. We had looked at every single item from what we thought our licensing fees would be, to our staffing requirements, to our cost of building the technology, to the cost of our office space, and more. We had done everything to be well prepared, and then I get this essentially cold response.

I was very quiet as we drove as we drove to the airport, which was a bit unusual for me. Instead of giving everyone high fives and praise for their incredible contribution, I drove in silence, and as I focused on the road ahead, my vision seemed to narrow to a dark tunnel.

We stopped briefly at a shopping center so that Peter could buy a Beanie Baby for his daughter.

Karim turned to me as everyone got out of the van.

"Are you okay?" he said. "Do you want me to stick around with you?"

After knowing me for over 15 years, he had picked up that something was really bothering me.

"No, I'm fine," I said. "You guys go in. I just need a few minutes to think."

He went with the others, but I felt touched by his concern.

I sat in the van trying to collect myself. I felt like I had just lost the 400-meter city quarter-final to Brad Lomheim in grade eight again.

After a few minutes, the rest of the team returned from shopping, I put on a poker face, and we flew home to Vancouver. Now we had to wait to hear from Keyur and the other partners at Comm Ventures.

A couple of days later, Keyur called. He made no mention of my suitability as a CEO.

"We really do like the deal, Mark," he sad. "We think it's strong. We're very close. But it would really help if you just had one client."

This was a huge relief for me. Suddenly the aspect of everything shifted again, and I was scrambling in my mind for what to reply to Keyur.

We hadn't signed any deals at that point, but I knew we were close. Vered was back in Toronto working with a couple of prospects, so I asked Keyur to give me one day to catch up with her.

I hung up the phone with Keyur, and I called Vered.

"I just talked to Keyur, and it looks like we're very close, but we just need one client to seal the deal."

Vered hesitated for a moment as she seemed to collect herself. I could tell that she had news.

"Well, how about Pepsi?" She blurted out the words as though she could hardly contain herself.

I laughed. "That would do!"

It turned out that an agency that represented Pepsi had approached Vered the day before. They had chosen Hip Digital to power a new promotional program for them.

Under the promotion, Pepsi customers would scratch a product card for a chance to win a song. Winners would find a pin code that enabled them to go to a Pepsi promotional website to download the music. We would build the music download site for Pepsi, and there would be 30 songs to choose from.

They also had plans for Pepsi listening stations on the walls of subway stations, where people would be able to plug in their headphones and check out tracks from all of the different artists if they wanted to.

I had the pleasure of calling Keyur back later that same day.

"How about Pepsi for our first client?" I said.

That was it. We were funded.

Keyur never mentioned the CEO thing again. I suspect they might have been trying to throw me off my game a bit as we headed into figuring out how much of our company $3 million dollars would buy. It was a negotiating tactic along the lines of "the deal looks pretty good, but you're a little weak".

The important thing is that we were able to close the deal. We had landed our first big deal by signing the contract for Pepsi, and Comm Ventures invested $3 million into Hip Digital. We were now seriously in business.

When people ask me about some of the hardest moments I have encountered in business, I would have to say that one of them was that moment with Keyur on the street in front of the Comm Ventures building in Palo Alto. I thought that I had blown the deal. It all ended well, but it was a very hard moment.

After signing the Pepsi deal, we continued working hard to get licensing agreements with the other major labels. Throughout the process, I remember being quite surprised by their reactions to our approach. They were very critical of our model and they questioned whether or not it could really deliver value.

But they also projected a sense of righteous indignation. It really bothered me. It was like they were saying, *What gives you the right to sell our music and make money doing it? Don't you realize how valuable our library of music is?*

I thought to myself: *Of course we appreciate the value. That's why we're here to help monetize it.*

Frankly, I was dumbfounded. Last time I checked, if you manufactured a product, in this case music, and someone opened up a retail store to sell your product, that was a good thing.

Had the business model changed? And I missed the memo?

I think I actually said this at one point to a licensing executive at one of the labels. I was so completely struck by the arrogance of some of the business affairs executives. Sure, they were the gatekeepers for their content, so they had a certain right to be critical in performing their due diligence, but they seemed to overlook a few obvious facts. Namely, the music was made to be sold, the artists wanted it to be sold, and we were offering them a channel for getting it sold and providing promotional exposure for the artists as well.

We totally understood that the song libraries were the "crown jewels" of the labels, and we didn't expect them to hand them over without a good dose of due diligence on any licensee. But their holier- than-thou behavior was at bit excessive at times.

Nonetheless, arrogant licensing managers aside, we jumped through the necessary hoops and obtained the licenses for Canada. Now we could start working on the U.S. and U.K. labels.

While all of this was happening, we encountered some early challenges related to the media. The first round of licenses provided us with songs in Windows Media file format (.wma). When you clicked to download a song, a window popped open to ask you to identify a destination drive and seemingly numerous other overly technical questions. The .wma format was a digital rights management (DRM) system, and was designed to restrict the number of times a song could be shared or copied. The user experience was horrible. Unless the user was a total techy who thrived on managing files on their hard drive, one attempt to buy a song would send most people running for the hills—or more likely, running to

Napster who had created a "painless and brainless" interface that made it simple to download any unlicensed song for free.

Meanwhile, the record industry was giving a different set of rules to iTunes. If you went to iTunes and downloaded a song, you would see exactly how the process should work. It was seamless, friendly, and easy.

But back in 2006, we were stuck with the old Windows Media format.

Not much later, the industry started to shift decisively towards the MP3 format for music files. This made sense, so it was a good move. But now we found that we needed to go back to the labels to negotiate new licensing agreements for MP3s.

This proved a hard pill to swallow. Because when the labels did grant us MP3 licenses, we were forced to pay additional cash advances against future sales of those MP3s. This was tough one to explain to Comm Ventures as our original round of financing did not take into account that we would be paying twice for content licenses—first in WMA format and then in MP3 format. Consequently, I found myself having to head out on the road to raise another few million to pay for these advances.

Generally speaking, this was not a Herculean task. However, in our case, not being cash flow positive, raising capital was much more difficult and always proved to be very dilutive to our capital structure.

After Pepsi, we continued to work hard at pitching and landing big clients. One of our new customers ended up being Aeroplan, Air Canada's loyalty points program. They were looking for new ways that members could utilize their Aeroplan points for things other than airline seats, so we created an offering where members could redeem their points to purchase songs. It was so successful as a promotion that the Aeroplan music store became a permanent offering. An airline loyalty points redemption program for songs: it was a first in the music industry.

Again, we were just trying to find new and innovative ways to monetize music at a time when the music industry was in a severe state of decline. The Aeroplan promotion exemplified the kind of out of the box thinking that we brought to our clients.

We also did programs with Best Buy and Samsung. With the Samsung program, the customer would get a free Beyoncé track and others when they initiated their account. I think we had a picture of the Hansen Brothers or Cold Play on the side of the packaging. It was a huge campaign for us and a big success for Samsung.

All the while, the Hip Digital business model was proving successful. In addition to generating revenue from downloads, we were also earning fees by creating promotional campaigns. We basically became an agency. We would build sites for our clients where their customers would go, enter their pin codes and download the songs they wanted. We would skin each website differently according to each client's brand and promotional offering, all powered by our backend.

Accounting and reporting were critically important. Every time a song was sold, we had to ensure everyone was paid what they were due. Whether a song was purchased with points, or redeemed as part of a promotion program, it had to be accounted for meticulously, and everyone had to be paid in respect to copyright and rights ownership.

Let me give you an example.

Imagine a song written by four different writers, and each of them happens to live in a different part of the world, and each of them is associated with a different performing rights organization. Typically, performing rights organizations monitor airplay and sales, and then they issue quarterly royalty cheques to the musicians, songwriters, and publishers. And of course, the record label has to get paid as well. All of this meant that our system had to provide accurate accounting to make sure every penny was paid to the right people. It was extraordinarily complex.

In addition, our servers had to have a 99.99 percent average up time without failure. No pressure!

I have to admit, when I got the idea for Hip Digital, I didn't realize just how extraordinarily complex it was going to be. It didn't seem that daunting at the outset, but when I look back at the process we eventually undertook to develop our architecture, and then all of the wrestling to get licenses and sign promotion deals with clients, it seems staggering. As always, the devil is in the details.

As we continued to sign deals and build promotions, my role seemed to focus more on raising money and managing our investors more than anything else. No surprise, but everything took more time to build and always cost more than we anticipated. Sales lead times also took longer and as a result our actual revenue was lower than our projections, so subsequent rounds of financing were essential in order to survive.

This is pretty typical for young entrepreneurial companies like ours. This is how boundless optimism and enthusiasm can become a double-edged sword. It can cloud reality and precipitate the downfall of a young company.

The last thing a CEO of any startup wants to hear is, "Things are not going as well as we had hoped." Still, my typical response at the time was, "Are you kidding me? If things were going any better we'd all be on the beach."

However, secretly, I took these warning signs very seriously. I was lying awake and stressing at night as I tried to come up with ways to increase sales and create the next big strategic move that would have us turn the corner towards being cash positive.

One of these late night mind melds and a conversation with Vered gave me clarity on an idea of creating our own content management system, or CMS. What if we could build a system that would allow clients such as ad agencies and record companies to create their own promotional campaigns in-house? This would really reduce the need for us to produce custom campaigns for every program we launched. These were proving to be very labor intensive and provided very low margins.

So we came together as a team with the goal of creating a CMS that would allow clients to choose from a series of templates and cover art, import their own graphics, and populate the site with whatever songs they wanted to be part of that particular campaign. We called our content management system PACE—Promotions and Artist Campaign Engine.

Attempting to convince the board that investing $250,000 into developing the engine was the right thing to do was almost my demise as CEO. I had to threaten to resign if they did not approve our request. After much wrangling, the board finally agreed to approve it.

PACE ended up being one of the best things that we ever did. We were suddenly licensing and charging for a piece of software over and over again. Our operating costs dropped significantly, and we were powering dozens of new sites. All built by our clients on our platform. This was my dream. Hundreds of sites accessing our backend repository of nearly 6 million songs at one time.

It was my first experience being the CEO of a VC-backed company, so I was getting an MBA in street smarts as I worked to secure funding and manage the expectations of our shareholders in Silicon Valley. And we ended up doing some extraordinary things to raise capital.

In late 2008, financing suddenly became especially difficult. The U.S. subprime mortgage crisis and ensuing financial collapse had thrown the markets into the toilet again. Suddenly nobody was interested in investing in an early-stage digital media company.

Feeling the heat and knowing that we had to find a way to float the company, we heard of a possible acquisition of a company that had $3 million cash in the bank. We moved quickly to broker an acquisition. We liked the company, and we liked what they had in terms of technology and personnel, but more importantly, the merger would secure new capital for Hip Digital.

We closed the deal on December 28, 2008, and it was a win-win for both parties. They had raised about $25 million during their brief existence, but they had already spent about $22 million of it. From their perspective, it was a good bet to merge with a company like Hip Digital because it meant that their investment would find new legs. From our perspective, we had raised another $3 million and would live to fight another day.

We turned a lot of heads. People were asking how on earth we managed to accomplish this during such a dismal period in the financial markets—particularly at the end of December, which is a period typically referred to as "Siberian winter" in terms of getting financing. The answer is that it was a combination of good luck and seizing the opportunity, but the upshot is that 2008 went out with a bang for Hip Digital.

The company continued to grow, and we ended up with offices in the United Kingdom, Toronto, Palo Alto and Vancouver. However, all of our basic system development was done at our North Vancouver office, which was always buzzing with positive energy and enthusiasm.

One of my best memories of the North Vancouver office—believe it or not—was playing ping pong. I had a Kettler ping pong table at my house that we weren't using, so I took it to the office and we installed it in the lunch room. I figured it would be good to give our team the opportunity to unwind from time to time with some physical activity rather than just staring into their computer screens all day.

The kitchen was just around the corner from my office. It used to give me great pleasure to hear exclamations of excitement and triumph as members of our staff engaged in a quick game. It did wonders for company spirit. At our Christmas party in 2007, we gave everyone their own ping pong paddle with its own carrying case. Each case was embroidered with the name of the employee, and each had a little pouch with three ping pong balls inside. It was a bit geeky, but everyone loved them.

That period probably represented the high-water mark for me at Hip Digital. As the company continued to grow, I started to feel increasingly that my role as CEO was beginning to shift. I had always felt that my strength was my ability to use my ideas, energy, and relationship skills to motivate people, raise capital, and get new companies off the ground. Starting with an idea on the back of a napkin, making it a reality, and taking it to a certain size. We were now approaching 40 employees and starting to feel as though it required the discipline of hardcore management. I knew it wasn't my core strength.

There are great CEOs out there who are experts in the day-to-day operational stuff. They aren't interested in blue-sky stuff or big ideas.

They live, eat, and breathe the small details. And I knew that I wasn't one of them.

I was also spending close to 35% of my time simply managing the expectations of our shareholders and VC partners. Spending countless hours generating reports and updates, and this took time and energy away from building the business. I knew it was just part of the animal, but it wasn't me.

One morning in June 2009, as I arrived for work, I was met at the office by fellow board member and Comm Venture partner Baris Karadogan. I knew something was up by the look on his face and his body language. He seemed anxious and uncomfortable.

And for good reason: He had come to replace me.

I wasn't surprised. As I left the building that morning, he shrugged and offered me some parting words.

"Hey, Mark, don't feel bad," he said. "The average life expectancy of a CEO of a VC-funded start-up is 18 months. You lasted three years— that's impressive!"

Baris would not have been my choice for CEO. He did not believe in relationships, and in the music business, it's all about relationships. Actually, I believe relationships are the underpinning of all business, but it's particularly true in the entertainment industry.

Baris took over the helm as CEO. Peter Diemer, our VP Development, left that day, and Vered Koren left a few months later and joined EMI Canada. Henna Patel, another great staff member, left shortly after Vered's departure as well.

Hip Digital is still going strong today. The company now has offices in Vancouver, Dallas, Toronto, and Palo Alto, and they still focus on promotional programs. In addition to their core focus in music, they have added other digital goods such as mobile apps, movies, and e-books. Comm Ventures have changed their name to Fuse Capital and they are still major shareholders.

For me, I remember Hip Digital as five very challenging but rich years.

I am proud of the path that we carved, and I'm grateful for the richness of the friendships that sprung from those years. I'm also proud to see that the company is still surviving and thriving. It's like seeing one of your kids grow up.

NINETEEN

Wheels, Wetsuits, and Water Bottles

Running helped me to maintain my health and sanity during my years in business startups, the music business, and the film industry. It has always been a mainstay in my life. In the course of time, running also drew me into triathlon and ultimately the Ironman distance.

It all started in 1991 when I was challenged by a good friend of mine, Jesse Dylan, to compete in an Olympic-distance triathlon in the city of Kelowna, British Columbia. This came on the heels of me challenging him to run the New York Marathon with me in 1990, and he agreed on the understanding that I would do the Apple Triathlon in Kelowna with him the following summer.

"Done," I said.

We ran the New York Marathon together, and then as agreed, we did the Apple Triathlon in Kelowna. The Apple Triathlon is a popular Olympic-distance triathlon—1500 meter swim, 40 kilometer bike ride, and a 10 kilometer run. For me, it was my first time swimming in a wetsuit while surrounded by 500 other athletes thrashing like fish fry and frothing up the water. But I made it through that first race, and soon I was signed up for more triathlons with my buddy Jesse.

Before long, I was hooked. And I wanted to start competing in long-distance triathlons.

In 1997, I got my wish.

That summer, having established myself as a competitive triathlon athlete, I found myself competing with Jesse in the long-distance World Championship triathlon in Nice, France as part of Team Canada. It was a reasonably civilized set of distances: 4 km swim, 120 km bike ride in the mountains behind Nice, and 30 km run along the shore of the Mediterranean to the finish.

Two months later, I did my first Ironman in Penticton, British Columbia. The Ironman is a slightly less civilized set of distances. However, the compelling beauty of the competition course through the south Okanagan valley makes it special. It's the perfect place for long-distance triathlon. You start with an incredibly beautiful lake for the swim, and then you pedal a spectacular bike course through the hills of the south Okanagan. The bike route rolls and climbs as it goes south through Oliver, Osoyoos, Keremeos and back to Penticton. After the cycling portion of the race, the run is dead flat with the exception of a few small hilly sections along the shore of Skaha Lake from Penticton down to Okanagan Falls and back.

After my first Penticton Ironman in 1997, I returned every two years to do it again. Each year that I raced, Jane and I would take every available opportunity in the final months leading up to the event to drive to Penticton for a weekend of training. We would leave Vancouver on Friday afternoon, drive four hours to Penticton, and check into a hotel. On Saturday, I would ride the bulk of the bike course, usually ticking off in the range of 150 kilometers, and on Sunday I'd do something close to the full marathon-distance run. On Sunday evening, we would drive back to Vancouver.

On a particular training weekend in June 2007, while preparing for my fifth Ironman, something very strange happened that mystifies and intrigues me to this day.

It was Friday afternoon around three o'clock, and Jane and I had just set out from our home in Vancouver to drive to our hotel just north of Osoyoos. We had gone through our usual routine of loading our bikes onto the roof rack of the car and I had packed the rest of my training equipment into the trunk. We sped off from our house as we had done so many times before, and we were soon crossing the Port Mann Bridge over the Fraser River.

Suddenly, I heard a loud clunk at the back of our car.

I looked in my review mirror.

For a second, what I was saw didn't register. There was a bicycle toppling and cartwheeling across the pavement behind us. Then it struck me: it was my $6000 carbon-fiber Cervélo. To my absolute horror, my time-trial competition bike was flipping topsy-turvy-end-for-end across four lanes of highway traffic. It looked like something out of a *Terminator* movie, with cars and trucks swerving left and right to dodge the flying wreckage and debris.

My next thought: *I pray to God that it doesn't fly through a windshield and kill someone.*

Luckily, no other vehicles were hit, and no one was killed.

In shock, I pulled over into a service area at the east end of the bridge. There was a small office where permanent staff monitored the traffic through a wall of video screens and took care of general maintenance on the bridge. I walked into the office and found a guy who hadn't seen his feet in years sitting behind a desk. I explained what had just happened.

He was a comedian.

"Yeah, we saw it all happen. Well, you won't be riding that bike anymore!" he snickered almost gleefully.

"I've notified the guys at the other end," he continued. "The truck's on its way."

They had a flatbed truck always ready at the other end of the bridge for this very purpose. Apparently it's not uncommon for objects and debris to fall off vehicles as they cross the bridge.

So Jane and I waited while they collected what remained of my bike. I was pale and numb with shock as I tried to process what had happened.

The truck arrived shortly with the remnants of my bike. It was utterly shattered, and so was I. The frame had snapped, so when you picked up the bike, it basically folded in half like a limp dishrag. The handlebars were still intact, but the little levers for the gears at the end of the aero bars were snapped right off. The carbon fiber brake levers were also broken off, along with the rear derailleur, which was now dangling on the chain like a jewelry pendant. The seat was still there, but it was completely shredded after taking several bounces on the pavement. Remarkably, the forks hadn't snapped, but the front wheel had come flying off, so the guy with the truck had to collect it separately.

Grimly, we threw what remained of my bike in the back of the car, and we continued driving. Gathering myself, I decided that I was not going to let this get in the way of my training weekend. We had set this time aside, and we already had the hotel in Osoyoos booked for two nights.

As I drove on, a thought occurred to me. I had bought the bike from my friend Greg Timewell one year earlier when he had owned a bike shop in Port Moody near Vancouver. He had since sold his bike shop and moved to Kamloops, British Columbia, which was more or less at the north end of the Okanagan valley above Penticton. Though he had sold his shop, I knew that he had taken a bunch of bike parts with him and set up a small operation in his basement in Kamloops.

I decided to call him. It was now about 4:30 p.m.

"Hi, Greg. It's Mark. You won't believe what happened," I said, and I told him the story. "By any chance, do you happen to have another frame?"

It was a bit like hoping to find a needle in a haystack. The odds of him having another Cervélo frame in my size were not great.

"You're a 56 cm frame, right?"

"Yes."

I heard him put the phone down, and there was silence for a couple of minutes. Then he came back on the line.

"This is just incredibly bizarre," he said. "Was your frame blue?"

"Yes."

"I came up to Kamloops with only seven frames from my old shop, but I actually have one of those. A blue Cervélo 56 cm frame. What are the odds? It's just bizarre."

"The other funny thing is that they've discontinued that color of blue," he continued. "You can only get this frame in red, white, and grey now."

"Can you build me another bike?" I asked hopefully. "I'm definitely going to need one." I tried to muster some humor in my voice.

"Sure—no problem," he replied. "But how am I going to get it to you? Do you want me to put it on a bus?"

"No, don't bother," I said. "We're on the highway now. We'll come to you. We can be in Kamloops in about 3 hours. If I come to your place, can we finish building it tonight?"

"You bet" he replied. "We'll see you when you get here! I still can't believe that I have that exact frame."

Jane and I arrived at Greg's house around 7:30 p.m. We immediately went down into his basement to work on the bike, and by about 10 p.m. we had finished building it. We were only missing the pedals, but I was hopeful I would be able to pick up some at the bike shop in Penticton the next day.

Jane and I said goodbye to Greg and his wife Yvonne, and we set off down the road again. Our hotel in Osoyoos was nearly three hours to the south. I phoned ahead to let them know that we would be late, and I explained about the mishap with my bike.

When we arrived around 1 a.m. and checked into our room, we found a beautiful bottle of red wine already opened and breathing. It definitely helped to ease the pain. It tasted absolutely sublime. We then collapsed into bed exhausted. As I closed my eyes that night, I remember thinking: "Did today really happen?"

We woke up the next morning around 8:30 a.m., and it was cloudy, windy and rainy. It seemed to add to the drama of the whole situation. So much for a nice, warm, windless series of hill climbs!

Still, I remained determined. After all, I had long since learned the value of training under diverse and adverse weather conditions. For example, at the World Championship long-distance triathlon in Nice in 1997. For a number of reasons, our coach had asked us to arrive at the race location a week in advance. One reason was to swim in the Mediterranean every day leading up to the race, so we could get accustomed to the different types of conditions that might be present on race day. In the days leading up to the race, we faced everything from two-foot chop to five-foot swells. When race day arrived, the sea was as smooth as glass. We had prepared well for the worst, while hoping for the best, and in the end we were rewarded.

Now I found myself facing a similar challenge in Penticton. I was still prepared to go and ride the course because I knew that I wouldn't be able to choose the weather on race day. If I prepared for the worst and ended up with great weather on race day, then it would be a bonus.

But I still needed pedals for my new bike.

I called the only bike shop that was open within a 50 kilometer radius, the Bike Barn in Penticton. I told them of my mishap on the Port Mann Bridge, and then building my new bike, and that I still needed pedals. I told them that I was looking for Speedplay pedals, and specifically the Platinum model. Again, I was looking for a very specific item, so I wasn't expecting that they would have that precise model by that manufacturer. I had to be prepared to take whatever they could offer.

"Let me check," said the sales clerk on the other end of the line, and the line went silent for a minute or two.

Then his voice returned.

"Wow, I'm surprised," he said, "but we have one pair."

"Awesome," I said. "Please put them on hold for me."

So we loaded me up with four water bottles—which was the maximum that I could carry on this bike—and a bunch of energy gels and bars—and we drove up to Penticton from Osoyoos. We bought the pedals, I put them on the bike, I said goodbye to Jane, and I headed out onto the bike course. After everything that had happened, here I was pedaling south through the town of Penticton without having missed a beat.

As was typical of my training rides, I was riding by myself because it was much harder mentally. As well, the rules of triathlon don't allow drafting, so the typical road racing technique of riding together in a group or peloton doesn't apply in competitive triathlon. You have to keep a minimum of three bike lengths in front of you, otherwise you're penalized.

So I figured there was no better training than to be on my bike for 5 to 6 hours to toughen up my mental game and prepare me for race day. And on this particular training ride, I was challenged from the outset. The headwinds were pretty cruel, and the rain came off and on. My maximum speed was about 11 km/h all the way from Penticton to Osoyoos. You want to talk about grinding it out? That was me.

At one point, I went around a bend in the road halfway between Okanagan Falls and Oliver, and the wind hit me on my left side at 90 degrees. It almost blew me off my bike.

I started to laugh.

I thought to myself, *someone is trying very hard to make me not do this ride.*

But I continued. And when I arrived in Osoyoos and turned right at the Husky gas station to ride up the Richter Pass, the wind was suddenly behind me.

Now it was even more comical. The tailwind was so strong that I was doing about 24–28 km/h up the 7.5% gradient beneath me. It was crazy.

After the Richter Pass, you normally continue to Keremeos and then turn northeast on another road to return to Penticton. However, on this particular day, I simply rode to Keremeos and turned back the way I came to complete an "out-and-back" route that covered the requisite 150 kilometers. Why is this significant? Because it meant that I would now be riding *down* Richter Pass on my return.

This proved to be equally amusing. Despite pedaling hard, I found myself only doing about 20 km/h downhill into the headwind, whereas I would normally be doing around 70 km/h.

However, when I made it back to the Husky station in Osoyoos and turned north again on Highway 97, the wind was still blowing hard from the south. It was the sweetest thing on earth. On my return to our hotel in Oliver, I found myself cruising at about 55 km/h on the flat for the final 10 kilometers. Cycling nirvana!

And as I turned off the highway onto the small country road leading to our winery hotel, the sun suddenly broke through the clouds. After a day of brooding overcast and semi- darkness, the sun shone over me as I rode the final stretch between fields of grapevines back to the hotel. It was near magical.

Sunday ended up being a beautiful sunny day without wind. Jane and I got up early, and I did a training run along the soft path that follows the canal along the length of the valley floor from Penticton to the U.S. border at Osoyoos. Jane rode alongside me on her mountain bike the whole time.

I ran an hour-and-a-half north from Oliver towards Penticton, and then an hour-and-a-half back to get my three-hour run in. I stopped every half hour to eat a power bar or a gel pack, and Jane and I chatted all the while. In all of my years of running, cycling, and training, these are some of my fondest memories.

One month later, I completed my fifth Penticton Ironman. It was another epic day. I was up at 3:30 a.m. to start eating breakfast, and my body was not ready to accept food. It was the middle of the night and my stomach was nervous, but I had to eat. I knew the race would burn between 12,000 and 14,000 calories, so it was critical to consume as many calories as possible.

I will never forget the ominous feeling in the air when I made my way down to the body marking zone to get my race number applied on each arm and each calf. As always, I was attended by one of the hundreds of race volunteers who had signed up to help at the event. All of the competitors seemed to be walking around like zombies. Kind of like, "Holy shit—this is really happening."

By start time, there was close to 3,000 athletes standing on the beach, waiting for the starting gun to be fired. When the shot finally rang out, we plunged into the water in one seething mass and the months of preparation and waiting were over. As always, I said a small prayer as I submerged my head under the water and took my first few swim strokes.

It was 12 hours, 28 minutes, and 58 seconds later when I crossed the finish line and collected my finisher's medal. It ended up being one of my best times in the Penticton Ironman, but it's not the main thing I will remember about training and competing in Penticton. Instead, I will always remember that surreal afternoon when my bike came off the car on the Port Mann Bridge, and how we found my replacement bike and continued on.

And there was a funny thing about losing my bike that way. That Friday in June 2007, I had loaded the bike onto the roof rack exactly as I had always done. To this day, I am certain that I hadn't done anything differently or wrong. When I got out of my car after my bike flew off on the bridge, the first thing I did was check the rack to see if something was broken. I expected to see the strap that held the rear wheel to be snapped, but it wasn't. It simply looked like it had been undone. And the mechanical arm that swung upwards and clipped to the frame also looked perfectly fine. Nothing was broken anywhere. It simply looked like the roof rack had "released" the bike.

And here's where it gets even more interesting for me. I had always had trouble with the front derailleur on that bike. It would never shift gears properly, and it was really fidgety. I had bought the bike a year before, and I had ridden it for a year already, but I had been forced to take it back to Greg three or four times to try to adjust it— always without success.

"I don't know what the problem is, Mark," Greg had said, "but it shouldn't be doing this."

So this thought lingered in the back of my mind after the mishap on the bridge: Maybe it had happened for a reason. Maybe the frame of the bike had a hairline crack or some other significant structural defect that could have caused a catastrophic failure. Maybe the universe had actually been helping me out by dumping my bike on the Port Mann Bridge.

"You know, I think somebody may have done me a favor," I said to Jane. "Who knows what would have happened to me if I was going 70 km/h down a hill and my frame suddenly failed."

The bike wasn't covered by insurance—it was a one-hundred-percent write-off—but I took it as a sign. It was just too strange that this rack had let go of my bike in that manner.

It will always intrigue me. The fact that Greg had a matching frame available, and the Bike Barn had the exact pedals that I needed to fit my shoes. Once again, the stars had aligned for me in my hour of need.

TWENTY

Conversion Experience

I t was August 2009. I had just caught my breath after leaving Hip Digital, and I was now ready to turn my sights towards finding a new project.

As I started to think about possible avenues of opportunity, I recalled that in 2001, my old friend Dan Lowe had started a technology company in Calgary called Conversion Works. It was interesting startup: I knew that at one point they had seemed to be at the leading edge of a new technology in 3D film production.

From my intermittent conversations with Dan during that time, I understood that Conversion Works was developing a software technology that would convert regular 2D films into 3D films. If standard films represented 2D images as they were seen by both eyes, then the task of 3D conversion software was to analyze that single left eye image information and generate the right eye perspective with its respective offsets, thereby creating the 3D image. While 3D is standard industry fare in Hollywood today, 3D and particularly 3D conversion was still in its infancy in 2001.

Conversion Works had subsequently spent many years—and many dollars—trying to develop their technology. They had expert developers and solid R&D teams, and it seemed like they were doing all of the right things. However, they couldn't seem to commercialize their process at a price that would make sense for Hollywood Studios. By January 2009, they appeared to be still spending a significant amount of capital to try to get their technology to work, and by summer 2009, I had heard that

Conversion Works might be closing up shop. I decided to call Dan to get the full story.

"What are you guys doing?" I asked him.

He said they weren't sure. He gave me a breakdown of recent happenings with the company, and how they had basically ceased operations. They had run out of money, and they were unable to find more investment capital. The plan had been to use their new technology to win lucrative contracts to convert Hollywood feature films into 3D. However, despite their best efforts to garnish interest from the big studios, they had not landed any feature film projects.

Yet they had created a couple of amazing 3D demos. One of them was a clip from the movie *Titanic*. On their own initiative, they took a short one-and-a-half-minute segment from the film and converted it to 3D. Then they succeeded in getting an audience with James Cameron, director of *Titanic*, so they could show him the clip. He was apparently very impressed and spoke to others about the demo, stating it was some of the best 3D conversion he had ever seen.

And then they went bankrupt.

I had a very strong hunch that 3D was going to be huge, as it would not only give studios an additional asset to generate revenue from, but I could imagine what could be done with archival movies. Classics like Star Wars, Raiders of the Lost Ark, and the Bruce Lee movies being converted and re-released. It would be found money.

I had a hunch that it might be possible to dust off the project, create a new company with a strong team, and make it work. I told Dan as much, and I asked him if he would mind if I talked to some other people about the idea.

I went to talk with my friend Rory Armes who had just left Electronic Arts in Vancouver. We were running buddies, and we also knew each other from the M-Sound days in the early 1990s. He had originally been part of a Vancouver gaming software company called Distinctive

Software, which eventually became Electronic Arts Canada. Rory ended up being a senior executive at EA studios in Vancouver for about 20 years.

When I presented the idea to Rory, he had the same thoughts as me and figured it was an idea worth pursuing. We talked about the potential for finding new investors and setting up shop in Vancouver.

After a few more exploratory conversations with Rory and Dan, we decided to go forward with trying to resurrect Conversion Works, and I went to Calgary in February 2010 to meet with Dan so we could start to refine our plans.

Conversion Works had fallen into complete disarray by this point. The former management had taken the computer drives home, and Dan assured me that those drives came up empty when you tried to find anything of the code left on them. Undeterred, I made an arrangement with Dan that Rory and I would nonetheless dust off the project and start anew with whatever we managed to recover of the old workstations. We agreed to preliminary terms on what percent of ownership each of us would have, and we agreed that we would form a new company based in Vancouver.

In April, I went to Paris to run a marathon, and then I stopped in London afterwards for a couple of meetings. Then the Eyjafjallajökull volcano erupted in Iceland.

We had planned to meet that week in Calgary for the final negotiations with the old owners of Conversion Works, but the eruption changed everything. The volcanic plume extended across the entire airspace of the North Atlantic and Western Europe. Transatlantic flights were grounded for a week. I couldn't get home, so we ended up negotiating the terms of the agreement by phone. For the call, I was in London, Rory was in Vancouver, Dan was in France, and the rest of the owners were in Calgary. (Dan was stuck in France for the same reason that I was stuck in London.)

Under the agreement, we would create a new company called

Conversion Works Inc. and the original owners would be partners. We went back and forth as we negotiated precise numbers and terms.

One week later, I flew direct from London to Calgary. Our negotiations had gone well and I decided that I should try to take any of the workstation computers they had out to Vancouver. Even though we were told that the hard drives had been wiped clean, but I figured there might still be some code on the drives that we could recover. I cancelled my return ticket, rented a van, drove out to the facility where the computers and workstations were piled up, loaded them into the van, and then drove 11 hours straight to Vancouver.

When I finally arrived into the outskirts of Vancouver just after ten o'clock that night, I called Jane and asked her to stay up and help me unload about fifteen Mac computers and five workstations into our living room. The next morning, we loaded them up again and drove them to a small office space on Dunlevy Street in Railtown in Vancouver. This would be the birthplace of the new Conversion Works.

The space was actually a small recording studio with a small control room and a recording room of equal size, owned by a good friend of mine, Brad Lintott. He believed in what we were doing and agreed to let us "squat" in the space temporarily until we got settled into new digs.

Now we needed the software developers and expertise to staff it. I felt that they only way that I could this back on the rails was by putting the original team of developers back together, so I began the task of tracking them down. To have any hope of putting any of the pieces back together, I learned from Dan Lowe that the number one guy was Trevor Rowland, who at the time was living in Toronto. So I called him up out of the blue.

Trevor let me know that he had an extremely bad taste in his mouth from his whole experience at Conversion Works. In fact, the entire crew of developers that had worked for Conversion Works were all extraordinarily unhappy.

It turned out that when the company folded, none of them had been given proper severance. They had been laid-off with weeks of unpaid salaries. Trevor had been forced to scramble back to Toronto to find work, and he and his family had just been settled there about one year when I called. He was still deeply disgruntled, and I could hardly blame him.

Through a series of conversations, however, I managed to convince him that we could put this back together and create the greatest 2D to 3D conversion company Hollywood had ever seen. I also managed to convince him and his wife Shea to fly out to Vancouver at our expense. I told him that I wanted to discuss seriously a new offer with our new company, and I wanted to sell him and his family on Vancouver as a wonderful city to live and raise a family. .

In late May, Trevor arrived with his wife—who was five months pregnant with their second child—and their little boy at Vancouver International. I picked them up at the airport and booked them into the Westin Grand Hotel. Over the next few days, I picked them up every morning and drove them around Vancouver so they could get to know the city. All the while, Trevor and I discussed potential terms for him to rejoin the project as part of a new company.

It was a long shot, but it worked. Trevor had many misgivings, but I convinced him that this time would be different. We agreed to salary terms and he and his wife were sold on Vancouver.

But we would need more developers. Trevor directed me to a couple of the other previous team members to see if I could also bring them on board.

Along with Trevor, three guys named Pablo, Ben and Warren had also been part of the main development team at the original Conversion Works. Pablo was still living in Calgary and Warren and Ben had moved to Edmonton. I called them.

I was met with the same level of bitterness as I had experienced with Trevor. They had equally bad memories of their exit from Conversion Works. And I quickly discovered the toughest part of convincing them to return to the project—the knowledge that it might somehow benefit the former managers and owners of the company.

They each asked me in turn, "Are those guys going to benefit from this?"

We couldn't avoid it. Under the terms of our agreement with Dan Lowe, the old shareholders would still have a stake in the new company.

"Yes, they will all be shareholders," I said. "But so will you. You're going to be part of something much greater. It's going to be different."

"If we can shake off what has happened," I continued, "and move forward with you as owners and make something of this, then all of your previous work won't have been wasted."

Understandably, it was emotionally tough for Trevor, Warren, Ben and Pablo. They harbored a lot of enmity towards the previous owners and management. However, I managed to convince them that they would be treated fairly this time around. We agreed to terms with Warren and Pablo, and soon they were on their way to Vancouver as well.

As we successfully negotiated the return of Trevor, Pablo and Warren, I began to work on attracting investment in the new company. Between May and October, a corporate finance guy from Calgary named Rick Yuck and I raised $2 million through brokerage firms and individual investors.

Rick and I wore out a lot of shoe leather in the process. One evening in September, we drove from Calgary to Innisfail, Alberta so we could visit one couple in their home. We took with us a large flat screen television and set up a demo and a presentation for them right in their family room. They were impressed with what they saw.

As I finished the presentation, they excused themselves and went into the kitchen, returning after about 30 seconds to announce that they were interested in investing a low six-figure sum into the company. I was not expecting the commitment would come so soon. Usually, it would take folks a few days to process the information at which time they would let us know if they wanted to invest and if so, how much.

The next night, we drove from Calgary to Brooks, Alberta and I presented to about 20 people made up of oil field workers, trucking company owners, road construction builders, doctors and ranchers at the Heritage Inn. It was an interesting cross section of individuals. I showed them our demo, and talked about what we were trying to accomplish and our vision. In the end it was a successful trip with a number of them deciding to invest in our company.

It was never easy. I found the process of raising capital mentally, emotionally, and physically draining.

Meanwhile, Rory was on the hunt for a CTO for the company. He approached his good friend, Tim Bennison. Tim had been the CTO at Radical Entertainment, so he would bring considerable experience and expertise to our team. In short order, Rory had him sold on joining us.

With a couple of more staff additions, there were soon nine of us crammed into our tiny two-room office in Railtown at 45 Dunlevy St. It was very hot with all the bodies and equipment running. So for the next three months, we literally sweated as we attempted to cobble together bits and pieces of the old software as the workstations whirred like crazy in about 700 square feet of office space.

Our plan was to create a company with two divisions: 3D conversion and software licensing.

The 3D conversion division would be the services part of the company. It would receive film footage from studios, convert it to 3D, and then spit it back out. However, we knew that there were a lot of other companies getting into 3D conversion as well. We were convinced it was a viable business, but the business of visual effects and post production is highly competitive, and it was notorious for having very low margins

We knew that we could build significant value if we developed our own proprietary conversion software and then licensed it. If we could get our technology to scale so that other companies could use it, we would make serious profits in licensing fees. That was the Holy Grail.

We brought in a third partner, Nilo Rodis, who Rory had worked with during his time at EA. Nilo was a very talented art director who had an arsenal of film credits to his name, including a few of the Star Wars movies with George Lucas.

One particular day in August, Nilo indicated that his partner Cari Thomas was very interested in what we were up to. Cari had just been hired as part of the visual effects team that was just beginning work on a new *Spiderman* movie. The studio had decided they were going to be releasing the film in 3D as well as native 2D, and Cari was approaching a few different 3D conversion companies as part of her due diligence. She was looking for each company to produce short 3D demos of some test footage. Whoever produced the best demos would get a shot at doing the 3D postproduction for the film.

The head of visual effects was Jim Rygiel, who had recently won the Academy award for his work on *The Lord of the Rings*, so this was serious business.

Cari introduced us to Jim, and then I flew to L.A. to meet with him, equipped with some demo footage on a portable drive. We were set to meet at the Sony studios in Culver City where Jim had booked a screening room.

The morning I arrived, Jim met me on the lot and explained that the screening room had been double booked by some of the studio brass, so we were not going to be able to screen our footage. Somewhat disappointed, and sensing this was really a special one-on-one opportunity to show our stuff, I asked Jim if there was a 3D television that we could use.

He thought for a moment. "You know, there are a few of them running trailers in the Sony merchandise store."

So we walked across the back lot, passing recognizable facades from many different feature films, as well as the set of the hit television series *Glee*, as we made our way to the store.

The Sony store was a sea of souvenirs from every Sony film ever made—everything from pencil cases to princess capes. And there we were, unplugging cables and plugging my laptop into the 3D TV on one of the walls as the staff looked on in disbelief.

My heart began to race as I went to hit the "play" button on my computer after plugging everything in, thinking, *please God, let this work.* Beads of sweat were actually rolling down my back.

Shazam. It did work. In fact, Jim was so impressed that he suggested a follow-up meeting one week later.

A few days later, Jim called our Vancouver office.

"We're not sure if we want to shoot the test shots in regular 2D and hand that over to you," Jim explained, "or if we are going to shoot in native stereoscopic with a 3D camera and then give you the left eye to convert from."

I suggested shooting with a native 3D camera was an excellent idea as it would allow us to compare our conversions of the shots directly with original 3D footage.

Jim went away to discuss further with his team. A few days later, he called back to let us know that they would be shooting the test shots in native 3D and they would send us the left eye information.

I hung up the phone. *Was I nuts to suggest this?*

At this point, our developers were still just trying to squirrel together a complete set of software tools that would allow us to complete the shots. However, under an umbrella of incredible uncertainty, we agreed that this was too good an opportunity to pass up.

A few weeks later, they sent us the *Spiderman* test clips and we set to work.

They purposely sent us shots that were very complex in nature. I remember one of them was looking straight down from the top of a very high building. The shot really gave you a sense of vertigo, and had numerous lines that converged together, making it very challenging. Another shot was a big explosion that produced thousands of small objects and dust particles flying at the camera lens. Again, very technically tough because each piece of debris had to be identified and tracked as it came towards the camera.

We set to work, but we quickly discovered the bits of software that we had managed to recover didn't provide an end-to-end solution that could complete the job. Just when we thought we had cobbled together a solution, we discovered that it simply couldn't deliver. It was a daunting situation.

We only had a few days to turn the test footage around and get it back to Jim and the folks at Sony. How the shots looked was only part of the test. Equally important was how quickly we could complete the shots. Turnaround time was critical. Inability to deliver in the allotted time was simply not acceptable. Creating beautiful converted 3D footage was one thing. Doing it within Hollywood production time frames was another.

We worked frantically to cobble together our 3D conversions of the *Spiderman* clips any way that we could. We pulled out all of the stops— and we finally managed to piece together a set of tools and series of solutions to get the demos done.

Then we submitted our clips to Jim, and we waited for word back.

About two weeks later, Jim phoned us. Not only was our 3D the best that they had seen from the different companies, but in some cases our converted 3D shots were better than the native stereoscopic 3D captured on their cameras during original shooting. We were now on the shortlist for the *Spiderman* movie.

It was high-fives all around. We had only been able to complete the demos through the incredible resourcefulness and commitment of our development team, but we did it.

Then in October, we got a phone call from Cari Thomas. She said, "I've just recommended you guys to my friend in London."

The name of her London friend now escapes me, but he was the head of post-production for the film adaptations of *The Chronicles of Narnia*. The company that he had contracted to do the 3D post-production was falling short on deliverables and they were on a deadline, so they asked if we could take on several minutes of the film. And of course we said yes.

This would be our first film. Not a bad place to start.

By this time, we had moved our offices to a building called The

Landing at 368 Water Street in the Gastown district of Vancouver. We were on the third floor at the time, and in the process of renovating the basement so we could get everyone moved into the same space. We were a pretty small crew, maybe about 20 people.

On this particular Saturday, Rory was out of town, but I called him and told him that we had this opportunity to do *The Chronicles of Narnia*.

Tim Bennison our CTO came into my office. "Mark, I don't think we should do it," he said. "We're not ready yet. We're going to crash and burn. It's just too soon."

"I know how you feel," I said. "Rory and I have talked about it, and I think we should go for it."

"Okay, then you should probably talk to everybody."

So we called a little town hall meeting, and I told the group about the offer before us. I explained that we had received this call from London, and that they were interested in us taking on this project. I told them the deadline and the number of frames involved.

I talked about fear and how it could prevent us from doing it, and how none of us wanted to stumble, but at the same time, even if we tried and we came up short, and we weren't able to deliver all seven segments, but we do an amazing job on five pieces, I don't think it will be seen as a failure. Just the fact that we said yes, we are going to help you, was in our favor.

"It is my firm belief that we should do this," I said at last.

I must have given quite a persuasive speech, because Tim and the team agreed. "Okay, let's get to work."

So we set about the task of converting these seven shots into 3D. Each shot varied in length, and they were hard shots. They had given us the most difficult minutes of footage from the film. It may have been that they kept getting pushed out by the company who were working on the 3D conversion for the film, so they just had to pass them on to us. There were all kinds of complicated visual elements that we had to render, such as particulate matter. Every frame had countless elements that had to be identified, and each element had to be given a unique value on the x, y and z axis for the right and left eyes in 3D.

I remember we had some serious challenges with our internet connection at the building, and it was problematic because we were back and forth with the *Narnia* post production group in the UK through the entire process. We would submit a shot to them and they would review it. Then they would come back to us with their comments and notes for improvements. To ensure we didn't have a break in service, we had guys working on a few Saturdays to beef up our connection and get everything where we needed it.

And this is one of the typical challenges of these types of projects. The client doesn't want to know about your difficulties. They don't care if you're having trouble with your internet. You've committed to doing the work, and they just want to see the work finished.

Our technology challenges weren't the only difficulty at this time. While we were working on *Narnia*, I connected with a respected patent and trademark office in Vancouver and a lawyer name Gavin Manning. As part of our pending acquisition of the original Conversion Works, there was a series of software patents, partial patents, and applications at various stages throughout the world, so we set out to create a complete scrub down of all of them.

Through the month of October, Gavin created a 35-page document that showed where all of the patents were and what they described. It was extremely complicated and labyrinthine, but it allowed us to determine what was there, whether or not they represented a real value or a liability, and if necessary, what would be required to bring them into good standing and maintain them.

Furthermore, chasing after these patents globally could easily have burned through our start-up cash faster than we could raise it, and potentially burn through everything we needed to run our business on a day-to-day basis.

At the core of all of this was the financial pressure of trying to raise more funding. My pitches to investors were being met with the sound of doors slamming. After raising close to $2 million dollars, we had stalled.

Feeling a bit helpless and very frustrated, Rory and I discussed the situation, and we decided that I should fly to Calgary to meet with Dan Lowe. It was now November, and we were thick into the work on *Narnia*.

It was a Thursday and a classic cold prairie morning when I arrived at Dan's office. However, it was the end of the day before I was able to meet with him. I basically spent the day in the kitchen area, sending emails and trying to be productive with my time. He was in a string of meetings, but I felt like there was something strange about it. We were friends, and I felt like I was being shoved aside.

When we finally sat down in his office in an old red brick heritage building in Southeast Calgary, it was about 4:30 PM.

"Dan, I've come to a screeching halt in my ability to raise capital," I explained. "The market is just not being receptive to what we are selling. People are looking at our proposed offering and calling into question our valuation of over $25 million".

"We're also concerned that the patents could require a staggering sum of money to complete and get them to a point where they're strong and defendable. Meanwhile, we're fighting to cobble together a solid suite of software tools that will allow us to scale our output to a profitable level. To fund any of this, we would have to sell off a highly dilutive amount of equity in the company. Very hard-earned, expensive and valuable capital."

Remember, this was 2010. After the financial markets crashed in 2008, no one was investing in anything that wasn't backed up with measurable sales or assets. During the dot com boom of the 1990s, companies could say, "We think this company will be worth $200 million in three years, so we're going to value it at $50 million today." You could show people a chart with income projections that looked like a hockey stick, and if people liked the story, they were likely to buy into it. In 2010, they would just laugh at you. "Do you have any sales? No? Then I'm going to value you at zero." That was just the reality of it.

"I can't do this," I said to Dan.

"Mark, the company is worth that," said Dan. "People will pay it."

"Dan, I just can't agree with you," I said. "I wish there was some way you could help me out here."

He said, "Well, write down what the structure is."

I wrote down the structure on his office white board.

"Okay, fair enough," he said. "I have to go now." He said that his wife was there to pick him up.

We walked out to the front of the building together. It was dark and there was some snow on the ground. It wasn't a warm goodbye. Dan got into the car, gave me a wave, and drove away.

I was left standing there in the cold with the crackling sound of his car tires driving away on the snow. That's what the snow sounds like when it gets to minus 20 degrees on the prairies. A very distinctive and lonely sound.

As I stood there watching Dan and Dianne pull away, a flood of memories came rushing back to me like a wave of cold air. I remembered all of the times we had spent together as friends—working together through the hungry years, making records together, our struggles, the insane laughter, sharing our dreams.

There was a security guard in the front foyer, so I walked back into the building, ordered a cab to the airport, and flew back to Vancouver. Feeling a bit numb.

I tried to call Dan for about three weeks, but he didn't return my calls.

Meanwhile, still on the hunt for new investors and cash flow to allow us to keep the doors open, work was continuing on the *Narnia* project. We were on tight deadlines with the studio, and the client wasn't interested in hearing about our problems. My partner Rory was stepping up in a big way, writing six-figure cheques to bridge finance the company.

The irony and the cold reality was that we were working on one of the biggest movies to be released in 2010, but the revenue generated from our work was a fraction of the cash burn rate for our team, which had now ballooned up to more than 65 people.

In the end, we met the challenge and we delivered the *Narnia* shots on time. And the studio loved what we gave them.

When the movie opened in Vancouver in December 2010, everyone in our office walked over to the Scotiabank Theatre at Burrard and Smyth to watch the film. There were about 35 of us, so we were a big group as we arrived at the theatre. We watched the movie, pointed excitedly when we saw one of our shots on the screen, and then cheered when we saw our name in the credits at the end. It was a great moment for our team.

For me, however, the joy was a bit short-lived. As 2011 began, new developments started to affect my role and future in the company.

The phone rang in my office. It was now the first week of January, and this was the first time I had heard from Dan since my unsettling trip to Calgary several weeks earlier.

"I've got a couple of guys here with me," Dan said. "So, what's going on."

"Well, Danny, I was really kind of hoping that you and I could just talk together in person."

"Well, all of us are talking right now," said Danny.

"Okay," I said. "I'll go and get Rory."

I got Rory and brought him into my office.

"Okay, here's where we are at," I said to Dan and the others in the room with him. "It's not working. We have thrown all our might into pulling a set of functional and usable tools together and have fallen short."

I just laid it all out, expressing our concerns and the challenges ahead of us, including hitting a brick wall as far as raising additional capital was concerned—capital that was absolutely critical to pulling the pieces of the technology together.

"We just can't seem to justify the company's stated valuation to the investment community," I concluded.

And the meeting just went downhill from there—with all order of sabre rattling and the threat of a lawsuit.

This immediately flipped everything upside down. Suddenly the idea of raising any additional capital was pretty much over. The call was finished, and the room went dead quiet. What had just happened? A twenty-five year friendship suddenly felt like it had never existed. And we were boxed into a corner.

We knew that the company had to restructure to continue doing business. We also had new projects in the works that could be at risk if we became mired in a lawsuit. We needed a new plan, and we needed it fast.

We had a series of meetings to figure out our next steps. There were potential new investors, advisors and consultants who weighed in on the strategy as well. It was decided that a new company would be created.

The new company would be called Gener8. But as we continued to meet, hour after hour behind closed doors, I started to feel a disconnect. It was becoming difficult for me to see a clear path to the other side and what the new corporate structure would actually look like.

So I decided to resign. To be truthful, it broke my heart to resign. I had such plans and high hopes. It was time to reinvent myself...

I stepped down as co-CEO on February 14, 2011, and resigned from the board of directors.

To be fair, there were also practical management considerations. When Rory and I started the company, we both agreed that we would co-CEO as long as it made sense. We couldn't continue with two CEOs forever. Rory was clearly the killer operator, and I was really the start-up guy with ideas and energy. As the company continued to climb towards over 100 employees, the CEO role was really in Rory's sweet spot and not mine. Rory would continue on as CEO.

Although it hadn't worked out precisely the way I had imagined back in 2009, the restructuring process provided a logical juncture to depart. In the end, we created a successful company, and that was the important thing.

Gener8, now operating under the name Eight Solutions, is going strong today. The company now has close to 200 employees and contractors, and it has worked on some great films. I enjoy the fact that it is now recognized as one of the leading 3D conversion companies in the world, and I will always be proud of what we created.

TWENTY-ONE

Dedicated Creator of Fashion

By the time I exited Gener8 in February 2011, I was pretty much fried. You probably could have wrung the stress out of me and mopped the floor with it. With half of my stomach lining now gone, and years of flying in the realms of finance and high tech, I wanted to come back to earth. And I knew what I wanted to do.

For a number of years, I had a notion that I might one day venture into the world of fashion and design. I wasn't sure precisely in what capacity, but I had this sense that if the planets ever aligned themselves at the right time, I could see myself entering that arena. Looking back, it may have started with me buying my green suede boots when I was 10. How many 10-year-old boys become obsessed with a pair of green suede cowboy boots they see in a department store? And then go to such lengths to get them?

Just as my discovery of music in my pre-teens inspired my desire to create my own music, my connection with fashion at an early age probably forms the basis of my desire to express myself through that medium.

I have always held an appreciation for expressing who we are and what we are feeling through what we wear and how we wear it, and I have always been intrigued by fashion as art. And for me, it's easy to see the relationship between music, writing, art, and fashion. They are simply different manifestations of the creative process taken in different directions.

When I left Gener8, some of my fashion design ideas had started to take shape. I had been thinking about a particular business idea for a few years, but it had only ever been given space in the back of my mind. The idea was simple. I wanted to create a collection of scarves that would incorporate my interpretation of the peace symbol, with a view to shine the light on the possibilities for peace: inner peace, peace on earth, peace of mind. Part of the concept also involved taking a portion of the sales and giving back to the planet through a foundation affiliated with the company.

I have always loved scarves, and I wear them all the time. It goes all the way back to me delivering newspapers as a kid. In Calgary, it would often be minus 30 when I was delivering papers, so I would have to wrap the scarf around my face just to keep my nose from freezing. Years later, still in Calgary, I would often visit vintage clothing stores and rummage through the boxes and racks in search of cool silk scarves from the '40s or '50s. For a few dollars, I would be nice and warm, and I would look stylish as well in a timeless classic.

But why peace symbols? I simply felt intuitively that I wanted to feature the peace symbol and incorporate it into my designs. There were also a couple of good reasons why I would want to embrace that image.

One is that I have always liked what the peace symbol stands for, and I like how it is universally recognized around the planet. Another is that I have often lamented its decline through the 1980s and 1990s, when it was often relegated to the shelves of dollar stores and tacky accessories shops in strip malls, frequently in the form of sparkly rainbow-colored stickers or neon iron on patches. I think the peace symbol carries an important message that we need to remember, and as far as I'm concerned, peace is never out of style.

But would it work to use the peace symbol in my designs? There was the danger that it might be seen as unoriginal or tired. And would it work to base a business on the concept of peace? Perhaps people would find it naïve or overly idealistic.

I have always believed that difficult and important decisions require hard questioning and several "wake ups" before you make your final decision. After a number of wake ups, I knew that this was the right way to go.

Peace: it was meant to be.

So I started to imagine. And the image came to me: a scarf, made of silk chiffon, with a beautiful hand-rolled edge, in multiple colors.

As my thinking began to evolve, I realized that there was nothing to prevent me from connecting all of it with music as well. I started to imagine that if I started a foundation in addition to a fashion company, we could form a separate foundation website that sold the scarves for fundraising, and we could also sell songs donated by different artists, along the lines of what we had done at Hip Digital.

Why not? After all, I knew a lot of people in the music business, and I could approach artists I knew and ask them to donate a song for one year. With every song sold from the foundation website, the foundation could earn 10 or 15 cents off the transaction. Over time, the funds could be used to make a difference to the planet.

Was I dreaming?

Make scarves. Sell music. Use the proceeds for important causes. Promote peace on the planet.

The more I thought about it, the more it felt deeply right. It seemed like a custom fit for everything I had done to this point in my life— every relationship, every job, every situation since I was four years old. I decided to move forward by starting with the fashion collection, and once I had established the brand, I would leverage it to launch the music component and other complementary products as part of the funding plan for the foundation.

I am sure that it was just lack of objectivity that had caused by my burned-out state, but it seemed that all I had done for 30 years was start things and raise money. Along the way, I had a wonderful rich journey where I met amazing people, but I felt like I had been living my life on an IV drip of cortisol. With my stomach almost constantly in knots, I had developed burning mouth syndrome, which I still have.

To some extent, I had been my own worst enemy. I had always possessed the kind of energy that I just continued to push forwards regardless of how exhausted I was. People would often comment, "Where does this guy get all of his energy? I want some!" Or, "Whatever he's on, I'll take some of that!"

But it took its toll on me. At age 53, I found myself unable to see a clear picture any longer, and I was starting to question what was really important to me in life. So as I mused about creating a fashion company and a philanthropic foundation, I thought long and hard about how I would approach it.

As I surveyed my history in music and business, the picture slowly became clear. I was an artist and a creator at heart, and I needed to return to my creative roots.

It was like therapy for me. I began by dusting off my paintbrushes, and I went out and bought a new supply of paints. I built some canvases, and I created a painting easel by taking a small aluminum stepladder and using two C-clips to clamp a piece of three-quarter-inch plywood to it. And I started to paint.

I painted hundreds of peace symbols. My aim was to create one that was truly fresh and communicated the feeling I wanted.

The idea of "reintroducing" the peace symbol was a bit intimidating. I figured people would be skeptical, but I felt that the symbol was needed again more than ever. Not only was it a strong design, but it still represented something that everyone on the planet really wants:

Peace. With ourselves, our families, our friends, our neighbors—our fellow citizens of the planet.

I thought to myself: *It may be a gutsy move—who knows what will come out of this—but I'm going to go for it.*

So I painted and painted and painted. And I experimented with different techniques, including painting with a trowel. I especially liked how the trowel invited a looseness of expression similar to Japanese calligraphy.

I finally created one peace symbol that really resonated with me. It was so far from being "perfect" that it was just right. I knew I was ready to put it to use.

In December 2011, I launched Mark Holden Fashion as a company, and I set to work in creating our first scarf.

I imagined the scarf in silk chiffon—black fabric with white peace symbols on it. That was my first vision.

I connected with a friend named Christine Morton who was a successful lingerie designer in Vancouver. I went to her and I told her what I was trying to accomplish, and she introduced me to a fashion design firm in New York garment district called The Style Council. One of their specialties was creating textile print samples.

I called The Style Council and I spoke with a woman named Louise Altese. I told Louise what I wanted to do, and she asked me to send her a high-resolution digital file of my designs. I took the canvas painting into a local print shop and they created a very high-resolution scan. Next I recruited Joel McCarthy—a young film student and Photoshop graphics wunderkind—and we began the process of layering numerous graphical components into what would be the final design for each scarf.

The design layout was one thing, but it was the color that required a lot of going back and forth to get it right. In doing so, I learned a lot about the process of creating print textiles, as all of it was new to me.

Soon I was on the plane to New York to meet with Louise. She took me to visit a very famous fabric supply house in Manhattan called Mood Fabrics. We looked at what seemed to be an endless sea of silk chiffon fabrics, and after settling on a beautiful choice of fabric, we created a set of samples and suddenly we were on our way.

During this time, I travelled in April 2012 to Nice, France with Jane. I had been thinking a lot about the message behind what we were doing.

I wondered how best to articulate it. If I were to write it down on a piece of paper, what would I say?

I had been ruminating for several days on the idea when we found ourselves in a little restaurant in old town Nice one afternoon. As we sat there with our menus, words suddenly started to come to me like a lyric for a song.

"Sweetheart, can you excuse me for just a second?" I said to Jane. "I have to write something down."

I turned over my placemat, and I started to write. And the following words came out:

It is sometimes not easy to understand what went wrong.
Why things became unraveled.
We can all take solace in going to that quiet place that exists within us all.
At peace with ourselves, our friends, our neighbors, our fellow compatriots.
Citizens of the planet, find your inner peace.
Wrap yourself in it.

The words just seemed to flow out of me through my pen. It was like divine intervention. I felt my eyes starting to well, and something in my chest swelled.

I showed what I had written to Jane.

It was then that I realized that this was what I was meant to do. The scarf was just a vehicle, and these words defined what it was really about—the possibility of creating something that would touch people on an individual level.

It immediately reminded me of my earliest desire to pursue songwriting, and some of the questions that have been put to me over the years.

For instance, I remember being challenged by Erica Ehm on MuchMusic during an interview in 1988 when our song "Never Give Up" was in the top 10 in the Canadian charts.

"You know, I am not sure about the message behind your music," she said. "It's pretty poppy."

Some of the media loved to take potshots at us because we were signed to a major label—MCA Universal—and we were managed by Bruce Allen. Everybody loved to hate Bruce because he was so outspoken.

I looked at Erica.

"You know what? We're not necessarily trying to solve all of the worlds problems or create world peace with our music, but hopefully it can still make the world a better place to be," I said. "We're trying to create music that has a positive impact and makes people feel good. If we can make one person look at things slightly differently, then the rest is gravy."

Funnily enough, all these years later, I was now making a scarf dedicated to peace. I felt the same now. If one of our scarves could inspire someone to think about creating peace—with themselves, with a family member, with a friend—then that would be incredible. It would mean far more to me than simply selling a scarf. So I knew I was on the right track.

We returned to Canada, and we prepared for the next step. I began the arduous process of trying to find a suitable manufacturer for my modest collection. I sent files of the designs to factories in China, India, Portugal, Vietnam, and Turkey, and I waited to see what came back. This process takes weeks upon weeks, and months upon months, of back-and-forth to narrow it down to one or two trusted suppliers. There were months of disappointments as we received some very nasty sample scarves that were not even close to the level of quality that I wanted.

Completely unsatisfied with what I had received to date from the four corners of the earth, I was introduced to a Vancouver designer named Rosemary Cuevas. I had been introduced to her though my friend Deb Nichol, a well-known Vancouver retailer. Rosemary in turn introduced me to a textile agent in Florence, Italy named Stephanie Pugelli. I connected with Stephanie and told her that I had pretty much exhausted the options to manufacture elsewhere, and I wanted to look at producing my scarves in Florence. I asked her if we could meet and source a suitable manufacturer.

In September 2012, I flew to Italy to meet with Stephanie. She introduced me to two different mills in Prato near Florence. We visited the factories, me dragging along my rolling suitcase of sample chiffon scarves. I also wanted to produce a new line of scarves in a modal-silk blend, and I was able to source the fabric in one particular factory called Ottotredici.

I remember walking into their huge warehouse-looking space with very high ceilings, white walls, and small checkerboard-style windows. I looked across the floor to see a well-dressed gentleman in his early sixties working at a high table, hand finishing a pile of beautiful scarves. He was actually wearing one around his neck. It had incredible volume and a beautiful sense of lightness and softness in it. The way it draped was amazing. From 50 feet across the factory floor, I could see this was the fabric that I wanted. I loved it as soon as I touched it. We came to an agreement on price and I returned to Canada to start creating the designs for the first Italian samples.

I knew manufacturing in Italy was going to put the retail price of my scarves into a luxury brand level. It would definitely impact how we would build the MH-Mark Holden brand, as we would now be competing with global powerhouses such as Louis Vuitton, Gucci, Versace, and Hermes.

Things began to progress quickly from that point. We sent designs back and forth with the manufacturer in Italy, we started to create samples, and they looked very good. So we made our first order and we started to create a small collection.

Our first office was in a small warehouse that belonged to Deb Nichol. Her company was called The Latest Scoop, and she created pop-up stores all over Vancouver. She had exceptionally good instincts around the retail business, and she loved what I was doing. She offered me this very small windowless room in the back of her warehouse, and that's where Mark Holden Fashion was born.

There was no heat that winter, and there was no bathroom. If we had needs, we had to go downstairs to the Italian restaurant.

Once I came back upstairs to find Joel McCarthy with four scarves wrapped around his neck, trying to stay warm. We looked at each other, and we both started laughing.

Our only heat source was a tiny 8-inch space heater that produced about 1500 watts. We would try to position it as best as we could so that it would hit both of us as we sat in opposite corners of the office.

One day, I remember losing all feeling below my knees. I thought to myself, this is getting ridiculous. It was about five o'clock in the afternoon, and Joel had left for the day. I figured it was time to get a better heater, so I went out and bought one.

It was a very humble beginning, but I have fond memories of those days. We had our samples hanging on a rolling rack, and we had a huge 8-foot-by-8-foot canvas graphic of our peace symbol hanging on the wall. We did a lot of very creative work while we were there, and I remain grateful to Debbie for giving us that space.

It was now December 2012, and I started to think about building our web site and creating a bit of an online presence. Naturally, I thought, *wouldn't it be great if I could get Mark Holden dot com?*

I typed it into my browser, and I found a plain landing page that was empty except for the resume of a Mark Holden in Minnesota. There was a contact cell phone number, so I called it.

He answered.

"Hello, Mark," I said, "This is going to sound a little strange, but my name is Mark Holden."

I explained to him what I was up to. I told him that I was a designer, and that we had a foundation, and now I was looking to create a web presence and build my brand

"Would you be interested in selling me your URL?"

"Well, I've never even thought about it," he said. "What were you thinking?"

"I don't really know. I haven't done this before. Maybe two thousand dollars?"

"Well, let me think about it," he said.

I thanked him for his consideration, and we said goodbye.

Six weeks passed, and I heard nothing from him. I began to think that maybe he wasn't interested at all, and that maybe he just wanted to hang onto it. I had a feeling that this was a long shot, and I figured that he must have decided against it.

Finally, I phoned him.

"Hi, Mark, I just wanted to check in and see if you had given it any more thought."

"Yeah, I was thinking about this recently," he said. "I was out with a friend just the other night. I told him about it, and he helped me to think about it."

"He said, 'Well, would you sell it for a million dollars?' and I said yes."

"And then he said, 'Well, would you sell it for a hundred thousand dollars?' And I said yes, absolutely I would."

"And then he said, 'Well, what about ten thousand dollars?' And I said yes, I would sell it for that."

I breathed a silent sigh of relief. Now we were getting into a workable range. For a second, I thought he was going to ask me for a million dollars.

"Then my friend said, 'Well then, would you sell it for five thousand dollars?'"

Mark hesitated a moment, and then he continued. "Well, I might sell it for five thousand dollars."

I could hear in his voice that five thousand might be a bit low, and I might be risking the opportunity if I offered anything lower.

I was sitting in my car on Powell Street in east Vancouver on a dark night. I had pulled over in my car to make the phone call.

"What if we said six thousand?" I said. It was still a lot of money, but in the overall picture of trying to start a company and a brand, the web domain was very important to me.

"Okay," he said. Done deal!

Cue silent fist pump from me. "Great," I said.

It was a great relief to get the domain. Having Mark Holden dot com was like Giorgio Armani having Giorgio Armani dot com. Not that I thought I was in the same league, but my hope was that maybe one day

I would be. And of course, the bigger we became as a company, the harder the negotiating would be. If we had been an established brand, it could have been very difficult to get that URL.

It would take another two weeks to make the official transfer of the domain. It would also require an incredible amount of trust because I didn't want to use a lawyer or a broker. Typically, we would have made the transaction through an agency that holds the funds in escrow, and waits for one party to release the passwords, and this and that. But the two of us just did it.

At one point, when I had sent the money to him, he could have said, "Thanks, it's been a pleasure," and I wouldn't have had a leg to stand on legally. But I knew from talking with him that he was a good guy, and I put my faith in him.

I remember saying to Jane, "I'm going to do it. And if this guy decides to take me to the cleaners, it's just money. It's not going to ruin our lives. It will be very disappointing, but we're not going to have to sell our house."

But it all worked out, and it happened at just the right time. Because we were now preparing for our first big trade show—the Magic/ENK fashion show in Las Vegas in February 2013.

I had recently connected with two people, Treya Klassen and Simon Levin, and they were instrumental in helping me prepare for the Las Vegas show. Treya and Simon both had 20-year backgrounds in manufacturing and sales, and they had both been involved in big fashion and textile manufacturing companies, so they joined me on the trip.

Treya, Jane and I travelled down together. We had all of the samples packed up and shipped via FedEx to the hotel in Las Vegas, and then we flew on a very early flight out of Bellingham.

I was quite nervous in anticipation of the show. It had been quite a process to ensure that we had all of the right paperwork and insurance in place, and there were always some feelings of uncertainty when you shipped your samples by courier.

We arrived at the hotel, and the samples were there, so we took them in a taxi to the convention center to set up our booth. I also stopped and bought a computer monitor along the way, so we would be able to run the promotional video that we had shot and the images from our Look Book catalogue.

When we arrived at the convention center and our booth for our load-in, we discovered that the shelves weren't the ones that we had requested, so we had to get them swapped out. We spent the whole day just getting our booth organized and whipped into shape. I was exhausted by the end of the day, and I still felt nervous about how our collection would be received. The show opened the next morning, and it was scheduled to run through to Thursday.

We got up early and we arrived at our booth at 8:30 a.m. For the next four days, we would receive people as they walked past and show them our line.

The first order that we wrote was for a couple who had a two boutiques in Newport Beach, California called Novocento. Treya and I high-fived each other after we finished writing it up. It was a confirmation that we had product that people liked and would buy, and they understood the message behind it.

The show was great for us. At one point I recognized two women who were buyers from a boutique in West Vancouver called Kiss and Makeup. I had tried to see them in January before we went to Las Vegas. They visited our booth and fell in love with our scarves and our message. We agreed to meet when we got back to Vancouver, later that night, they posted on Instagram, "We came all the way from Vancouver and wouldn't you know it, the coolest thing we've seen so far is a designer from Vancouver."

They would eventually become one of our first retailers, and they did great work in promoting our line.

Following the Las Vegas show, and a very successful trunk show in Vancouver in May 2013, I went to Paris in June 2013. I wanted to get into a European show so we could start to open up that market, and my first target was a show called Premiere Classe.

Premiere Classe runs twice a year, once in September and once in February, and it's one of the biggest shows on earth. It happens to coincide with Paris Fashion Week, so it's a very big deal to exhibit there. In June 2013, I wanted to meet with one of their organizers and try to get into the show.

I managed to set up a meeting through my new friend Serge Baccaria whom I had met in Las Vegas. He was with a French men's design company called Billtornade, and he said he could introduce me to some people. When I arrived in Paris, he actually connected me with the assistant of the managing director of Premiere Classe. Her name was Sylvie Poirot, and she agreed to meet with me on a Thursday at two o'clock in the afternoon in the Saint Germaine district.

The meeting was in an incredible sixteenth century building with tall vaulted ceilings and old wooden beams. It had all been completely remodeled with tons of glass and steel, and it radiated modernity and style. I was led to a large boardroom table in an open office area, and I sat down with my samples and waited. On one side of the large room, there were about 30 people working feverishly at their computers, presumably preparing for the next show.

Then I saw Sylvie Poirot emerge from an upstairs office. She was in her mid-fifties and elegantly dressed in business chic. She came down the stairs, slowly with a casual unrushed grace, introduced herself, and sat down across from me.

"Mark, I'm very pleased to meet you," she said, "but I just want you to know that we have no space for you. We have no possibility to have you exhibit at Premiere Classe. We already have many scarves, and there's no possibility."

I was stunned. But I didn't say anything. I let her continue to talk.

Sylvie talked for about twenty minutes, and during that time she explained to me that she had been doing this show for 15 years. I didn't say anything. I just listened.

She explained that she was very knowledgeable and that she knew what it took to operate a successful show.

"Every year I get comments and emails from the big brands saying that we must keep the show fresh and alive and dynamic and moving forward," she said. "This means I have a huge responsibility to make sure that this is the case."

She explained that she also had to ensure that the big brands were well represented, and that they were surrounded by other good brands. I simply continued to listen.

When she was finished, I nodded thoughtfully to acknowledge everything she had said, paused for a long few moments, and then I adjusted myself in my chair to speak.

"Thank you, Sylvie," I said. "Thank you first of all for taking the time to meet with me today. I know how busy you are, and I'm very grateful for the opportunity. I understand everything you are saying. If I may, I have just a couple of thoughts that I'd like to offer."

She smiled patiently and simply nodded.

"First of all, I started my career many, many years ago as a musician and songwriter, and the music business provides a very good training ground in rejection. So I am very comfortable with rejection."

She smiled again, nodding in acknowledgment.

"I just wanted to start by saying that," I continued. "The other thing that I would like to comment on is something that you said earlier. You made a comment about keeping things fresh and alive and moving forward."

"Yes."

I gestured towards our scarves as they were laid out on the boardroom table in front of us. I was very proud of them.

"These are beautiful scarves," I said. "They're made in the finest mills in Italy. To me, it is extremely important to create a product that is beautiful and makes no compromise. However, I don't imagine for a second that I can walk in and compete with the Chanels and the Ferragamos of the world. I look at the market, and I see an absolute sea of gorgeous fabrics and powerhouse brands known the world over. I can't compete in that arena."

"But to me a brand is something that people buy because it makes them feel a certain way. And our brand is about creating a sense of peace within someone who sees the scarf, or who buys the scarf, or who wears it. So it has to be beautiful and soft and meaningful. And when you wear it, it should feel like the physical embodiment of peace. That's the only way that I have a hope."

"Our price point is higher than some of our competitors, but I think our quality is incomparable, and I think we can hold our own with some of the biggest brands in the world."

"In addition, the core vision of our business is to make a difference in the world, so a portion of the proceeds of every single item that we sell will go into our charitable foundation, called the Just Imagine Foundation, which will be used to make contributions to different charitable causes and provide micro loans to new entrepreneurs throughout the world."

I paused. "This is actually what it's all about. This is really the important work that I think we as business people and citizens of the planet need to do. Each of us needs to help to make a difference."

At this point, I prepared to drop the big one. It was risky, but I figured I had nothing to lose since she had already said that I had no possibility of making it into the show.

"As far as being fresh and dynamic and new, I just walked through your door a half hour ago."

She paused and smiled, clearly moved. "I really appreciate your words, Mark," she said finally. Then she reached over to touch my arm. "I would like to offer you a place in the show."

"Thank you very much," I said. "We will be honored to be in the show. I think we can do some wonderful things together, and I thank you for being part of what we are all about."

That was the end of our meeting. We said our goodbyes, and I went outside with my rolling sample case in tow. I took a deep breath and watched the bustle of Parisienne traffic passing by me.

I was exhausted. But I felt like a million bucks. Because I had gone from a no to a yes in 45 minutes. I grabbed a taxi, jumped in, and headed back to the hotel.

When I arrived back at the hotel, Jane was waiting for me. I told her the news, and we walked around the corner to our favorite little bistro on the corner of Rue de Castiglione and Rue St. Honoré to toast our first Paris show with two glasses of house rosé. It was sweet.

My experience with Sylvie reinforced the idea to never give up. You have to believe in yourself and what you are doing, and you have to continue to push forward.

The meeting had actually been a little atypical of me. I've never been quite that forward and assertive. I have always tended to err on the side of being more modest, and maybe wrongly at times. "Okay, that's fine, maybe I'll circle back in six months and we can talk again." But on this occasion, I figured I had nothing to lose, so I took the plunge, and the outcome was overwhelmingly positive.

From Paris, we went to Milan to visit another mill, and then we returned to Vancouver and continued working to grow our collection.

During June and July 2013, I went into a 6-week period of heavy design work. I had to deliver all of my new designs in our new Imagery series collection to the factories for printing before the end of July because they all shut down for the month of August.

It was a big push for us. I created almost 30 new designs and sent them to Italy. It actually ended up being too much for our suppliers. Our agent came back to us and said, "Mark, we can't sample all of these. We'll shut the factory down. We don't have the capacity." The idea that our little Vancouver-based company had threatened to shut down the mill in Prato with our over-sized order made me smile.

We reduced our number of designs, but it was a real blitz for me to create the designs for our spring and summer 2014 collection. This was the collection that we would be showing in Paris in September 2013 at Premiere Classe.

The samples started to roll in. As we made preparations to leave for France, we faced a number of challenges.

For starters, we were going to Paris during Fashion Week. There are three big Paris shows: Tranoi, Premiere Classe, and the Box. In addition, there is the entire Fashion Week and all of the associated events. So the hotels triple or quadruple their normal rates, and we couldn't afford those prices. The average hotel room was going for about 500 euros per night, which would make it about $800 per night for us for only one room. Meanwhile, there were going to be three of us attending the show: myself, Treya, and Natasha who worked in our office.

I decided that we would rent two apartments. We were able to find two in the colorful Marais district which was about 30-minutes walking distance from the venue.

We decided this time that we wouldn't ship our samples as we had done for the Vegas show, because we weren't staying in a hotel, and we were concerned about sending things by courier. We decided that we would carry them on the plane with us. When we caught our flight in Vancouver, we checked four very large roll-up suitcases full of samples.

We arrived in Paris in the late afternoon on Wednesday, and the show started on Friday morning. None of our bags arrived.

We had no suitcases, no samples, nothing. The airline told us they would be coming—it wasn't like they had been sent to Zimbabwe or Argentina—but you never know for certain until you receive them.

This fell soundly into the category of "what can go wrong will go wrong." Again, I felt the familiar lump in the throat stress and anxiety of preparing for a big show.

The three of us jumped into a taxi and went into Paris. We set up Natasha and Treya in their apartment, and then I checked into mine. Then Natasha and I took a taxi back to Orly Airport at around eight o'clock in the evening. By now we were cross-eyed. We hadn't eaten for several hours and we had been awake for 36 hours straight.

Three of the four bags had arrived, so we took them with us back to the apartments. The fourth bag ended up being delivered in the middle of the night to Treya and Natasha's apartment. So we finally had everything we needed.

I awoke early the next morning and walked from my apartment to the venue on Rue Cambon to see how long it would take. The show venue is located across the street from the famous Coco Chanel Apartment and the beautiful flagship Chanel store. During these shows, I very much enjoy being able to walk to the venue each morning as it is a great way to think through the day, and it's also a great way to take in the sights and sounds of the city. Thirty minutes after starting out, I arrived.

We loaded into the venue at six o'clock that night. Our booth location was in a corner of the very large pavilion room, and after months of imagining and hoping that we would be assigned a good location, our concerns were dashed. However, we were very visible from each end of two very long corridors.

After spending several hours setting up, and steaming the collection ready for presentation the next day, we went out for dinner around 11:30 p.m. at a bistro in the Marais district. My first beer tasted very good. By midnight we were dizzy with exhaustion as we made our way back to our apartments to catch up on sleep before our first big day of the show the next morning.

Although we didn't end up writing any new business during the show, Premiere Classe was a good success for us in many other respects. First of all, we had "gone to school" on this show. We made some excellent industry contacts, and we connected with a lot of very good people. We also learned a lot about the market.

I learned that the market for scarves in Europe is saturated. It is saturated with great product from India, from China, from Africa, from all over the world. I discovered that most of these scarves were at a lower price point than ours, and although they differed in quality, they were certainly acceptable to most value conscious consumers. I realize that if I really wanted to sell any degree of volume, we would have to place our scarves at a very low price point. This would be tough for us. A beautiful quality scarf will always find a buyer somewhere, but not everyone can afford to pay the higher price, so the market will be smaller and more competitive. This was just one of the many lessons learned early on.

Following the Paris show, I began working very hard to reduce our costs while not compromising the quality of the fabric and the final product. The ultimate goal was to have an amazing line of products at the best price point possible, with a meaningful social message. That's the sweet spot.

I have always believed that whatever you do, you should always start with why. *Why am I doing this; not what am I doing or how am I going to do it.* In the case of Mark Holden Fashion, our intention was to create something that would illuminate the possibilities for peace.

On the eve of finishing this book, I heard a moving story from a friend of mine. We had given one of our scarves to her sister when she was in the final days of a very brave fight with cancer. She had taken such comfort from wearing the scarf that she never took it off. In the end, she passed away wrapped in it. I was very moved when I heard this. I felt very proud knowing that one of our scarves had given her some comfort and peace.

TWENTY-TWO

Boulevard: Never Give Up

For anyone who knows me, it's no secret that I always carried a lingering regret after Boulevard's demise in 1990. Boulevard represented the culmination of a dream I had had since I was kid, so it was crushing to see everything implode just when the dream was coming true.

In the 25 years that followed the breakup, I hardly spoke to any of the guys from the band. We all moved on with our lives as we pursued various careers, and other things simply took over. During that time span, I talked a couple of times with David Forbes, the lead vocalist, but there were a couple of guys with whom I hadn't talked in over two decades.

I once called David from Las Vegas during a business trip in 2009. For some reason, I had been thinking a lot about the band. We talked for a while and caught up, and I asked him at some point if he would ever think about getting the band together again.

"Yeah, I might think about it, but I don't know how it would work," he replied. "I'm a firefighter now, and I'm married—I've got a whole other life."

And that was the truth for all of us. We had all moved on in 25 years, and all of us had new lives, so the idea of getting the band together again didn't seem to hold much promise. Even the call with David brought back a somewhat discomforting mix of dark feelings about how things had ended up. So I felt strangely both relieved and disappointed after we spoke.

Five years later, in the spring of 2013, David and his wife Karen came up to Vancouver from their home near Seattle to have lunch with Jane and me. In the course of our conversation, the idea of reuniting the band surfaced again. We agreed that it could be cool, but we didn't say much more than that. We finished lunch, said our goodbyes, and the notion more or less evaporated again.

Strangely enough, when Dave and Karen returned to their home in Washington State that same night, they got a call from our keyboard player, Andrew Johns. He was heading south from Vancouver and passing by their town, and for some unknown reason, after more than 20 years, he decided to call David. He had passed by their town many times before, but this was the first time that he had decided to call them.

The idea of a band reunion lay forgotten. Then out of the blue, in October 2013, David received a long-distance phone call from Europe.

It was a guy named Kieran Dargan calling from Ireland. He explained that he was a concert promoter and the producer of Firefest, an annual retro music festival in Nottingham. It was three-day festival that brought together 80s bands, and in the past year, Kieran had received numerous requests and inquiries from fans wondering whatever happened to the band from Canada called Boulevard. Apparently, enough people had written to him that Kieran finally decided: *I'd better look into these guys!*

He searched Boulevard on Youtube, found a couple of our videos, and then managed to track down David Forbes' phone number. And he called him.

"Myself and the other festival organizers sat down and created a list of the top bands that we'd love to have at next year's final fling event, and Boulevard is high on our list," he said. "We're wondering if you guys would consider reuniting to come and play at the festival?"

Of course, David was taken completely by surprise, but he told Kieran that he would check with the rest of us and then get back to him.

David sent a couple of emails to me and the other band members, and all of us expressed interest in discussing the idea. I was especially pleased, even though I had no idea how or if it would really happen. But somehow it felt right to look at the possibility.

All of us met in late October 2013 in Vancouver, and the only guys who weren't there were Tom Christiansen, the base player, and Randy Gould, our former guitar player. Tom was now living in Houston, and Randy's whereabouts was unknown.

We met at the Fairmont Waterfront Hotel on a Wednesday night at 10 o'clock. There were myself, David, our drummer Randall Stoll, and our keyboard player Andrew Johns. It was the only time we could manage to meet. Andrew had to fly in from Vernon, British Columbia, and he was also enroute to Los Angeles where he was playing a gig. Randall had some family commitments to deal with, so timing was challenging for him as well. Still, we managed to pull it off.

We greeted each other with exuberant hugs, and then we sat down and ordered some beers. It felt great. It was as if no time had passed between us. We were quickly gabbing and catching up, and soon Andrew and David were at the piano in the lounge playing one of he songs from our second album "Rainy Day in London".

A woman in the bar actually approached us. "Who are you guys?" she said. "I know that song." That was cool. It felt like a positive omen.

We continued gabbing and catching up for about an hour, and then I more or less called the "formal" meeting to attention. Before we started discussing things too deeply, I felt that I needed to get something off my chest. The one thing that had been troubling me around the idea of a band reunion.

"Guys, I've been thinking a lot," I began. "I have to say, as excited as I am about the opportunity to get together and play at the festival next year, I just can't do it if Randy Gould is involved. I just can't do it."

"I have lived with a dark cloud over my head and a lump of sadness in my chest for the last 25 years since the band came apart. And every time I think about the band, or Randy, I get the same feeling. If I don't follow my feeling, I know that I'll be making a big mistake. I'm sorry, but that's basically where I'm at."

To my surprise, there was a collective sigh. Everyone's shoulders suddenly dropped, and all of the guys looked visibly relieved. It was a collective sense of: *Thank God*.

And then the stories started to come out.

It turned out that all of them felt the same way as me. All of them had felt bullied and manipulated by Randy all of those years ago, and they talked about how miserable he had made them feel. He had actually intimidated a few of the guys by suggesting that any one of them could be fired at a moment's notice. Apparently, he had told them that the band's front line—composed of him, David Forbes, and me—was all that really mattered. He had told the rest of the guys that the drummer, keyboardist, and bassist were basically expendable.

It made my blood boil to hear this.

"If I had had any idea whatsoever of what was going on, I would have fired his ass," I said.

It was horrible. How could such a simple thing have completely derailed us? But we had all been young guys at the time, and we weren't necessarily equipped to deal with the kind of subterfuge and manipulation that Randy had apparently orchestrated.

"My God," David said. "I had no idea that any of this was happening."

David had been a great band member and friend to everyone during that entire period, but he hadn't really been around enough to see what was going on behind the scenes. Other than when we were touring, he would typically just come up to Vancouver to do a vocal or rehearse, and then he would go back down to Kent, Washington where he lived. He was quite separated from the day-to-day events.

I had known this at the time—I had known that David had no idea what Randy was doing—but I didn't feel right reaching out to him to say, "Hey Dave, can you support me here? Randy's being a dink." No, I figured that it was up to me to try to resolve it, and of course the band ended up imploding in the end.

So we talked about everything that October night in 2013, and we agreed that the band would get back together, but we would find another guitar player. We also agreed to talk to Tom in Houston to see if he wanted to join us, but if he didn't, we would find another bass player too.

When I drove home at 1:30 a.m. that night, I felt like 10,000 pounds had been lifted off my shoulders. Everything felt resolved and 25 years of brooding regret basically evaporated. During our meeting, I had learned that the guys had truly appreciated what I had done—how I had started the band, and all of the work and effort I had put into it, and how tough it had been on me and my young family, how much I had had to scramble, and how unfair it all was in the end. They all saw this.

I felt a beautiful sense of redemption.

In the days that followed, we quickly set forth with vigor and purpose. We found a new guitar player—a guy named Dave Corman—and we set up a couple of rehearsals throughout the spring of 2014.

Soon we were preparing to play our first warm-up gig. It was a summer festival in Vernon, British Columbia.

It would be our first show in 27 years.

The last time we had played live together was in December 1988 at the Pacific Coliseum in Vancouver during our tour with Boston. Now we were playing on a big stage together again, but we were more or less isolated from the outside world. This was premeditated. We knew that if we sounded bad, which was a distinct possibility after years of not playing together, we could manage a bit of damage control. It was a great way to cut our teeth again without embarrassing ourselves.

We played the Vernon gig, and it went well, but then we all scattered again.

We soon discovered that our biggest challenge in preparing for the Nottingham festival was simply bringing everyone together. Andrew was playing gigs up and down the coast between Vancouver and California, and Randall was one of the most in-demand drummers in Vancouver. Dave Corman was also a pro guitar player in three or four different cover bands, and he also ran his own studio, so he was a busy guy as well.

We rehearsed in a very small windowless room in what looked like an abandoned single-story building on Third and Main Street in Vancouver. Our twelve-by-twelve-foot room was just big enough to fit all of us and our equipment, with blankets and other materials hung on the walls to dampen the sound, as well as a few tattered old tour posters from previous bands. It was quite a sight.

And amidst the madness and the challenges of coordinating ourselves, we managed to do one more small show in Vancouver in October 2014 about a week before Firefest.

It was great gig at a really funky venue on Granville Island called the Backstage Lounge in the Arts Club Theatre. There was a small crowd of about 120 people, and they were really enthusiastic and positive. We felt like a band again, and we felt ready for Nottingham. The next day, David left for England, and on October 22, the rest of us flew from Vancouver to join him.

We flew overnight and arrived in London on a Thursday morning. Randall and his family had decided to head over a few days earlier to join David in England, so it was me, Jane, our daughter Ashley, Dave, Andrew, and our cameraman-director, Joel McCarthy whom we had hired to document the band's reunion. We landed at Heathrow, and we were picked up by veteran driver Chris in a small bus that had been organized by Firefest to drive us to Nottingham. Chris looked the part of a classic English lorry driver: Pear shaped, bald except for a very long bit of rock and roll mane on the back of his head, and "summer teeth"—some are here, some are there.

We were accompanied by a cast of characters. Riding with us was a heavy metal band from Greece called Red Rum. These guys looked rough. They were in their fifties, and they were totally unshaven and disheveled. Still, in keeping with their genre, they were wearing leather vests and lizard skin cowboy boots. Their long hair, tattoos, and five-day beard growth paid complement to their middle-aged paunches. They looked like they had been drinking and smoking their entire lives and loving every minute of it.

They turned out to be great guys. However, as there were about thirteen of us in this little tiny bus with luggage and gear, it was a bit cramped. We had a three-and-a-half-hour drive to Nottingham, and after flying and travelling for several hours already, all of us were probably a bit ripe and needing a shower.

We finally arrived in Nottingham and checked into the Crowne Plaza. About 25 bands from all over the world—Spain, Greece, Germany, Italy, Australia, and more—were scheduled to play at the festival, and the Crowne Plaza had been identified as the host hotel for the festival. Most of the bands were staying there, so it was a busy place.

Over the next three days, the hotel lobby and bar became the ultimate meeting place. While hanging out there, fans would frequently approach with phones, cameras, and pens to get autographs on all forms of band swag, including vintage posters and album covers.

It was something from another world. It was a blend of young and old, from hardcore heavy metal rockers to pop artists like ourselves. Just an incredibly colorful mix of ethnicities and characters. Some seemed to be from another era altogether.

The festival was taking place in an old established nightclub called Rock City that held approximately 2,000 people, and we were scheduled to play on Saturday. Tom arrived on Friday night—one day before our performance—so we ended up running over the tunes together in the lobby of the hotel on Saturday morning.

Tom had spent the sum total of perhaps one hour rehearsing the tunes since the gig in Vernon four months earlier. It wasn't optimal preparation, but it was going to have to do. I've got a picture of Andrew with his ear pressed against the tuning head of Tom's bass, trying to hear what he was playing so he could guide him through the chord changes.

When it came time to go on stage, we were feeling reasonably confident. Our biggest concern was that we might actually be a bit light for this festival. I mean, we were rock, but we weren't heavy rock. We might be compared to a cross between Toto and the Scorpions, but we weren't heavy metal like Slip Knot. Some of the festival bands were definitely serious heavy metal thrashers.

We prepped ourselves in the green room in the basement of the venue as we waited for the band before us to finish their set. The room was permeated with the unmistakable stench of stagnant cigarette smoke, stale beer, and bleach. It took all of us back to the hundreds of similar gigs we had collectively played in years past. As we waited, we learned that epic bands such as the Clash, The Sex Pistols, B.B. King, Cold Play, Brian Adams, Billy Idol, Def Leppard, and countless others had played at this venue in the past. The list of artists was astounding, and it went on and on.

When our time came to go on stage, we had to walk along a long subterranean corridor and then climb a set of narrow, rickety old wooden stairs that had probably been there for a hundred years. As I walked up them, with my tenor sax in one hand and my alto in the other, I thought to myself: *Wow, imagine the artists who have walked up these same stairs in the last 60 years—The Clash, B.B. King—you name it.*

It was electrifying.

We walked out onto the stage with the curtain drawn—a massive black fabric tarp that was held up by giant, extendable light stands. Each stand was manned by a stagehand in a black t-shirt with "crew" stenciled on the back—standard issue for roadies the world over. Each of us absorbed in our own worlds, we busily made last-minute adjustments to mic stands, pedal settings, tunings, and set list placements on the stage floor.

The final few seconds seemed to play in slow motion for me as I looked around to make sure that everyone was ready. The stagehands were completely laser-focused on the stage manager, Paul, waiting for his signal to drop the curtain. Paul gave the nod, and suddenly we heard:

Ladies and gentlemen! We are thrilled—and quite frankly can't believe—that these lads are here with us at Firefest! All the way from Vancouver, Canada...Boulevard!

The curtain fell to a healthy round of applause and a few cheers and whistles. I stepped up to the mic and I talked a little bit to the crowd. I told them the story of how Kieran had phoned us and how we had ended up there.

"We are thrilled and honored to be here," I said with sincere humility. "We have to give kudos to Kieran for tracking us down and bringing us here, and to those of you in the audience who supported us in coming here."

We started to play our first song. As we played, the crowd seemed to watch in stunned disbelief. Was it dismay? Disappointment? Politeness? I couldn't tell. Were they asking themselves, *who the hell are these guys?*

Apparently, they knew us better than we realized. Because after we finished our first song, the place absolutely *erupted.*

As we started into our second tune, I looked down into the audience and I saw a lot of people actually singing the words. *Words that I had written in back in the 80s.* It was astounding.

Despite the fact that we didn't have time to do a sound check on stage, apparently the front-of-house sound was excellent. We played an awesome one-hour set, and the sound and lighting technicians were outstanding. When we finished our last number, "Never Give Up", we absolutely blew the roof off.

I talked with Kieran afterwards. "Mark, without question, this has been the best performance of the festival so far," he grinned.

We soon discovered that people were saying the same thing on Facebook and Twitter. We were stoked beyond measure.

Immediately following our show, we were taken downstairs for a "meet and greet" with some sponsors. We had about 2 minutes with them. Then another young production assistant appeared to usher us somewhere else.

"We've got to go," she said simply and firmly. "Follow me."

She led us down another corridor and up another set of stairs. We arrived in the front lobby where we had to cross a huge lineup of people that went out the front doors of the club and down the block. Glancing at them, I figured they must be waiting to see the next band.

We pushed through the line, which was more or less a crowd, and we were shepherded into the merchandise room. This was where all of the t-shirts and other bits of swag for the different bands were being sold. At the far end of the room, I saw three tables set up. They were just empty tables with Sharpie pens on them. And then I realized what was happening.

It was the meet and greet with our fans.

Of the 2,000 people who were there that night, there were probably about 700 people lined up to meet us. That was the lineup that we had crossed in the lobby. And it went out the front doors, down the block, and around the corner.

We dutifully stood behind the tables, and they started letting the fans in. People began to stream past us. We were signing photos and shirts and the odd body part as fast as we could, but we only had a half hour before the organizers had to clear out the room to get ready for the next band.

We were in shock and disbelief the entire time. Some of these people had travelled great distances to see us. There were fans from places like Sweden, Israel, Spain, Argentina, Germany, Italy, and the United States, and two guys had come all the way from Lima, Peru. They were carrying CDs and posters that they had bought in Peru, and they wanted us to autograph them.

But one guy completely blew us away. His name was David Pound. It was later that night, long after the meet and greet, and we were having a drink in the hotel lounge around 11:30 p.m. The place was a sea of big hair, denim jackets with the sleeves cut off, and all varieties of bandanas covering receding hairlines. This man and his wife walked up to me.

"Are you Mark Holden?" he said.

"Yes, I am" I said inquisitively.

"I wonder if I could ask a favor of you."

He pulled out our second album, on vinyl, still shrink wrapped, from 1990.

And he opened it.

There was a collective gasp among the people who were watching nearby.

"Don't open it!" someone said. "It's so valuable unopened!"

"This is worth way more," he said simply, and he handed me a pen. "Would you do me the honor of signing it?"

This was a very cool moment and perhaps one of the highlights of the festival.

The next day, I went into a local Starbucks with Jane and our daughter Ashley. I noticed a group of elegantly dressed people with olive skin seated at the other end of the room. They were obviously Spanish or Italian, and they looked to range in age from early thirties to early fifties. They were talking animatedly, and they seemed to be having a great time. You could feel the energy radiating from their small but very engaged group.

Moments later our lead singer David walked in. The group of Spanish-Italians suddenly leapt to their feet: "David! David! David!"

He talked with them for a moment, and then he turned and pointed at me. All hell broke loose. We were quickly surrounded this group of fans that turned out to be from Barcelona and Madrid, and they had come to the festival specifically to see our band.

Again, it was mind blowing for us.

It was now Sunday, and we had arrangements to go to London that day. Accordingly, at 11 a.m., our chartered bus pulled up in front of the Crowne Plaza. We loaded all of our suitcases onto the bus, pulled out of Nottingham, and three hours later we were checking into our hotels in the heart of London, and psyched to go into Abbey Road Studios to record backing tracks for the new album.

Prior to going to England, we had all felt that we had a lot of unfinished business as a band in terms of new material. Consequently, we had decided to record a new album to recapture some of the magic and provide a follow up to the festival. There were a number of songs that had been written over the past 25 years that had never seen the light of day—some because of the strained politics within the band during the recording of the second album just prior to our breakup. Some had been basically "voted off the island" because a certain guitar player had rallied support against them in his bid to take over the band and turn us into something we weren't.

But now some of these gems from the archives would get a shot. Bigger and better than ever.

In the months leading up to our trip, we had done an online crowd-sourced funding campaign to fund two things: a new album and a documentary film capturing the entire reunion experience, stretching from our first rehearsals in Vancouver to our final performance at the festival and our recording sessions for the new album. The campaign had generated contributions and support from fans all over the world.

To this end, we hired Joel McCarthy who had now become a seasoned documentary filmmaker. He seemed to possess this magical "right time at the right place" ability to capture rehearsals and other goings-on.

And as we had already decided to record a new album, the thought naturally occurred to us as we prepared for Firefest: *If we're going to be in England, why not see if Abbey Road is available to record some backing tracks for a few of the new songs?*

So I contacted studio manager Colette Barber to discuss rates, avail-ability, and whether or not it would be possible to do a single-day booking at the studio. Colette connected me with her assistant, Peach, and we made the arrangements.

Recording at Abbey Road was extremely cool. We recorded three new songs in Studio 2 where most of the Beatles albums and dozens of other albums such as Pink Floyd's "Dark Side of the Moon" had been recorded. There seemed to be this blanket of quiet, positive energy that emanated from the walls of this giant room. It had been built in the 1930s, and it was the oldest purpose built recording studio in the world.

The entire experience was all so rich. The band was back together, and all of us were excited. None of us expected that we were going to be the next big thing, but we relished the opportunity to finish what we had started. When the band came apart in 1990, we all knew that something had remained unresolved.

In the end, it seemed a fitting final chapter for Boulevard. But then again, maybe it was a new beginning? We had played our music for crowds of appreciative fans, and we were able to record new songs at one of the most fabled recording studios in history. We were together again, and we were more in line with our original intentions and aspirations than ever before.

After years of regret and remorse, I think all of us found resolution and peace. And it had all started with a simple phone call from England in the spring of 2013. For me, it represents just one more beautiful thread in the tapestry of life.

TWENTY-THREE

What It All Means

The days and the years tick past faster than we know. And in the process of living, I think we often overlook the obvious.

In my life, I can see that I have sometimes been so involved in surviving from day to day that I haven't necessarily stopped to reflect on the bigger picture of where I have been and where I might be going. Or if I have stopped to reflect, I haven't necessarily been able to get a full view of the trajectory of my life.

What have been the events, choices, and attitudes that defined me? I feel like I have an entirely new perspective now.

I look at who I was at age 25, and then age 35, and then age 45. I see things I wouldn't change in the slightest, and I see a few things I might do differently if I had a second chance. I see times when I may have misdirected my energies, spun my wheels, or deluded myself a bit about my situation or circumstances. But I can also see where I stayed true to myself. I have always come back to being me. It feels good to know that.

As well, in the instances where I lost my footing or suffered setbacks, I'm tempted to think that things had to be that way. Life is, after all, a learning process. And you can't know what you don't know. Sometimes you have to stumble a bit before you can rise up. And I have certainly stumbled on more than a few occasions. And that's okay.

When I retrace my ideas and decisions from the time I was three-years-old until now, I can see a thread that connects all of my lifetime yearnings into one fabric that is unmistakably me. I find that fascinating—almost like knowing myself for the first time.

For starters, I can see that I have always wanted to help people. My early experience in Edmonton with a boy who was trying to build an outdoor ice rink with scraps of wood and a collection of old bent nails. I remember feeling absolutely distraught as he burst into tears with the realization that his hope of building a skating rink for everyone was over. Even at my young age, I had known that he didn't have a chance of completing the task, but to see him weeping so inconsolably left a lifelong impression on me.

I also think it helped to set the tone for the person I would become in the rest of my life. I have continued to feel profound empathy and even pain when I see people thwarted in realizing their dreams. For example, it still troubles me when I see a closed storefront or a sign that has been covered over. I always think: *That's someone's broken dream.*

This is why I have always taken pleasure in helping people to get started in their own businesses and creative ventures. I am now hoping to do that work on an even greater scale through charity work associated with the various companies I have been involved in, the foundation, and what Jane and I have done on a personal level.

Throughout my life, I have also remained the four-year-old entrepreneur with the red wagon full of newspapers looking to launch a new business venture of my own. Like music, business entrepreneurism has always been a creative endeavor for me. It's about bringing something to life that didn't exist before. There are essential creative energies that are intrinsic to making a new venture come to life from concept to completion. That has always been exciting to me.

I'm still the same 10-year-old with a penchant for stylish clothes. It started years ago with green suede boots in the basement of the Bay department store in Calgary, and it has never stopped. The recent expression of my love for clothing and fashion continues to manifest itself in my latest endeavor.

I'm still the 12-year-old budding musician who wants to write a hit song. From my early days practicing clarinet, and then through my years as a professional musician, sound engineer, and 80s Rock band member, I have never ceased to be fascinated by the lure of creating a good pop hook or a strong riff that will stop people in their tracks and move them.

The foundation created from my years in the music industry naturally led me into developing M-Sound and Hip Digital. Each one of these ventures in turn became catalysts for other entrepreneurial ventures.

All of these interests and proclivities have been with me since I was kid. However, like most people, I don't think I ever stepped back to gain a full perspective on how much they were an integral part of me, or how they might one day come together into one defined purpose.

When I finally decided to recognize that I am principally a creative guy who needs to create things, it provided me with a new clarity of purpose that made it relatively "easy" for me to start new things that made "why am I doing this" obvious. Being crystal clear on *why* is the critical question for anyone wanting to start a new venture or get an idea off the ground.

In the end, the business processes are similar to those at M-Sound, E-Zone, Hip Digital and Gener8. And the same business fundamentals still apply: design, production, sales and marketing, brand creation, back office reporting, and accounting systems. But the difference now is that I am aligned with the product and the process more than I have ever been in the past.

The Just Imagine Foundation is a key part of this alignment. We created the Foundation in 2012 with the vision of making a difference on this planet through local and global actions, large and small, to alleviate human suffering. The long-term vision is to provide funding assistance to a wide variety of deserving individuals who are trying to get a new idea off the ground and charities that have a proven track record of success in helping those in need, whether it be a women's shelter, a disabilities organization, or disaster relief.

At time of writing, the Foundation is still very much in its nascent phase. One program we were involved in, along with my close friend Deb Nichol, the queen of pop up retail, focused on raising funds for the Greater Vancouver Food Bank Society. During Christmas one year for example, we created and sold peace-symbol t-shirts through various outlets in Vancouver to raise funds. With support from local retailers, each t-shirt was basically able to provide a family of four with three meals for one day. On another occasion, Boulevard played a small show in Vancouver where all the members of the band agreed to contribute 25% of each ticket to the GVFBS. Our drummer Randall Stoll and I met with them after the show and presented them with a cheque. They are amazing, beautiful people, and they are doing remarkable work for the good of their community. I truly feel inspired to do more every time I step foot in their very large but modestly run warehouse in East Vancouver.

Another objective of the foundation is to help entrepreneurs. I have a special place in my heart for entrepreneurs because I am one, and I have been all of my life, and I know how difficult it is to get great ideas off the ground. Just like an aircraft, many great ideas don't ever make it past that first 50 feet after takeoff because it's the hardest time to sustain your momentum and keep from being pulled back down to earth. This is called the "ground effect". Through the Foundation, my intention is to provide startup capital and mentorship to help budding entrepreneurs to achieve liftoff. It could be a woman in Vancouver who requires one sewing machine to start a seamstress business in the back room of her house, or a potter in Indonesia who needs a new kiln to expand their artisan pottery business.

I believe that if you can change the life of one person, you have done something significant to promote inner peace for them and make the world a better place. That has been part of the mission statement from the first scarf created at Mark Holden Fashion. The Foundation is a natural extension and will amplify that mission.

Deciding where to distribute funds, however small the amount may be, remains one of the most extraordinary and meaningful activities I have ever experienced.

I still feel like I am on a journey. I still feel challenged. And I am constantly reminded that there are no shortcuts. When you start a business, it's often tempting to think that you can create a short cut to instant success, but at the end of the day, you still need to come up with a good idea, create a well thought-out plan, and execute like mad to get it off the ground. There are a million good ideas out there, but only a very few ever see the light of day because the hard part is making them real.

You have to be smart about your choices and strategic in how you direct your energies, and you have to know how to use all of the resources available to you. One of your biggest assets has to be your previous experience. Whenever I have had to make big decisions, I call upon lessons learned in the past. From Sound West, M-Sound, E-Zone, Hip Digital, Gener8, and life in general. I just think, have I been down this road before? I also leverage the experience of others whenever possible. I am not afraid to ask for advice, or to be a bit critical of myself.

When we returned from the 2013 Premiere Classe show in Paris, I sat down with my team and we discussed the challenges that we faced as a new startup trying to break into the world of fashion and design. There was me, Natasha, Don Bull, and Karim Mitha, our general manager. We had just spent a whole bunch of money in Paris, and we were discussing how sales were taking longer, and how retail was tough and getting tougher, and so on. I gave an overview of where I thought things were at, and then I provided a bit of reflection:

"You know, sometimes it's hard for me to differentiate between indulging my unbridled enthusiasm for this project, and then having the presence of mind to say, okay, it's time to stop being quite so enthusiastic and time to be a little more pragmatic."

Sometimes it is difficult to know where you need to pull back a bit and be a little more critical. Blind enthusiasm can lead to making poor decisions if you're not listening or seeing what's really happening in your marketplace and in your business.

I think that is one of my greatest personal challenges as an entrepreneur, and I think it's one of the biggest challenges of any entrepreneur who believes completely in what they are doing. For sure, you need to be enthusiastic and committed, and you must be courageous—but you also need to be sensible and pay attention to the business fundamentals.

A few years ago in France, by chance, I was reconnected with a pivotal event from my past that helped to reframe my understanding of all of my thinking around business, purpose, and life in general.

In 2008, I travelled with some friends on a cycling trip to Saint Nazaire, France. It's a small town located more or less at the base of the French Alps. These guys had previously done a cycling trip in the area, and they invited me to join them on this excursion. One of the rides we did was l'Alpe d'Huez. If you are a Tour de France fan, it represents one of the epic climbs where some of the greatest cyclists in the world battle through twenty-one switchbacks to reach a summit over 1000 meters in altitude.

We got up very early one morning and drove for about an hour and half to get to l'Alpe d'Huez. We did the ride, and it was absolutely epic. It was incredibly beautiful and difficult, but when we got to the top, the feeling was fantastic.

We came back down and had some lunch, and then we began driving back to Saint Nazaire. We had been driving for about a half hour when I looked up and saw a craggy mountain lookout with a gondola above us. It gave me an eerie, familiar feeling. A feeling that I had been here before.

I looked at our guide, Phil, who was driving. "Where are we?"

"We're in Grenoble."

All of these years later, I was looking at the place where I had camped in 1975 as a 17-year-old.

It was a powerful moment. In one instant, I was transported back, remembering Cham the Lebanese university student and his incredible generosity. That experience had opened my eyes and set me on a path of compassion in a very visceral way. It had made me aware of some of the incredibly special people on the planet and the power of kindness and sharing. It was a pivotal life moment for me.

Since then, I have spent much time thinking of the people in war-torn countries like Lebanon and Syria and the struggles that they and so many people on the planet have had to endure. And yet a vast majority of them remain immeasurably compassionate and giving.

There is much good in the world, and much kindness that goes unrecognized.

If Cham only knew what kind of an impact his selfless acts of generosity had on me all these years later. Like the Butterfly Effect, it started with one simple act and continues to radiate outwards into infinity. And it reminds me of the words of anthropologist Margaret Mead: *Never doubt that a small group of thoughtful, committed citizens can change the world; indeed, it is the only thing that ever has.*

I believe that if we think deeply about it, all of us were born onto this planet with absolutely no expectations and no guarantees. As children, we were happy when we got our way, and we were sad when we did not. Simple.

I had big dreams as a child. I felt an unbridled sense of promise, and an innocence that harboured a sense of endless possibilities.

I have always tried to hang onto these feelings. I have tried to find that balance between what my heart is telling me and the noise in my over-crowded brain. I have tried to sift through that noise, often amidst a vast sea of emotions to seize the pure, heartfelt essence of each true idea and protect it.

Don Henley pretty much nailed it for me in his song "New York Minute": *What the head makes cloudy / The heart makes perfectly clear.*

This lyric has become one of the mantras in my life. I have learned to let passion guide me, choosing the activities and goals that inspire me with heartfelt desire and satisfaction. If I am doing something, it is because I believe in it and I am passionate about what it represents.

I just can't resist the draw to create. Focusing my energy on making things happen that I hope will have meaning. Things that have a greater purpose than just financial rewards—things that will make the planet a better place.

I hope you will also follow the path of your heart, and I hope you will trust the power of your imagination and live life through big windows. Where the journey takes you will surprise and delight you.